D A

HANGMEN

Riding with an outlaw
motorcycle club in the old days.

This book is dedicated to all of the members of the Hangmen Motorcycle Club who have worn the patch, whether in the past or the present, and who will do the same in the future.

~Reviews on Amazon~

With plenty of action, memorable characters, and club history… Dale has hit a home run with Hangmen.

Once you start reading, it's hard to put down. Actual events make it really fun to read. A must read for bikers that can relate to what the old days were like from a real old school biker.

This story takes you into the life of a motorcycle club member and lets you almost experience for yourself what it feels like to be young, reckless, penniless, and living on the edge.

From beginning to end, a great book! I wish it had 100 chapters because I was bummed when it ended.

It's an easy read, filled with excitement, comedy, and emotional drama! My only complaint is that it left me wanting more.

Thoroughly enjoyed reading this book. Each chapter has more adventure and unexpected twists than the last. I'm amazed at the life he lived and had no idea of the nuances of such a life. Makes me look at motorcycle riders/"gangs" in a different light. A worthy read.

A 1%er world very few could imagine living in. I literally couldn't set the book down once I received it.

Contents

Prologue

February 20, 1972. Having ridden all day from Northern California, I was tired. The night was approaching and the streetlights were coming on. Looking up at the tall palm trees, I could see the evening mist thickening overhead. My ass was sore. However, it was a comfort to lean back between the thighs of the eighteen-year-old girl behind me.

It felt good to be off the freeway, now in Anaheim, cruising down State College Boulevard, slowing with my right foot on the rear brake. Reaching down with my left hand, I started downshifting, steering the long front forks to the left onto East Virginia Street.

Immediately, I hung a right into an asphalt-paved alley. Staying in first gear, riding past the garbage cans and dumpsters, I listened to the satisfying galloping sound of the motor at idle as I coasted to my destination.

Arriving at our temporary clubhouse, a residential home rented by a club member, I pulled into the driveway and up to the back-yard gate. As I shut down the engine of my chopped Harley, the silence was numbing. The girl climbed off and stretched her legs in her tight bell-bottom jeans.

Distractedly, I stared at her ass as she bent forward, trying to loosen up after having spent the last eight hours and three hundred and forty miles sitting in one spot. It had been a while since our last gas stop.

I waited as she opened the gate. Then I walked my bike inside the backyard and put down the kickstand. Finally, the journey was over. For today anyway.

After striding across the yard and pushing open the back door, I was greeted with welcoming shouts, hugs, and hearty backslapping as brothers whom I had not seen in a few months surrounded me.

"What the fuck! Look who's here!"

"Well, I'll be damned, you found your way home!"

"Look what the cat dragged in!"

"Yeah, well, I knew you assholes couldn't do without me for long."

Led Zeppelin was on the stereo, dim light came from lava lamps, fake wood paneling covered the walls, and dingy, ages-old, stained shag carpet covered the floor. The drink choices were Budweiser or Boone's Farm wine. It was nice to be back.

Sue, the girl I had brought with me, sank into a chair in the corner of the living room. She looked like she was going to go to sleep right there.

I started to relax at the dining room table, putting up my feet, drinking a beer, and chewing on a piece of cold pizza someone had given me.

Barry asked, "What the hell have you been doing up north all this time?"

"Sitting on my ass in jail for the last two months, waiting for my hearing."

"How'd that go?"

"They're holding me over for trial, attempted murder for stabbing some jerk in a fight."

"That sucks. Good luck with it. I'm glad you're back. The shit is really hitting the fan down here. These Seekers have pushed us too far and we're going to take 'em out."

We were living the dream. All that mattered to us was what we believed in. The Club! The Hangmen. It was our life. It was our faith, like a religion. It had become the only thing that mattered in our lives. Our brothers, our bikes, and the patches on our backs. More important than family. More important than anything.

There were maybe eight of us in the room, just a small portion of the So.Cal. chapter. Charlie, Uncle Tom, DeVinch, Pooch, Pugh, Barry, Curt. Just hanging out. Looking forward to getting some rest after the long ride, I wondered where Sue and I could crash for the night.

So.Cal., Southern California, was my home, even though I didn't have one when I wasn't traveling on my motorcycle or staying with friends. I was homeless by choice, kind of a vagabond. The club was my home.

Then the phone rang. Hearing the conversation from our side, we all perked up. It seemed that one of our guys had some of the Seekers Motorcycle Club surrounded at a street corner just a block or so from Disneyland.

It was a Shell station on the corner of Katella and Haster streets. Right away, we all knew where it was. Not wanting to take care of business on our motorcycles, I told Sue to stay put and wait for me as we stripped off our colors and ran for three cars parked outside.

Seven of us were in two vehicles, while Pooch was by himself in his car. As we drove, there wasn't much talk, with each of us lost in our private thoughts as we raced to the location about ten minutes away.

It was just past 8:30, already dark, one of those foggy Southern California evenings when the marine layer had come in from the ocean and cloaked the city in a soft, surreal caress where nothing seemed real. Like a dream or a movie set.

I almost expected to hear a haunting soundtrack playing in the background. Nothing seemed real anyway. Maybe it was just the drugs. After all, it was the early '70s. Which, as some people have said, was more like the '60s than the '60s were.

During that short ride, my mind wandered back over the events of recent months. How had we gotten here? The Seekers had been pissing us off for a while now. One thing after another, it seemed.

Having been up north, I had heard only bits and pieces through phone conversations after getting out of jail. The root of the problem was the worst of reasons to fight and one of the most common.

One of our guys had an Ol' Lady, if you could even call her that. Her name was Sherri and she was pretty, a platinum blonde with big tits and a great ass.

She worked as a stripper. But still, there were plenty around like her. She was just a girl he had fallen in love with, and she was not faithful to him, although he thought she should be. She was not worth it, but honestly, neither was he.

To the rest of us, this wasn't about a girl. The problem we had with them was their disrespect for us. It was one thing for their president to be fucking an Ol' Lady who was supposed to belong to one of our guys. They should have respected that, but they didn't.

However, to flaunt it in our faces was unacceptable. Who the fuck did they think they were? The friction had been escalating, coming to a head for weeks, and we had decided that we would not allow it to go on any longer. The Seekers would pay with an ass whooping!

Already tired from the long day's ride, and now anticipating violence, I felt adrenaline build up in my system until I started getting a case of the shakes. To keep it under control, I casually looked out the window, hoping that nobody in the car would see that I was trembling, almost uncontrollably.

I was no stranger to fighting, but showing fear was out of the question. Even if adrenaline wasn't merely fear, it still looked that way. I had just gotten out of jail and didn't want to go back. In a situation like this, anything could happen.

Taking in slow, deep breaths, I tried to relax and make it look like I did this every day.

We blasted down State College to Ball Road, turned right, and headed west, underneath the Interstate 5 overpass. Then we turned left at Euclid and sped four long blocks to Katella.

Upon arriving, we parked the cars near the corner on the east side of the gas station and then piled out into the chilly, misty night. The low-hanging sky seemed to be painted yellow by the bright Shell sign.

We walked around the office with its big glass windows, almost floor to ceiling, to the west side of the station. There, the Seekers were waiting with their bikes against a tall cinder block wall. With our heavy boots clomping on asphalt and then concrete as we passed the gas pumps, we took our positions. Cars were at the pumps, getting gas.

Ordinary people surrounded us, not paying any attention to what was going down. Everyday life in Anaheim. But that everyday life was about to get very un-ordinary.

We took our places without discussion. In those days, we fought so much and everyone just seemed to know what to do.

We were facing ten Seekers standing in front of their bikes with their backs against that high cinder block wall on the west side of the gas station. They were waiting for us. Not like an ambush but waiting to see what we were going to do. Maybe they knew that they had pushed us too far.

The fog and the garish yellow glow from the Shell sign made the surreal scene seem even more strange and abstract. We had not brought any guns. We were facing them like we would go at it, a la West Side Story, but without switchblades, only locking blade 'Buck' knives.

No chains or pipes, as the police or news media would have you believe. Dan'l, who had made the call from the gas station, came over and joined our line.

The shakes had subsided. I picked out a Seeker opposite me. I didn't know his name and I didn't care. I focused on him; he was going to be my target for when the shit hit the fan. He stared back, knowing that we were about to become opponents.

My trusty knife, already bloodied from previous encounters, was open and held down along my side, ready for action. I thought we were going to fight it out. We were a team.

As we stared them down, I held my breath, waiting for the order to go. But the order had not come from our president, and we wondered why.

Our opponents just stood with their backs to the wall, waiting for us to make the first move. I could see knives in their hands. Soon, I found out what the holdup was.

What seemed to be a Mexican standoff turned out to be much worse. I thought we had not brought any guns, but I was wrong. Barely visible through the fog across the street was Pooch in his car.

Sitting at another gas station on the north side of the intersection, he had flanked the enemy as they stood against the wall. Pooch had a military surplus M1 .30-caliber semi-automatic carbine, and he was vowing to shoot these fuckers. In our position, we were not in his line of fire.

Knowing he was over there, Charlie, our president at the time, sent DeVinch, one of our So.Cal. members, across the street to tell Pooch not to shoot anyone. We would take care of this. He was only supposed to cover us, just in case.

But it was to no avail. Pooch was pissed off, had an itchy trigger finger, and had decided it was time to scratch it. Pooch was a bit crazy sometimes, but you had to be if you were part of this club back then.

We had been in position only a minute or so when big DeVinch strode back across Katella Avenue, waving his long arms. Exasperated, he yelled to us in his Missouri accent, "He's gonna do it! He's gonna do it!"

Swearing loudly, knowing that Pooch wasn't bullshitting, Charlie gave the word to get the hell out of there. Following his orders, we had no sooner turned our backs on the Seekers to head to the cars than the gunfire erupted. Gunfire, a block from Disneyland!

Thundering echoes resounded off the surrounding buildings and walls, while bullets impacted against the cinder block wall, around and against their intended targets. It was only semi-automatic, but you wouldn't know it. Pooch was pulling the trigger as fast as he could, emptying a thirty-round magazine at the objects of our anger.

Seekers were falling and diving for the cover of their motorcycles and rolling around in pain on the ground. We had started out walking away, but now we were running for the cars we had come in, wanting to get as far from there as possible, trying to pretend that we were not part of what was happening.

Diving into the cars and swerving onto the roads, we raced away in different directions, all swearing to ourselves as the evening fog enveloped us. The echoing gunshots faded into silence as we listened to the police sirens approaching from all directions.

We melted away into the night. That wasn't the plan. It wasn't supposed to go down that way, but it did. It was just the beginning of a rather bloody war.

Clark, Gentleman Jim, Skip and Gremlin, 1968

Introduction

Come along on a ride with the Hangmen Motorcycle Club during the exciting times in the '60s and '70s. For the most part, with rare exceptions, this is what happened to me personally. The story continues to this day. This book focuses on when its reputation was still being formed, even after its beginnings in Richmond, California, from which no written history and very few pictures exist.

These stories are true, and the characters are real, except maybe where some deniability is needed. I have changed some of the names to protect the guilty. I am hoping that most, if not all, of the statutes of limitations have expired. Too many of the people involved are gone anyway.

Most of the pictures in this book are fuzzy due to the inexpensive little cameras we used, usually a Kodak Pocket Instamatic 110 or Polaroids. But just like black and white photos accurately portray a distant past, to me, these low-quality pictures perfectly depict the times when cameras were cheap and low-quality photographers were even cheaper.

I consider myself lucky to have been involved with an extraordinary group of men at an unusual time – the '60s and '70s, in the Valhalla of biker lore, California. A place in time that is gone forever because of all the changes in our society.

Changes like cameras everywhere and databases. We weren't 'Old School,' we were the original school. Not just the Hangmen, of course. I am talking about all the bikers back then.

I was with So.Cal., which meant Orange, Los Angeles, Riverside, and San Diego Counties. I couldn't be everywhere when things were going on, and there was a lot of shit that went on. Plus, there were the No.Cal. boys in and around Modesto and the OKLA chapter in Oklahoma.

I spent a lot of time in both of those places. Others could tell many stories about those two decades, the '60s and '70s, but sadly many of those stories have been lost, along with the people who could have told them.

In this book, I can reveal only a fraction of the things that happened. There was never a dull moment. Many people helped to make a reputation for this club.

I always saw us as Shakespeare's Band of Brothers.

"We few, we happy few, we band of brothers;

For he today that sheds his blood with me Shall be my brother."

~Henry V, Saint Crispin's Day speech before the Battle of Agincourt~

I still see it that way. Times have changed, but brotherhood does not. We stood together. We always do, no matter what – us against the world. We were a little crazy back then, in a good way. But also, as you have already seen, sometimes in a bad way.

Fire it up and let's go. Enjoy the ride and the adventure before it is lost in time, like fading newspaper clippings.

Chapter 1
The Bikes

The coolest part about being a biker in the '60s, mainly as a Hangmen, was riding a far-out-looking chopper, whether by yourself or in a group of awesome bikes.

Either in a perfectly organized tight pack or racing recklessly and dangerously in and out of traffic, the bikes always turned heads.

Flashing chrome and colorful paint jobs. Thundering exhaust that made an approaching pack sound like a herd of stampeding buffalo. Long chromed front ends with skinny twenty-one-inch front wheels.

Riders stomped on clutch levers, grabbed gears, and popped wheelies, usually with a hot chick on the back. Long hair and beards framed devilish grins stemming from the sheer fun of it all. Our only safety gear was a pair of sunglasses.

Greasy Levi's called slicks, heavy boots, and, of course, the noose on your back, your coveted 'patch,' usually on a sleeveless Levi's jacket or a cut-down leather motorcycle jacket.

Modern-day barbarians and misfits, living by our own rules. Ignoring laws and spreading fear among the citizen public and loathing and disgust among the cops. We were the one percent of motorcycle riders, reveling in our outlaw, anti-social image. It was a way of life.

Hippies, who were so common then, treated us with awe, like we were a warrior class that was anti-establishment like them. They thought we would be their military arm when the shit hit the fan.

They were flower children, with an emphasis on 'children,' and we were the adults who might protect them, or not. It was okay with us; that attitude frequently prompted them to hand over their women and drugs, which we were happy to accept.

Yes, we were anti-establishment, but we weren't left-wing anti-American like them. We were pro-American, with many war veterans in our ranks. It's the same today.

The Hangmen were known for cool, state-of-the-art choppers. If you hung around and didn't have a good-looking bike, the guys would probably not even ask you to ride with us, let alone prospect for the club. The fashion of our bikes was crucial, and we took it very seriously. We were bike builders as much as bike riders. Other clubs often commented on how nice our bikes looked. They were a large part of our reputation, along with the fact that we had many members who were complete badasses.

The sixties were famous for radicalism in just about every way. Our bikes were radical, but not quite the bizarre creations that you see today, custom-made in high-dollar bike shops for well-off celebrities and businesspeople.

Our bikes were frequently showpieces, but the number one priority was that they be rideable and not just around town. At first, we didn't have custom-made frames, gas tanks, or sissy bars that you could order online or even in a catalog.

Initially, we fashioned everything ourselves, mostly by altering stock Harley Davidson frames, motors, and front ends. By the late sixties, AEE Choppers started selling custom motorcycle parts and, in the early seventies, Paco began making frames and gas tanks. A few people started building bikes with them.

Of course, fast was in, with eighty-inch strokers, Mikuni or S&S carburetors, and all kinds of cams to go faster. The whole idea was to make the chopper faster and lighter by stripping it down from the original Harleys or Indians with all of the junk on them, like turning an old car into a hot rod.

Besides, fast is fun. The original 'choppers' from the fifties and early sixties did not yet have long front ends. That was something that showed up in the late sixties and became very popular in the seventies. It didn't matter how hard the bike was to handle or how rough it rode. To us, the more challenging the bike was to ride, the tougher the man riding it. We wouldn't be caught dead with a windshield, but we did start making homemade leather saddlebags, which were handy on long trips.

Some of our guys rode Sportsters, which were very common back then. Initially designed for racing, they were already lighter and faster than the Panheads or Knuckleheads that most of us rode, at least the stock ones.

But even the Sportsters were customized, with extended forks, raked necks, and, sometimes, solid struts in place of the rear shocks. At time, we would re-weld the whole back ends of the bikes to make them real rigid frames, emulating the older big twins.

Part of the reason for that was to make them sit lower, with the rear fender just barely clearing the rear tire. Sitting low was mandatory, but what was even more critical was looking cool.

Most of the guys rode the big twins, Panheads and Knuckleheads. We never called them 'choppers,' as that sounded pretentious. We just called them bikes or scooters, or 74s for the 1200-cc, seventy-four-cubic-inch motors.

In 1966 Harley Davidson came out with the Shovelhead motor. It just so happened that the whole top end, cylinders, heads, carburetors, and valve covers would fit right onto a pan head lower.

They seemed to have more power and were quieter due to the thick aluminum valve covers instead of the thin tin valve cover of the Panhead, which had a hollow ring to it, and they tended to leak oil if the gaskets were not just right.

Most of us started running the Shovelhead conversion. For some reason, free spare parts always seemed to be lying around.

My red bike in front, Uncle Tom's gold bike, and Lurch's purple creation.

We ran 'Suicide' foot clutches with a 'Jockey' shift lever directly off the transmission. Added to that were a front end frequently over six feet long, no front brake, and no suspension in the rear other than the air in your back tire.

These bikes could be tricky to ride, but we practically lived on them. Most of us didn't even own cars. It was an unnecessary expense, and besides, it never rains in California!

Some of our bikes were fast for their day, but there were no sport bikes to compare them to. In the mid-1960's, the Honda 50 was becoming popular, and the fastest street bike out there was probably the Norton Commando or Royal Enfield.

I tried to go for reliability over speed. When you want to go somewhere, it is always preferable to keep riding instead of working on your bike in a gas station or alongside the highway. Hot rods are fast but tend to be unreliable.

For Hangmen, long-distance riding was a requirement. Before patching out with the club, I was doing a lot of that as a teenager. Over time, I had ridden in just about every state west of the Mississippi River. We didn't have people east of the Mississippi, so we had no reason to go there.

As we started riding longer distances, our bikes morphed into a combination of street choppers and long-distance cruisers. However, these were not the kind of cruisers people ride today. They had no windshields, fairings, comfy seats, or saddle-bags other than leather ones that we made ourselves.

The bikes still had long front ends, suicide clutches, and rigid frames, but with pullback handlebars, highway pegs, and something to lean back on. Sometimes that might be a young lady along for the ride. Other times, it was just a sleeping bag.

Only four-speed transmissions were available on Harleys back then, so we used to change the gears on the crankshaft and the transmission sprockets. We called them Freeway Gears.

People had different preferences; mine was twenty-four teeth on the engine sprocket and twenty-six on the transmission. This allowed us to cruise on the highways at seventy-five to eighty miles per hour with ease.

It may sound high geared, but my motorcycle would do wheelies with no problem. The front end would come up effortlessly. If you wanted to get on it hard, like running from the police, doing wheelies became a problem, as it slowed you down.

In 1965 Harley introduced the Electra Glide with an electric starter. Of course, we didn't want anything to do with that. It was more manly to start the bike over with a kick-starter.

Tradition and style were paramount, but kick-starters were not always fun. Sometimes, on cold mornings, you'd stand on the kick-starter and it didn't want to go down.

That 1973 motor that I had bought from the Harley dealer was a delight – smooth, quiet, and well-tuned. I could turn on the key switch and push down the kick-starter with my hand like a downward punch. It would fire right up.

Our bikes were eye-catching and radical, but, at the same time, practical. We rode them every day, not only around Southern California but all over the Western United States.

Though they were challenging to ride with their long front forks and suicide clutches, we were proud of that fact, and it seemed that everyone in the club was a good rider.

The Bikes.

Chapter 2
"I'll Take It."

My folks split up when I was ten. I was stuck with my mother, who moved around a lot. Because I never spent much time in any one school, I didn't have any long-term friends.

But by the time I was fifteen, I had one friend who rode a motorcycle like I did. I needed to be able to get to work after I dropped out of high school. We stayed friends.

His name was Don, and for a teenager, he was a badass. He was older than me and a couple of grades ahead, I thought he was cool. I wanted to be like him. We rode motorcycles (Hondas) together while still in school. Though we couldn't afford one yet, we were intrigued by Harleys, choppers, and bikers.

We went to the movies a lot, mostly sneaking in the back fence at drive-ins and sitting on the ground with the car speakers from the posts blaring. If anyone caught us, we would disappear back through the same hole in the fence.

We were captivated by one Western: The Good, the Bad and the Ugly with Clint Eastwood. We must have seen that one ten times at the drive-ins, mainly on Beach Boulevard. We even started wearing long coats, emulating the dusters worn in those films – pre-Goth by a long shot.

Don graduated from High school in 1967, although they refused to let him attend the graduation ceremony because he was still on suspension for violence or threatened violence. They just wanted him gone.

When he left school, I did too. We were best friends, riding, working on the bikes, or just hanging out together. We got into occasional fights where I got to see his style, which consisted of winning.

He was so good that when the shit got started, at a gas station or a Taco Bell, most of the time he didn't need my help. He took care of it. Not that I didn't want to help; it was just that it was so much fun either watching him drive someone right into the ground or seeing him send them flying.

I always thought, 'I wish I could do that.'

Mostly, we went to the cheap biker movies that were so popular in the late sixties: Wild Angels with Peter Fonda (1966), Devil's Angels with John Cassavetes (1967), Hells Angels on Wheels with none other than Jack Nicholson (1967), and Hell's Angels '69 staring real Hells Angels like Sonny Barger, Michael Walter AKA Tiny, Magoo, and Terence Tracy, one of the most famous Hells Angels from Oakland, also known as Terry the Tramp.

These old movies can be corny, but they are a great place to see real old-school bikes. By the time that last one was released, Don was already a member of the Hangmen and I was hanging around on my own Harley.

Don found a Harley for sale. It was a basket case, meaning a pile of parts, sometimes without serial numbers, but the price was right: two hundred dollars. He was on his way. It was a rigid frame 1955 Panhead. While working nights in a chrome shop, Don started to chrome practically the whole bike.

One day, at Tom McMullen's AEE Choppers in Buena Park, he met a guy named Gremlin. It turned out that both McMullen and Gremlin were members of the Hangmen Motorcycle Club.

Don, nineteen at the time, was three years older than me. They invited him to a party that the Hangmen were throwing. I guess you could say the rest was history.

He was welcomed in after the usual hang around and prospecting requirement and, by the time he was twenty, was a full-patched member. Don was a tough guy! Standing six-foot-one, lean and hard as nails, not afraid of anyone, he fit right in.

For me, joining a motorcycle club seemed like a long way off. Besides, I wanted to join the Marine Corps and fight for my country in Vietnam.

Still, I envied Don, who got to hang around with a hardcore group like the Hangmen. I used to relish the stories that he told about partying and going on runs with them and about some of the bar fights that always seemed to break out.

I was kind of undecided about whether I wanted to be a Marine or a biker. Neither one of them paid very well, but because I was young, the call of adventure was strong. Both lifestyles seemed exciting.

In 1967, I was sixteen. Don had graduated. After briefly trying the tenth grade, I dropped out of school to find a job. I didn't feel I was learning anything, and it was getting in the way of my life of adventure.

My mother was the only one in a family of six who had graduated from high school. For me, the mere thought of going to college seemed about as remote as becoming an airline pilot.

I started working at odd jobs: valet parking, dishwashing, driving a truck, construction, whatever I could find, but I didn't stay at any one place for long. I was restless and didn't know what I wanted to do.

But I did know that I wanted a Harley so bad, I could taste it. I had just read Hunter S. Thompson's first book, 'Hells Angels," published in 1966, so I had at least a literary taste of the biker lifestyle. Plus, Thompson mentioned the Hangmen MC twice in his book.

By this time, I was riding a customized British Matchless 500. It looked pretty cool for a British bike. It was a single-cylinder thumper and sounded like a Harley, but it wasn't one, and no amount of paint or chrome would fix that.

It seems I am never one to do anything halfway. Even though it was a nice bike, it was still halfway, and it had to go.

September of 1968 in Anaheim, California: Just a couple of months after my seventeenth birthday, I found the bike I needed, and it wasn't a basket case. It was in one piece, and it was running.

It was a 1951 Panhead, in the original rigid frame, with a small peanut gas tank, a stock length wide glide front end with a narrow twenty-one-inch front wheel and a suicide clutch, fish-tail mufflers, and a chrome twisted steel sissy bar.

It was a '50's, early '60s-style bike. It was seventeen years old, like me. I saw it sitting for sale in a supermarket parking lot. The guy wanted seven hundred dollars for it, which seemed like a lot of money back then, especially with the unverified stories about fifty-dollar basket cases being available.

He let me take it for a ride. I had never ridden a suicide clutch before, but I was young, agile, and a fast learner.

It was an incredible feeling with that monster between my legs. The Harley, I mean. The sound, the weight, the feel, the throbbing vibration – it was magical.

I reached down below my left thigh to grab the jockey shifter and heard the solid clunk in each gear and that distinct coughing Harley exhaust note.

Hells Angels or Peter Fonda, eat your heart out! You got nothing on me! I felt like a real motorcycle rider now.

It was dark when I left the parking lot and probably hadn't gone more than ten minutes. After getting the heady feeling of the big Harley, heading westbound, I was coming back to the parking lot at Lincoln Avenue.

Just short of Knott Avenue in Anaheim, a car suddenly pulled out of a driveway from an alley right in front of me.

I locked up the rear brake and slid sideways. The back tire came around to my left. Just before I would have hit the car, I let off the brake, hit the throttle, and squirted behind the car, then bolted up and onto the sidewalk.

Fortunately, there was no one on it. I continued on the sidewalk for about another hundred yards, then swerved into the parking lot.

I was back where I had started with the guy waiting for me. He was wide-eyed, having just watched my little maneuver.

I skidded to a stop right in front of him and managed to get the jockey shifter into neutral. Remembering to put the kickstand down, I shut the motor off and breathlessly said, "I'll take it."

My life would never be the same. I said yes not only to a motorcycle but also to a new way of life – a life in which, frequently, my survival would depend more on luck than on skill.

For me, my formative years were motorcycles and the club, not college or the military like most young men. If I had known guys who were into other endeavors in life, would my life have been any different?

Who knows? But that is where I was and the path I chose.

Now that I had a Harley, Don invited me to come with him and meet some of the Hangmen. One day, we rode to Anaheim High School and pulled into an alleyway behind an apartment building that faced the school employee parking lot.

In the garage, working on his motorcycle, I met Gremlin. Don introduced us. Shortly after that, Uncle Tom came downstairs. They both had apartments side by side over the garages. They were the first Hangmen I met.

My "New" 1951 Panhead. September 1968

Chapter 3

Hangin' with the Hangmen

Gremlin's Sportster in 1968, before it was the Green Turtle.

Both Uncle Tom and Gremlin were cutting-edge bike designers and builders, not professionally for others, just for themselves. They were trendsetters. The Hangmen were known for having some of the coolest, most radical choppers around. Though Gremlin rode a Sportster, it was hard to tell at first glance. It was a work of art and took many trophies at bike shows over the years. Before that, he had an award-winning Panhead up in Richmond.

Just being around them made me want to customize my Harley even more. It was pretty cool just the way it was, and I wish I still had that bike today. I already had a lot of influence from Don, who had a head start learning from these craftsmen. First, I replaced the stock fork tubes with new ones, fifteen inches longer than stock. I didn't bother raking the neck to make the bike sit more level. Nor did I take the time to get the fork tubes chromed. The other thing I didn't do was wait to get a longer cable for the front brake. Front brakes didn't look cool anyway, so I just left it off. I would soon regret that.

Though I was only seventeen, I had a beard and looked older. I felt a little self-conscious about my young age and saw no reason to mention it. So far, nobody had asked. I was riding a HARLEY! What more could they want? Of course, Don knew, but he didn't say anything either. I had visions of signing up for a patch right away. I had a lot to learn. It didn't take long before I was invited on the run to Big Bear the next weekend. They said, "Just bring a sleeping bag. That's all you'll need."

On the appointed day, Don and I showed up, and off we went. It was awesome riding with a pack of real bikers. Well, I was at the back of the group, of course, but I was with them, nonetheless.

Stopping in gas stations and feeling everyone's eyes on me. Strutting around, thinking to myself, 'Yeah, I'm with them, what about it?' How fucking cool was that?

Blasting down the highway, hearing the thundering roar of the pipes from fifteen Harleys, the smell of the exhaust, the wind rushing past my ears, trying to stay in position, speeding eastbound out of town on Highway 91. It wasn't the 91 Freeway yet.

After Riverside, we went north to San Bernardino. Finding Highway 38, we turned east and started climbing into the mountains, blasting around the curves, grabbing gears, leaning hard, going way too fast. As we climbed higher and higher into the mountains, the roads got into tighter and tighter twisties. It was exhilarating riding a chopper with real outlaw bikers and I loved it.

The higher we went, the cooler it got, and the more beautiful the scenery became. It was amazing being in the mountains above San Bernardino with vistas of one hundred miles or more.

Sudden cliffs with a sheer drop-off were on one side of the road and giant trees reaching into the skies were on the other, with fresh, clean air we were not used to living down in the valley. The sky was bluer up there, out of the smog, Living in Orange County, I'd forgotten what it was like to see a deep blue sky.

I was a little disappointed when we reached our destination. It was just a clearing in the mountains with a fire pit. I wasn't disappointed in the campsite, just a bit sad that such a great ride was over. But there was always the ride back down.

There were only about fifteen of us besides me and my friend Don, who by now had been branded with the nickname Lurch, after The Addams Family character, because he was tall and thin, but muscular. He had a deep voice and he didn't talk more than he needed to. It fit him well. He looked a lot like Lurch, only younger and more handsome.

I don't remember who all was there other than Uncle Tom, Indian Dave, Charlie, and Gremlin, One big Hangman who stood out was named Skip; he was gregarious and friendly, liked to drink, and had a million jokes. Skip was very accepting of me as the young new guy. I liked him right away.

Dinner was cans of pork and beans, beef stew, etc. Refreshments were cans of beer and bottles of cheap wine. At one point during the night, while we were standing around the campfire, Skip gave me a gallon jug of Red Mountain wine. It was about a third full, and even that was way too much. I thought it was a cool gift and started drinking it right away. I was no wine connoisseur, so I thought it tasted pretty good. The more I drank, the better it tasted.

As I stood by the campfire, watching the light reflecting off the tall pine trees all around and sparkling off the chrome from the parked motorcycles, my head was spinning and I had a warm and fuzzy feeling.

That was the last thing I remember until I woke up with my face in the dirt. It was daylight, and my head was pounding and spinning – not so warm and fuzzy anymore. Someone had taken the sleeping bag off my bike and thrown it over me, although I had no memory of being cold. Hell, I had no memory of anything after the jug of wine.

All I wanted to do was lay there with my eyes closed for at least the next week. But before long, we were saddling up and heading out, back down the mountain. It wasn't quite as much fun as the way up. Riding with a wine hangover is not recommended.

When we finally stopped at a diner at the bottom of the mountain in Redlands, most of the group went in to have breakfast and coffee. I waited with the bikes because I had very little money and even less desire to try putting anything in my stomach. To this day, I am still not a big fan of wine. But I had been on my first run with the Hangmen and, despite my hangover, I felt pretty good.

At some point, they found out how old I was (or wasn't). It was made clear that I should go away and come back when I was a little older. The guys didn't exactly run me off but said I had to be a grown-up to join this club.

The minimum age was twenty-one, though I knew that Lurch had snuck in at twenty. He and I still hung out a lot along with Mark, our other high school buddy. The three of us frequently rode together, worked on our bikes together, and did our share of partying.

I wasn't ready for the commitment of joining the club anyway. I was enjoying the freedom of being a young man in Southern California, riding where I wanted. However, I still went out to bars with the Hangmen, which was allowed because, by this time, I had a fake I.D. that said I was twenty-two, although I never once got asked for it in a bar.

I wanted to be a 'brother,' I wanted to be one of them. I wanted to be like them, and I wanted to belong. I looked up to these guys like they were older brothers. They were tough, charismatic, fearless, fun-loving, daring. They were all the things I wasn't.

When I went on runs or just out to bars with the Hangmen, we were often around other clubs like the Hells Angels, Hessians, So.Cal. and Dago Outlaws, Iron Horsemen, Misfits, Chosen Few, Mescaleros, and others. They didn't seem like different clubs back then, except for the patches on their backs. It was like we were much more alike than not. But when we were around these other clubs, the Hangmen made it clear that I was on my own.

If someone decided to beat me up or steal my motorcycle, they would not get the club into a fight or, worse yet, a war with another club over a hang-around kid. I did get jumped a few times, but nothing serious, and no one ever tried to take my bike.

Mark's and the author's bikes. 1969

Chapter 4
Harley vs. Car

1968-1969 – I'll skip over the embarrassing events that led to my continually getting arrested when I was still seventeen. It seemed that my Harley and my high school buddies had a lot to do with it.

My parents had split up when I was ten, and I started running amok soon after, getting my first motorcycle in 1966, when I was fifteen. By late 1968, all the guards in the juvenile hall knew me by my first name.

After enough arrests, my father got the courts to release me to his custody since my mother had no control over me and hadn't for a long time. I loved and respected my father, but unfortunately, he didn't have much control over me either.

But he wouldn't be around much longer, and soon any remaining shackles on my freedom would be gone.

The year 1969 started with a bang; I spent more and more time hanging out with the club. One evening, the 16th of January, I was at a bar with Lurch and some of the Hangmen and Cypress Crew down in Santa Ana.

I might have splurged on one beer, which was all I could afford, but we needed to get going because Lurch's bike was down and I had packed him on the back to go to the bar that night. Back then, it was more important to be somewhere than to worry about how you got there. There was no whining about riding bitch like we hear today. Riding on the back of a bike was still better than riding in the front of a car.

Lurch worked the graveyard shift at the chrome shop, and I needed to get him to work. I was pulling out of the bar parking lot with Lurch on the back, popping the foot clutch and doing one of my signature wheelies down the street, keeping the power on so that the front wheel came down smoothly like the nose gear of a landing aircraft. It was about 10:30.

I was heading north up Euclid Street, not in a hurry, probably at the speed limit. There was very little traffic on the road and the pavement was dry. It never rains in California.

I was approaching the Hazard Avenue intersection. (With a street name like that, I should have been more alert.) Without a signal, a southbound car made a sudden left turn right in front of us.

As soon as I saw the headlights swing toward us, I hit the rear brake, the only one I had, as hard as possible, which locked the rear wheel. At the same time, I tried to drive the bike to the right to miss the car, but that was impossible.

The fact that the bike threw to the right with the rear wheel locked put all three of us – the motorcycle, Lurch, and me – onto the pavement instantly.

As soon as we hit the road, we hit the car – approximately one thousand pounds of metal, flesh, and bone, traveling at forty-five miles per hour.

The impact with the car seemed like an explosion – not only the noise but the stunning concussion. I lay there in the street, stunned, trying to get my breath and take in what had happened.

That was when the pain started. Suddenly, everything hurt: my back, shoulder, ribs, wrists, and right hip. Thankfully, I didn't hit my head, and neither did Lurch, but the impact had broken his left ankle.

The frame just below the motor had taken the full impact against the right front wheel of the car. I was told later folded the wheel under the vehicle like an aircraft landing gear and moved the car a few feet to its left.

I didn't intentionally lay it down. It just happened that way. It was probably a good thing, as if we had been upright when hitting the car, we both certainly would have been either slammed against the car or launched over it to fly through the air for a while until we came back to earth. That would not have been fun.

At least not the coming back to earth part. The flying might have been okay. Of course, we didn't have helmets on. We never wore helmets back then, unless we rode in states where it was required.

Suddenly, we were surrounded by people. There was a gas station or convenience store on the southeast corner of that intersection, and some of the people came from there.

Others stopped while passing by. I was feeling great pain in what seemed to be my whole body. Folks in the crowd around me were telling me to lay still and not get up. No problem there! I couldn't move, let alone get up. At first, I worried about being paralyzed, but soon I knew I could feel my feet and wiggle my toes, so I was pretty sure that was not a problem.

Hopping around on one foot, Lurch commandeered a ride with a passing car that had stopped. He had the driver take him back to the bar that we had just left. It seemed like I laid there a long time, but you know how time gets distorted in unusual situations.

More and more people showed up: bystanders, police, and a fire truck. I never saw or spoke with the driver, but someone later told me that he was Mexican and had no driver's license or insurance.

At about the same time the ambulance arrived, I could hear the comforting roar of a bunch of Harleys pull up. I looked up at the foggy night sky as the ambulance drivers loaded me into the back of it. Some of the guys came over and told me to hang in there; I'd be alright.

A couple of them gave me a comforting pat on the shoulder or the chest. It made me feel better, and I was confident that the boys would take care of my bike.

I didn't know it at the time, but it was unrideable. The left front of the motor had taken most of the impact of the car's front wheel. It had jammed the chromed primary cover into the engine sprocket, preventing it from turning. The frame underneath the motor also took a blow and had a nasty bend in it.

Greg Tripp, one of the Cypress group, which I also found out later, got on it and, hanging his arm on the doorpost of some volunteer's car, had ridden the bike to a friend's house not far away.

A tow truck had to haul off the car I had hit, while my bike was 'rideable.' Well, not really, but the guys all thought it was cool that a Harley had taken out the car.

All I could think about was the excruciating pain in my back while the ambulance took me to the nearest private hospital, which turned me away. We went to another, which also refused to take me because I didn't have any insurance.

After the third choice of hospitals, they gave up and took me to Orange County Hospital, which, just like the Orange County Jail, was always willing to take me in.

The result of the night was two fractured vertebrae (lumbar L4 and L5), a couple of broken ribs, a broken shoulder socket, and a hairline fracture in my right hip joint. But no cuts or scrapes and no blood.

Our clothes weren't even torn. We didn't slide on the pavement. As soon as we hit the road, we hit the car.

The doctor scared the hell out of me when he told me not to move around too much, as they didn't want one of those broken ribs piercing a lung. I was afraid to even breathe for a month, as I had stabbing pains with every breath. Anyone who has had broken ribs can relate.

There were no casts or traction and no pain pills. After three days in the hospital, the doctors sent me home and told me to lay still for about six months.

I didn't, of course.

I did my best to lay still on my mother's couch for about three weeks, waiting for Star Trek to come on. As soon as I was able to hobble around, I started working on getting my bike fixed.

The author's bike a couple of days before the accident. Jan. 1969

Chapter 5
The Hang-Around

As previously mentioned, the guys had made it clear right off the bat that, as a seventeen-year-old hang-around, I was a nobody and was on my own when it came to getting into any shit with another club.

Though they were relatively new, the Hessians were the largest club in Orange County at the time. The Hangmen were a little smaller but had been around longer.

One night, after riding with the guys to a Hessian bar, I was out in the parking lot watching the bikes when a very drunk Hessian came up to me and mumbled something about his Ol' Lady and me. I didn't even know who he was, let alone who his Ol' Lady was.

When I asked him what he meant, his only answer was to hit me with a slow, sloppy right cross. It was such a lousy punch, I wanted to say, "Is that all you've got?"

But I didn't want to insult a patch holder, so as he continued to swing away at me, I busied myself with ducking, dodging, and blocking the following punches, which wasn't very difficult.

It was kind of good practice even though it felt as if it was happening in slow motion. As I said, he was pretty drunk. I wasn't worried about him, but I was concerned about all of his brothers. A crowd was starting to gather. At one point, he swung and missed and almost fell.

I grabbed him and held him up, putting him back on his feet, not because I cared about him, but because I didn't want the gathering crowd to think I had knocked him down. He turned and came at me again.

I don't know if he was trying to show off by picking on someone he thought was a loner, since I didn't have a patch on my back. Or maybe someone had put him up to it as a joke and a little entertainment.

Or maybe it was just a case of mistaken identity. Either way, I knew not to swing on a patch holder. It would surely bring down the thunder and put me at the bottom of a rat pack complete with fists, boots, and chains.

My buddies in the Hangmen had already told me they would not help. It didn't matter, since there were no Hangmen in the gathering crowd anyway.

Finally, after missing a wild swing, he stumbled and fell. Once again, I worried the other Hessians would think I'd hit him. Some of them who had been watching came running over, and I thought, 'Here we go.'

But instead of them jumping on me, I think they realized he was embarrassing himself and would soon embarrass the club. They pulled him to his feet and led him away, telling him things I could not hear to either calm him down or maybe try to convince him it was over and he had won. After surprising me with that first punch, he never laid a glove on me.

Suddenly, it was over. Everyone seemed to forget about me and walked away, so I wandered across the dark parking lot to continue watching the Hangmen's bikes.

I was thankful that mine was still there and the previous few minutes of entertainment had not been a diversion that allowed someone to roll it away into the darkness.

The night the Hangmen tried to kill me

June 1969. Just rebuilt after the accident. The last picture my father took of me.

It was the 4th of July 1969. My father was in the hospital with Hodgkin's cancer. I went to see him every day. And, every day, he seemed to get worse. I was still recovering from the accident and yet another arrest

The juvenile court had released me into my father's custody with the promise that he would keep me out of trouble, which was kind of like trying to get Wile E. Coyote to give up on road runners.

After the accident, my dad had demanded that I sell the Harley. I said I couldn't sell it the way it was; I had to fix it first. But after several months, when I got it back together, I realized how much I loved that bike.

I loved it not just for what it was, but for what it made me and who it made me. I had read about how, throughout history, a man on horseback was superior to a man on foot. I felt that this was the same thing. Without the bike, I was nobody.

This radical chopper made me unique and made me accepted around the Hangmen, the local outlaw warrior class of society. It wasn't just a motorcycle; it was my status and freedom. At least that is how I felt about it.

Eventually, I told my father I was sorry, but I couldn't sell it. It meant too much. I had to pursue this life that I had just tasted and didn't want to let go of.

He sighed with great resignation, shook his head, and sadly said okay. At least I wasn't in Vietnam, but still, he just knew I would get myself killed – or worse, go to prison.

On the 4th of July, it was time for a big run and the Hangmen had invited me to come along. We were going to meet the Hessians for a run out in the desert. I had rebuilt my Panhead even better than before, with new chrome fifteen-inch overstock front fork tubes and a new frame.

The accident had badly bent the other one. I'd had the motor rebuilt because the main shaft had taken a blow. There were also fishtail mufflers and a lovely red paint job from a spray can.

The morning was misty, but already warm. Meeting in the alleyway at Gremlin's and Uncle Tom's apartment building next to Anaheim High School, we roared out in a loud, shiny, long-haired group of about twenty bikes.

In the back of the pack, I was happy to be going along with the big boys. I was riding with the Hangmen again! Life was good. In the back with me was another hang-around, called Sportster Jack (because he rode a Sportster – go figure!).

After gassing up at the corner gas station, we stopped at a light where a young woman was hitchhiking, wearing nothing but a tank top, a pair of Levi's shorts, and sandals. Someone invited her to get on, and she did.

I guess she was going our way because she stayed with us the entire hot journey to Blythe. We hit Highway 91 and headed eastbound.

We traveled through Corona and Riverside, then Highway 60 and, later, Interstate 10 out through the Banning Pass and into the desert just north of

Palm Springs. There were no big wind generators then, and much of today's Interstate 10 was then just a two-lane highway. Today on that road, I pass dilapidated remains of gas stations at which we used to stop and fill up.

The long front ends didn't do much to absorb the bumps in the road as we bounced along on our rigid frames. We stopped every fifty to seventy-five miles for gas because of the small two- or three-gallon tanks.

I never knew anyone who ran the old Harley stock double-sided gas tanks. They were more practical, but we were not interested in that. Besides, we always welcomed any chance to get off those choppers for a while.

We headed into the desert. It got hotter and hotter! In Southern California, there was almost no winter or summer. We rode year-round. However, as we pushed eastward into the desert, we started asking, "Who's stupid fucking idea was this?" This was July in the desert.

It turned out that it was the Hessians' idea, but none of them would cop to being the plan's originator. They were the ones who had decided to go there and they'd invited us along. We rode out separately and met up with them.

As we got close to Blythe, the bugs, grasshoppers, and insects of all kinds started making their presence known. They decorated the fronts of our bikes and our sunglasses with their gooey bodies. It is a vast agricultural area, surrounded by farmland as far as you can see.

Getting into Blythe's outskirts, we motored into town on the two-lane road, now called Hobson Way. We stopped at the first bar we saw because it had not only several Harleys parked out front but a big sign that said,

'Cold Beer.' More importantly, it had an even bigger one that said 'Air Conditioned!'

Feeling like that guy lost in the desert, dying for water, we lined the bikes and crowded into the little bar to cool off. But nobody ordered water. It was beer, beer, and more beer.

Dinner was hamburgers as we enjoyed the air conditioning and cold drinks. However, it didn't take long before an altercation started with a rather drunk local who seemed to take exception to us invading his bar. He exchanged some angry words with some of our guys before he turned and left. Unfortunately, he didn't just go home.

He backed up his old pickup truck and aimed at our line of motorcycles. It seemed that he thought he could mow down the whole line of them, but he made it over only the first three before his truck got stuck, high-centered on the fallen bikes. Suddenly, an entire bar full of enraged bikers was pouring out into the bright desert daylight. He came out of his truck with a baseball bat.

Someone promptly took it away from him and used it to beat him. Also used were several sets of boots and chain belts. Indian Dave and Uncle Tom were among those gently persuading the guy that he should not do something like that. Being a hang-around, I left all of the fun to the patch holders. I could see they didn't need my help.

For a while, I thought they were going to kill him. What worse thing could you do to a biker than hitting his beloved motorcycle? On purpose! He was lucky to survive. When the police got there, we told them that the drunk driver had sustained the injuries due to the crash.

The local sheriff's deputies seemed happy to accept that explanation and carted the guy off in handcuffs. Fortunately, my bike was at the other end of the line from the madman in the pickup truck.

We straightened some handlebars, sissy bars, and footpegs on the damaged bikes as the sun set. We rode in the dark to a prearranged campground. On a dirt road among the farmland and next to the Colorado River, we drank cans of beer from cases bought in town. Then, after the long day's ride, we crashed in our sleeping bags, in the dirt, late in the night.

We spent most of the next day either laying around in the heat at our campsite, swimming in the cold, fast-flowing river, cooling off in the air-conditioned bar, or visiting the Hessians at their camp, underneath the Interstate 10 bridge alongside the river. They were doing target practice by throwing beer cans in the river, then shooting at them as they floated past.

One memorable event involved a Hessian who, after shooting at a can, stuck the gun into his waistband and shot himself in the thigh. He was lucky to miss the femoral artery and other essential items.

After laughing at him, his brothers stuck him in a pickup truck and took him to the hospital to get him patched up.

Not having eaten yet that day, I rode into town by myself to find some grub. Passing the Denny's, I spotted Sportster Jack's bike parked there. After steering my bike into the parking lot, I parked in the space alongside his motorcycle. Walking in, I found Jack sitting in a booth with the hitchhiking girl we'd picked up the day before. I joined them and ordered a cheeseburger. I never did get her name.

After lunch, she climbed on the back of Jack's bike. They headed one way and I went the other, back to the Hangmen campsite. It was a dirt field between the river and the alfalfa crops, shaded by a few salt cedar and cottonwood trees. When I arrived near sundown, it got a little cooler, but not by much. The rest of the night was tolerable, at least temperature-wise.

I began to realize that trouble was afoot. I could hear angry discussions, but had no idea what the problem was. I figured it was none of my business. Soon, I found out that it was.

A couple of the guys had been snorting heroin and who knows what else. They were hopped up with delusions, accusing Sportster Jack and me of taking off with the girl we'd picked up the day before.

Somebody claimed to have seen our bikes parked in front of a local motel. They were assuming that we had taken the girl there. We didn't, or at least I didn't. I couldn't afford a motel room. She didn't belong to anybody, but we were just guests. Running off with her would have been a big mistake.

Unfortunately, Sportster Jack was nowhere around, and neither was the girl. That left me to take all the blame.

Danny was the one who was pissed at me the most. Clark, who was also getting stoned, was right there with him. Both wanted revenge for these hang-arounds running off and fucking 'their' girl. I found out what was going on when they called me into a circle of grim-faced Hangmen near the campfire. I was now the guest of honor on the hot seat to face Danny.

I had just turned eighteen a week before. By now, it was quite dark in this very isolated spot, miles from town, right next to the Colorado River. Surrounded by all the Hangmen, Danny confronted me about running off with the girl.

Confused, I told him I didn't know what he was talking about. However, the more I denied it, the madder he got.

The interrogation went on for a while when, finally, he calmly said, "Okay," then handed me a chain belt, a chromed Harley primary chain laced into a leather belt that could be worn and used as a weapon. Puzzled, I thought at first that he was rewarding me with a gift for telling the truth. I took it and was about to thank him when he said, "I want you to hit me with this… If you can."

I was pretty naive and taken by surprise when he started swinging at me. He connected with the first punch, which didn't faze me. I tossed the chain belt off to the side and started backing up, blocking, ducking, and dodging, knowing better than to hit back at a patch holder. If I had, they all would have been on me.

Although it seemed like an eternity, after probably just a couple of minutes of 'Rope a Dope,' not expending much energy, I had nowhere to go and could not fight back, as I knew what would happen if I did.

Scuffling feet created a cloud of dust, like a fog. The glowing campfire illuminated it with shafts of light and shadows. I started to wonder if I was going to make it out of this.

Out in the middle of nowhere, with that fast-flowing Colorado River close by and my bright, shiny Harley sitting parked under the trees, there was too much incentive for me to disappear. I was desperately trying to stay alive.

Maneuvering behind me with his Bowie knife to get an angle to stab me in the back, just in case I was stupid enough to throw a punch, was Clark. Gentleman Jim had walked up to him and quietly said, "You don't need that. Put it away."

In the dark periphery around the dust-choked melee, I had three allies in this one-sided fight: Uncle Tom, Lurch, and Gentleman Jim. Sometime during this scuffle, Uncle Tom yelled, "Come on, Danny, you know you're wrong!"

This immediately started a shoving and shouting match among themselves about how a brother is never wrong. I was left off to the side by myself, thankful to be ignored for a while. Trying to stay calm, I racked my brain for a plan.

Danny may have been happy for the break, as he was panting, totally out of breath from the exertion of trying to hit me.

Finally, after much arguing among themselves, Danny called me back to the campfire. As I reluctantly came front and center, he yelled, "Where is that chain belt?"

"I don't know. I dropped it."

"Find it!" he demanded.

Searching around in the dark, I finally located it as a hint of light from the fire reflected off the chromed links.

Picking it up, I walked back to the group of Hangmen. It felt like when your father made you cut a switch so he could whip you with it.

Only this could be much worse.

I took a deep breath and held it out to Danny, thinking, 'Here we go again.'

He took it. I was ready to throw up my guard again, and I probably ducked when he threw his arm around my shoulders and said, "Okay, I believe you."

Just like that, it was over.

The crowd of Hangmen dispersed, talking among themselves as if nothing had happened.

A few minutes later, standing in the dark by myself, I was trying to get my bearings, almost surprised that I was still alive.

Gentleman Jim came over and, handing me a can of cold beer, elbowed me in the shoulder. Smiling with that twinkle in his eye, he said, "If you had gone down, I would've had to kick you, but I'd have done it lightly." Then he laughed and walked away.

That was Jim, charming as always.

As I grabbed the pull tab to open the beer can, I suddenly realized how dry my mouth was. Putting the can to my lips and tipping it up, I drank almost the whole thing in one guzzling pull.

You might wonder why I would continue to hang around these guys after an incident like this. Maybe they were just testing me to see what I would do, but there was never any explanation.

I was still enthralled with the whole image of the club and the lifestyle. Despite what had just happened, the fact that I had friends who stood up for me made a huge difference.

It gave me a sense of brothers having my back. They saved me from a bad situation. I already felt like I belonged.

Six weeks later, my father died of cancer.

Mark and Barry. Photo by T.F. Pugh

Chapter 6
Falling in Love

Early in 1970, I hung out at my buddy Mark's upstairs apartment in Anaheim. We spent a lot of time getting stoned and listening to Led Zeppelin or Grand Funk Railroad on his stereo. One night, his Ol' Lady, Linda, had a neighbor over, a cute little redhead named Sheri. We started talking.

It turned out she was married and miserable, wanting to leave her husband and go back to her hometown of Tacoma, Washington, with her one-year-old baby. We saw each other on the sly several times. She had a plan. If she went back to Tacoma, would I come up and live with her?

I had nothing keeping me in So.Cal., so I said, "Sure, why not?" I was still eighteen years old, and I think she was too. When she got to Tacoma, she would send me an address, and I could come up, move in with her, and… well, we didn't make any plans after that.

We were both very young, but we thought we were grown up. A couple of weeks went by. I was still enjoying the exciting life of hanging around the Hangmen. Then I got a letter from her with the address of a duplex apartment she had rented. I wrote her back, telling her I was on my way,

The longest ride I had been on was to Ensenada, Mexico with some other loners, not long after I got the Harley in 1968. Next had been the trip to Blyth the year before with the Hangmen.

Leaving behind everyone and everything and heading into the unknown should have involved more thinking and planning, but I guess that wasn't my style. I decided to go, and I did.

I wore my riding gear, the only clothes I took, packed my sleeping bag and toothbrush, said my goodbyes to everyone, and told them I would see them whenever.

Moving out of the occasional residence on my mother's couch in her one-bedroom apartment in Los Alamitos, I hit the road into the unknown.

Interstate 5 northbound was the Santa Ana Freeway in Orange County. Then I went up through the middle of Los Angeles. I was lucky, as traffic was light and I kept moving. Going up over the Grapevine early in the day was no problem. It was April and already warming up.

With good weather, it was a pleasant ride up Highway 99. Some Hangmen had told me that Gentleman Jim just moved to Modesto, which was on my way north. I planned to stop there and maybe get a couch or a floor for the night at someone's house.

Nobody gave me a phone number for Jim or anybody else in Modesto. They just said he wouldn't be hard to find. "If you go to the Classic Cat strip club, they're always there."

After four or five gas stops in the small towns lining 99, I arrived in Modesto at about eight o'clock at night and found the bar with no problem.

There were no other bikes in the parking lot as I backed mine in, threw out my kickstand, and went inside. Not seeing any Hangmen patches or bikers, I asked around with the waitresses. Yes, they all knew him, but no, they didn't know how to get a hold of him or any of his crew.

They said if I waited a while, he might show up. So, I picked a table by myself and spent some of the little money I had on a beer. I nursed it for an hour or so, having to endure watching pretty girls dancing naked, but that was okay; I could handle it.

I hoped that one of the waitresses or dancers would volunteer to take me home, but that was too much to hope for. Besides, I never asked. Maybe that would have helped.

I got one more beer and nursed it for another hour, still enjoying the scenery. It was almost eleven o'clock. I wasn't getting anywhere, so I decided to saddle up and go north again.

After another hour riding up 99, I stopped at an all-night gas station in a town called Lodi. The attendant came over while I was pumping gas and admired my bike. I got all the usual questions. "Did you build this?"

"Yes."

"Where are you from?"

"Down south."

"Where are you going?"

"North."

It had been a long first day, and I was ready to call it quits, so I asked him, "Is there any place to camp around here?"

I began to learn that those were the magic words. If someone was inclined to offer you anything, that would usually do it.

The attendant said, "No, but if you need to get some sleep, you can climb into the back of that U-Haul truck right there and crash. I'll be here all night, and I'll watch your bike."

Thanking him, I happily unstrapped my sleeping bag from the sissy bar, threw it in the back of the truck, closed the door, kicked off my boots, climbed into the bag, rolled up my leather jacket for a pillow, and went to sleep.

Or maybe it was more like passing out. The last thing I remember was the words to the Creedence Clearwater song echoing in my head: 'Oh Lord, stuck in Lodi again.'

Waking bleary-eyed in the morning, I emerged from the back of the truck, long hair hanging in my face. I proceeded to bungee cord my sleeping bag back onto the sissy bar.

A different guy came out of the office and said, "Hey, nice bike. The all-night guy told me you were in there, so we've been keeping an eye on your scooter. We've got some coffee going. Ya want some?"

Not having had any dinner, I said, "You bet!" They had donuts too. The coffee and a free doughnut were quite a feast.

This friendliness from strangers was the first I learned of the 'rules of the road' as a solitary biker. Not only were a lot of people interested in you, but they also wanted to help in any way they could. It was a constant thing that I was to find repeatedly as I rode from state to state. I was always amazed at how friendly people could be.

I came to realize this only later on, but in the late '60s, Hollywood had started making biker movies. Of course, it started with The Wild One with Marlon Brando in 1953, but it continued after Hunter Thompson's book Hell's Angels in 1966 and all the press coverage bikers were getting, most of it bad,

Hollywood took notice. Almost all were low-budget films. It's fun to watch them now on YouTube. Some of the movies were not that bad, and they're a great way to see real old-school bikes. Many people had seen these films. It was part of American culture at the time.

The year was now 1970, and both Easy Rider and Hell's Angels '69 had come out the year before. They were pretty big hits.

Then there was the television show Then Came Bronson, which had been out for about six months. Now here I was, from out of town, a long-haired biker on a radical-looking chopper with a California license plate.

Perhaps they – at least the small-town people I met – thought I was like someone in those movies. I was in no way trying to pretend to be anything, Hollywood or otherwise. I was using the only mode of transportation I had and being who I was, but I think the friendly small-town folks I met along the road saw more than that. Perhaps I reminded them of those bikers in the movies and on T.V., but I was there in real life. It wasn't so much me, of course, just the image that they saw.

I could be wrong; that's just my impression. Probably they were just nice people and didn't need a reason.

At the very least, people were curious about me and always seemed interested in the bike. Every time it happened, I was surprised at how friendly and generous strangers could be. I had never been out on my own like this before, and it was a pleasant surprise.

Traveling on very little money requires some creativity. I learned a few tricks from some of the Hangmen. As a farewell gift, they had given me a couple of stolen gas credit cards: one Shell and one Texaco.

Our tanks held only about two and a half gallons at that time. So, we'd pull in and get two gallons of gas at forty cents a gallon – eighty cents total. This was when they would rack the card through that machine. For a buck, nobody would run a credit card to see if it was hot.

They had to make a phone call to do that, probably long-distance. Sometimes you could ask for ten dollars cash back and put it on the card. Then you could get something to eat.

Still, that was not a big deal. If you were charging one hundred dollars' worth of tires on a car, that might be a different story.

For years on and off, I traveled that way. Only once did a gas station attendant call and check the card. When it came back bad, he said, "This card is no good. I'm going to have to keep it."

I shrugged and said, "Damn, my father must not have paid the bill." I jumped on the kick-starter and rode off. I had more.

Back then, you didn't have fast food on every corner in every town in America, so most places where you could get something to eat were diners. I also learned from Gremlin that if you went into a coffee shop and asked for two cups of hot water, pulled a tea bag out of your pocket, and put it into one cup of water, you'd have tea.

If you took a bottle of ketchup and poured it into the other cup, you'd have tomato soup. It wasn't the best, but it was edible. Add some crackers that were available off the counter, and you had a meal, and it was all free. They wouldn't charge you for the hot water.

It wasn't like you were a bum or homeless, even though technically I was. Instead, you were a traveler on a motorcycle. It was a different dynamic altogether. Usually, the waitress would just look at you and shake her head, but frequently, the waitress or the diner's owner would feel sorry for you and give you a free hamburger or sandwich.

Sometimes that worked, but at the very least, you got some 'tomato soup' and tea. When you were hungry enough, that was a pretty good deal.

Day two on the road, I left Lodi after the free breakfast of one doughnut and coffee and pointed north on I-5 again. I was surprised at how warm it was in Redding, way north in the state. I was expecting it to cool off, and it did later as I came abeam Mount Shasta.

Having spent most of my young life in Florida and then Southern California, I had seen the San Angeles Mountains occasionally topped with snow, but that was only when the smog cleared out enough for me to see them.

I was impressed with Mount Shasta, so I pulled to the side of the highway and took a picture of my bike with that snowy backdrop. That was the only picture I took on that whole northbound trip. Guess I was kind of in a hurry.

When I crossed over the Oregon border, a little north of Grants Pass, it started to rain. Of course, it did; it was Oregon. To a motorcycle rider, rain presents all kinds of problems. The road gets wet and sometimes brings oil to the surface. Both the water and the oil reduce traction. Traction is always necessary for any vehicle. On a motorcycle, it is critical!

Getting wet means getting cold. Even on a hot day, it is surprising how cold you feel once you get wet. On a cold day, it is even worse. The accelerated air creates wind chill, which turns uncomfortable into intolerable.

Probably the worst is visibility – being seen and, more important-ly, seeing. No glasses at all creates obvious problems. Raindrops in the eyeballs at seventy miles per hour make seeing a challenge, and it hurts, feeling like stinging needles in the face.

In the eyes, it's even worse. A pair of sunglasses, which was my choice at the time, helps. However, raindrops build up on them, blurring and distorting what little vision you have left while you try to keep yourself safe in the middle of your lane, not hitting anyone and hopefully not getting hit.

By this time, it was late in the day, about six o'clock, and starting to get dark. I had been riding for eight hours with numerous gas stops. It was time to look for a burrow to crawl into for the night.

Getting tired of being cold and wet, I saw a sign that said Canyonville, so I pulled into a small, ancient-looking town with buildings that looked like they could be used in an old Western movie if it wasn't for the paved street.

I pulled up and parked the bike at no place in particular. It had a wooden sidewalk with a covered porch. I just wanted to get out of the cold rain and the chill of the wind. Standing on the sidewalk under the porch, I was shivering and soaking wet, but happy to be off the bike.

I was trying to decide what to do next when a guy walked out of the door of the general store behind me. He was about thirty-five years old and wore a blue apron. He said, "Hello."

"Hello yourself."

"A little wet out. Nice bike. Where are you from?"

We chatted, I answered his questions, and then I said, "I need to dry out. Where I could spend the night? Is there a campground near here?"

"No need for that," he said, poking his thumb over his shoulder. "I own this store. My family and I live upstairs. It used to be a hotel, and there are extra rooms. You can stay here tonight. We'll put your bike in the back."

I couldn't believe it. I never expected this kind of hospitality from strangers, especially to a biker, but I had a lot to learn. This kind of generosity turned out to be more common than not. He had a wife and three small kids, and he trusted me, a wild-looking stranger, to stay in their home for the night.

I thought, 'This guy is insane, but I'll keep that to myself.'

The walls of the room were old, dark wood panels – real wood. The room's brass lamps looked like they belonged in an antique shop, and there were glass doorknobs on the door. The bathroom was down the hall.

The one window looked out onto the rain-soaked roof of the building next door. In the distance, low clouds were merging with the thick pine forests of the surrounding mountains.

I figured that the building was close to one hundred years old. The bed had a metal frame, and the floor was that same dark wood, worn smooth from many years of guests. I was about to spend the night in a room, in a bed! For free!

I unrolled my sleeping bag, which I covered with a military poncho to keep it dry at times like this. I carried some spare clothes and tools, so I changed into my extra pair of jeans, a T-shirt, and dry socks.

I had just placed my wet boots on the windowsill over the heater when there was a polite knock on my door. My host asked me to join them for dinner.

Still not believing my luck as I walked down the hallway in my socks and dry clothes, I joined them in their kitchen dining area.

After eating a fantastic homemade meal of beef stew and hot, fresh-baked bread with gobs of melted butter, I sat at the table and answered questions from the whole family, mostly the kids.

"What's it like in California?"

"Are you an Outlaw?"

"Are the police looking for you?"

"Do you know Jack Nicholson?"

After dinner, I peeled off the T-shirt and my clean pair of jeans. The springs squeaked in the old bed as I snuggled under the covers and thick blanket. It was warm and dry in the old hotel. What an unexpected pleasure.

The next morning, I woke to the smell of cooking bacon and coffee. As soon as I walked out of my room, the wife stuck her head out the door and hollered down the hallway, practically ordering me to come and sit down. Breakfast was ready. Who was I to argue?

An hour later, when I was packed up and backing my bike out of the storeroom at the back of the store, my host handed me a brown paper grocery bag with a loaf of white Wonder Bread and a jar of Skippy peanut butter. I think they were just barely getting by with that little store. I was humbled that they had taken me in and fed me two meals and that now he was giving me a going-away present that could keep me fed for days.

I accepted the simple gift with much gratitude. This was just the beginning of my newfound faith in mankind, especially Americans. What was it about taking care of strange travelers? Or traveling strangers? Was it the bike that inspired that kind of curiosity and generosity and friendship?

I found out much later that it is more like an ancient worldwide tradition in many cultures around the planet. Perhaps a kind of quid pro quo: 'If I take care of you now, you may take care of me later.'

Day three. Blue sky, no rain, life was good. Oregon was uneventful other than beautiful, forested mountains on both sides of the lush, tree-lined highways. It was such a difference from busy, crowded Southern California and the vast expanses of farmland and ranches in the San Joaquin Valley. Just gas stops and more slogging up the asphalt and concrete slab of I-5 North.

But I didn't mind. It was a new adventure and I was traveling on my motorcycle, the future uncertain. There was nowhere else I wanted to be. I spent hours cruising up the interstate, sunglasses, and gloves as my only protective gear. The weather was nice and my leather jacket was rolled up and strapped onto the front forks. My long hair flew in the wind as I leaned back on the sleeping bag tied to my sissy bar. My feet were kicked out on the forward pegs. The bike was comfortable. I could go for hours and I did, day after day.

Having crossed into the state of Washington several hours ago, late in the afternoon I was passing through the town of Olympia, the state's capital. I was cruising along, minding my own business, when suddenly a pickup truck pulled up beside me. The driver, with long hair, a beard, and aviator sunglasses, started honking his horn and gesturing, pointing to the side of the highway. I thought, 'What did I do to piss this guy off?'

Searching my recent memory, I came up with zero. What could he want? I just shook my head and waved him away, like 'no thanks, never mind, go away. I don't need what you're selling.' But he wouldn't give up. He kept yelling and pointing, so I finally pulled to the side of the freeway, not knowing what to expect.

When we stopped, his truck in front of me, he jumped out and ran back toward me. Oh shit, he was a big guy! Lean and lanky, about six-foot-five! I threw my kickstand down, left my gloves on, and jumped off the bike, trying to get ready for action. When he got up to me, I could finally understand what he was saying. It was something like, "My brother and I both ride Harleys. Where are you from? Where are you going?" He had seen the California plate. "Here's my phone number. We gotta get together and ride, man!"

His name was Larry, and he was so excited to see a chopper from California up there in Washington State. We chatted a bit alongside the noisy interstate. I answered some of his questions and he gave me his phone number. I didn't think I'd call, but I took it just to get rid of him. Pretty soon, he was on his way, and so was I.

It was only another hour or so to Tacoma. It had been three long days, and I was anxious for my journey to be over. Later that night, I pulled up at Sheri's rented duplex. It was nice to get off the bike and stay off it for a while. I took my sleeping bag, the jar of peanut butter, and a squashed loaf of Wonder Bread off the bike and moved in.

The reunion with her was beautiful, sensual, and magical... in between the wails of her baby.

Chapter 7
Life in Washington

The honeymoon with Sheri was great, and it lasted about a week. I'm not sure what she expected of me. To settle down, help raise her child, get a job, and support them? Live happily ever after? That might have been a wonderful life for someone else, but, sorry, 'It Ain't Me Babe!'

I was the wrong guy for that. The truth was, I had not thought about it either. What was I going to do? Especially after the freedom of the open road on my trip up there. She was cute and sweet, but the idea of being tied down to a job and a family was second only to my desire to die and go to hell. At the ripe old age of eighteen, I had been on my own for several years, as I had dropped out of high school about halfway through the tenth grade.

Things were getting a bit testy in the little duplex on Kitsap Circle in Tacoma. Remembering Larry down in Olympia, who had stopped me on the interstate, I called his number, and he said to "come on down!" So, on a Friday afternoon when he was getting off from work at the auto parts store, I met him there. Sure enough, he was riding his custom chopped Harley.

I followed him a couple of miles through Olympia to his home on the shore of the inlet outside of town. It was a rather old but very homey wooden home surrounded by big trees on one side and water on the other. It was beautiful. His brother Steve was there. Steve also had a Harley, and the three of us hit it off right away. It didn't hurt that they liked to drink beer too. We proceeded to ride around town to their friends' houses, mostly people who also rode. They wanted to show off their new friend from California on a bike like theirs. After being cooped up in Tacoma, I didn't mind. I was having a great time riding and meeting new people.

Back at Larry's house, and after a few more beers, he said he had a spare bedroom if I wanted to spend the night. His pretty, slender, blonde wife didn't mind, so I said why not, since it was getting late. I called Sheri and told her I would be back in the morning. But one thing led to another, and I wasn't back in the morning. Saturday stretched into Sunday as Larry, his brother, and I kept thinking of things to do and places to go on our bikes. I finally got back 'home' Sunday night.

It didn't take long for Sheri and me to agree to part ways. It was painfully obvious that we had widely diverging visions of the future. I was aware of no vision for my future. I was just having fun riding my motorcycle and being free. Falling in love with a cute girl and having fun was nice, for a while.

Settling down and staying put? Uh... NO! My total stay in Tacoma was about six weeks. About a third of that time was spent down with the boys in Olympia. Soon, I packed my sleeping bag onto my sissy bar, put on my sunglasses, and moved out.

Before heading south to California, I spent a week in Larry's spare bedroom. At night, I tried to sleep as Larry made love to his not only beautiful but very vocal wife. This made it rather hard to sleep. Soon, it was a weekend and they were off work, so Larry, Steve, and I hit the road again. Taking off for another trip on the bikes, heading west out of Tacoma, we picked up Highway 101.

Then we turned south until the town of Raymond, where 101 points west until we hit the coast, and then south again through towns like

Bruceport, Nemah, and Chinook. We motored through lush evergreen forests, sometimes with the water off to our right, literally within feet of the side of the highway.

Another hour south, we rode through more beautiful country and more small towns and communities until we arrived at Cannon Beach, our destination. We were able to ride our motorcycles right out onto the hard-packed beach sand. That was great fun until we were surprised to see a police car behind us with its one red light on.

We had missed the signs. It turns out the speed limit on the beach was only fifteen miles per hour, and we were quite a bit over that. All three of us got speeding tickets. As I was using a fake driver's license, I never paid the ticket.

Caught speeding on the beach.

After hamburgers for dinner at a bar and grill, we bought a couple of six-packs of beer and headed for a campsite on a beach they knew, where we built a big bonfire out of the plentiful driftwood. Then we took some psychedelic they had brought, which caused me to almost panic all night, as I worried about the tide coming in and swamping our bikes and us in our sleeping bags.

I don't remember getting much sleep, but Larry and Steve kept reassuring me that the tide would not come in that far. I was not convinced, but the next morning, it turned out they were right. I couldn't believe it. We were still high and dry.

Steve and the author on the beach in Oregon.

Washington to California.

Back in Olympia, for my planned trip south, Larry and the boys wanted to throw a going-away party. They had already planned it, so it was hard to say no. About a dozen friends came over. Most were people I had met at some point.

Larry cooked hamburgers on the grill, and we drank beer, although I had only a few because I planned to leave that night. There would be fewer cops on the road and less traffic. Finally, as it was getting dark, after saying goodbyes, I pointed my long front end south on Interstate 5 at about six o'clock in the evening and settled into the ride.

Other than getting back to Southern California, I had no plan. Somewhere during a gas stop, I pulled out my map and decided to do something different. I wanted to get off the interstate and ride down the coast again like we had the week before. I wanted to ride along the beaches and through the redwoods.

At Grants Pass, after my second gas stop, I cut west on Highway 199. It was well past midnight. Traveling at night was less of a hassle in some ways: less traffic, fewer cops. The downside was the greater chance for close encounters with wildlife like deer, and in some places, elk or even bear.

I tried to be prepared for that possibility, staying as alert as possible for ambush attacks by critters. However, what I had not planned on was fewer gas stations being open off the interstate.

Two hours down the winding forested Highway 199 in the dark, I had crossed back into California. I was heading toward the coastal town of Crescent City. I knew I needed gas, so as soon as I reached civilization, I pulled into the small town of Hiouchi. Not surprisingly, in the middle of the night, the only gas station in the whole village was closed. Not wanting to run out of gas on a dark, curving road in the forest with no shoulder, I stopped next to the pumps and threw out my kickstand.

The sign on the door said they would open at 6:00 AM, so I sat down with my back against my bike, pulled my knees up, rested my head on my arms, and prepared to wait, trying to get some sleep.

I might have been there for an hour meditating when I heard a vehicle pull up next to me. Lifting my head, I could see, in the soft blue light of dawn, two guys sitting in an old Chevy pickup with a grey primer paint job. They were looking at me. Not knowing what they wanted, I just stared back.

Finally, the driver said, "You need gas?"

"Yes."

"We've got some gas cans at our place. Follow us, and we'll fill you up."

Glancing at my watch, I saw that it was not yet five o'clock. Another hour to go, so I said, "Okay."

I felt stiff as I got up, zipped up my jacket, pulled on my gloves, and kicked over my bike. They peeled out of the gas station, and I followed them, wondering what I had gotten myself into.

I didn't have much time to come up with many possible scenarios when they pulled off Highway 199 onto a dirt road winding through the redwood forest. Oh well, too late to back out now.

I followed them until they pulled off into a large, rock-covered driveway in front of a log cabin in a clearing. Swinging out my kickstand and turning off the key, I stepped off as they practically fell out of the pickup truck. I could tell they had been drinking, probably all night long.

I covertly slid my U.S. Army bayonet, razor-sharp in its G.I.-issued fiberglass sheath, out of my sleeping bag and into the back of my pants. It was my only weapon other than my fists or my smaller Buck knife.

One of them came stumbling over to me and said, "Wow, nice bike. Where are you from? Where are you going?" As we made small talk, the other guy emerged from the old wooden one-car garage with a five-gallon gas can. Five gallons was more than enough.

Standing on the crunching gravel of the driveway, we chatted in the pale blue pre-dawn light filtering through the vast forest of redwood trees as I filled my tank.

When it was full, I said, "What do I owe you?"

The taller one said, "Ah, don't worry about it. Hey, do you like trout?"

I was not much of a fish person, but I said, "Yeah, I guess."

"We caught a bunch of trout yesterday and still have a lot left over in the fridge. Would you like to join us for breakfast?"

My stomach growled at the mention of food, so I said, "Sure, why not?"

Still hiding my G.I. bayonet in the back of my pants, I followed them into the cabin, where we spent the next hour sitting around their kitchen table. They put yesterday's trout into the oven to warm it up on a big plate under tin foil.

I was surprised at how good the fish tasted. It was a surreal atmosphere as I sat there with a couple of strangers, drinking cold Coors out of a can and eating fresh trout in a place I never expected to find myself in.

The old cabin was toasty warm as we sat at an oak table. A dying fire in a stone fireplace smoldered nearby in the living room. The slanting morning sun was trying to break through the tall redwoods outside the window.

They talked about their fishing adventures from the day before, how one of them had fallen in the river and nearly drowned when his waders filled with water. The other one had saved him.

Their stories progressed to their heroic drinking exploits from the previous night, with plenty of laughter and embellishment.

You had to have been there to understand. They were so enthralled with their adventures that they didn't ask any more about my travels.

That was fine with me. I happily ate their trout and drank their beer. Free breakfast and free gas. I couldn't help but smile behind my beard. Life, for the moment, seemed perfect.

A full gas tank and a full belly, a little tipsy after three cans of beer, at six-thirty in the morning: It was a strange way to start the day, even for me.

Finally, I was saying goodbye to my new friends, whom I would never see again. I never even got their names. With a final wave goodbye, I whacked the jockey shifter into first gear and popped the foot clutch, throwing gravel behind me as I shot out of the rock-covered driveway. I marveled at the friendliness and generosity of strangers while also wondering about my suspicion and lack of trust.

I figured that this was still day one, given that I hadn't slept yet. I followed Highway 199 to Crescent City on the coast of California, then turned south on 101. It appeared that the sun was up, but the low marine layer kept a lot of the light out in the misty morning.

The morning was still a soft blue as the highway wound out ahead of me along the beaches and through the redwood forests. With hardly any traffic and no cops, I cruised effortlessly through the deep, dark woods, passing through small towns with names like Klamath, Orick, and Big Lagoon.

Beach, forest, beach, forest, repeat. Right on the coast, sometimes foggy – it was like a dream. The Simon and Garfunkel song "Scarborough Fair" played in my head for some reason. By then, I was getting tired, and the beer had not helped. I was afraid I would fall asleep, and it really would be a dream – a permanent one.

At about eight-thirty, I found a dirt road leading from the highway into the forest. Off-roading on choppers is something we did routinely. We weren't afraid to take them anywhere. Either you could ride, or you couldn't.

After I steered that long front end off the highway, with my butt bouncing on the rigid frame up a dirt road, the pathway turned into a single-track trail about a quarter mile from the main road.

I followed the single-track a few hundred yards more, then pulled off the path and parked in a Garden of Eden with towering redwood trees all around and lush ferns with soft mossy ground cover padded by eons of decaying vegetation.

It was peaceful, tranquil, and relatively dark, deep down under the canopy of all those trees.

Throwing my sleeping bag down over my military poncho for a moisture barrier, I took off my boots and snuggled into the bag on the soft forest floor. It was like a mattress. I got in the bag and pulled it up over my head. Instantly, I was in dreamland.

I wish I could say I slept like every other log in that forest, but it was not to be.

Not long after drifting off, I heard the sounds of people coming up the trail. I was annoyed, as I didn't want to be bothered. I could hear their footsteps and them talking.

Huddling inside my sleeping bag, I hoped they would not see me, which was not likely. Or maybe they would just pass by and leave me alone. No such luck. I listened as the hikers spotted me lying next to my motorcycle. They stopped. I heard their angry voices, and suddenly they rushed to attack me.

I came up out of my bag, yelling and stabbing with my old G.I.-issue bayonet, only to find that no one was there. The forest was empty and silent except for the idiot biker who could not seem to sleep quietly.

Tree squirrels and blue jays stared at this foreign invader that must have seemed to them like he was from outer space, or maybe he had just lost his mind. They were probably wondering when he would leave their peaceful forest so it could get back to normal. They're probably still talking about it.

I kept having the same nightmare. After the third rude awakening, not just for me but also for the forest inhabitants, I decided to pack up and head down the road again. It was about noon when I hit pavement and turned south.

After I passed through Eureka, Highway 101 turned inland, still curving and winding through the hills and mountains, heading for San Francisco. It was a great ride. The temperature got warmer as I traveled southbound.

I lost track of the gas stops, and both lunch and dinner were something out of a vending machine. After passing through Santa Rosa, I got to the Golden Gate Bridge at about rush hour, five o'clock.

For a long time, I had been looking forward to riding across the Golden Gate Bridge. Now, finally, the long-awaited opportunity came.

It sucked! Traffic was heavy, the wind was blowing hard off the ocean, coming in from right to left, and it was foggy. What I didn't realize was that the bridge moved. It was swaying in the wind. This was not what I had expected.

Traffic was running fast and tight, so I had to keep up. The lanes were narrow, and there was no shoulder. There was a divider in the middle, and a fence on the right to protect the pedestrian walkway, so there was no place to stop if you had a mechanical problem or ran out of gas. You don't want to be a roadblock on a bike. Some car drivers didn't seem afraid of concrete barriers, so why would a little motorcycle stop them?

The fog was coming in, so visibility was about one-quarter mile, and the bridge was swaying left to right. There I was, flying along at about seventy miles per hour in tight, fast traffic, with low visibility on a moving platform.

It was not fun, and I couldn't wait for it to be over. Being shoved back and forth by the wind gusts and let-offs, I had to fight to stay in my lane. After about ten minutes of that, finally, I was on the other side. I am sure the local bikers who ride across that bridge think it is no big deal, but it was a new and unexpected experience.

Passing the old fort and the Presidio, I entered San Francisco. I'd never been there before. After days of nothing but two-lane highways and small towns, Highway 101 spat me out right into the middle of downtown.

There is nothing flat about San Francisco, except perhaps the transvestite strippers. Maybe not even that. Certainly not the taxes. The city is charming, with that big city mix of both ancient and new buildings. From a distance, it looks clean and shining. Up close, not so much.

And the hills! Stopping at red lights and stop signs, which appear every one hundred feet or so, it seems you are always pointed either uphill or downhill. In these conditions, riding a bike with a suicide foot clutch and no front brake could be, well... suicide. Maybe San Francisco is where it got the name.

It's challenging. When you stop, you need to have your right foot on the brake and put your left foot down, but the bike must be in neutral before you stop. When you need to put the bike in gear to go, you have to use your left foot to push in the clutch.

But, if you are on a hill, you need to have your right foot on the brake. Choices, choices! And I didn't have a front brake. You have to make a rapid switch from right footbrake and left foot down to left foot-clutch and right foot down before you fall over so that you can get the bike moving.

As I struggled from stoplight to stop sign, I wondered, 'Where are all of the friendly hippies and Hells Angels that I had heard about?' (Friendly Hells Angels?) I was hoping to meet someone I could start a conversation with and maybe find a place to stay for the night. But I didn't know where to look, and no likely suspects seemed to be around. I kept riding.

The official motto of San Francisco is The Truth Shall Set You Free. I don't know about that, but I thought fewer hills and stoplights would be a good start at setting me free.

Highway 101 takes you right through the middle of the city and not in a straight line. If you miss any of the '101 South' signs for the turns, which I did, you'll get lost, which I did. A couple of times. I had to stop, park the bike, and ask for directions.

Asking about a place to camp in the middle of a city seemed like a silly idea, so I didn't. And people in San Francisco didn't seem to be very friendly. I tried my best to be sociable, but it didn't do any good. I wasn't good at it, so I kept moving.

Eventually, I reconnected with the signs that said 101 South. I was glad to have survived 'The City' and to be accelerating out of second gear for the first time in an hour or more. It was getting late, and the sun was off my right elbow as I found my way on 101 with the San Francisco Bay at my left elbow.

I passed Candlestick Park, also on my left. A short while later, I passed San Francisco Airport, where you had to be careful. A Boeing 747 might be taking off and blow you right off the freeway.

Later, I drove through San Mateo, San Carlos, Redwood City, and, finally, Palo Alto and San Jose, all with heavy traffic. Fortunately, it was not stop and go, but it was still crowded, slow, and tedious. Very tiring.

South of San Jose, the roads and the traffic thinned out and the speeds got back to normal as the scenery turned to the farm country of Morgan Hill, Saint Martin, and Gilroy. It was dark by this time, and I kept motoring south, not knowing where to stop and not wanting to go on.

Since having gotten up the morning of the day before and leaving Olympia the evening before, I'd had just a little bit of fitful sleep in the redwood forest. The long ride through the night and the tension of the Golden Gate Bridge and the maze through the streets of San Francisco had exhausted me.

Fatigue was chasing me like a pack of police cars. I tried to pretend they were not there, but I was losing that battle. The later it got, and the farther I went, the heavier my eyelids became. At about eleven o'clock, the fatigue was so bad that I started hallucinating. I was seeing strange naked humanoid creatures scurrying on all fours across the highway in front of me.

I thought I had left them back in San Francisco. It was like they were tempting me to hit them. More than once, I swerved or slammed on my rear brake, trying to avoid these apparitions.

Eventually, I realized that I was going to have to either stop and offer a ride to these demons or pull off and get some sleep. I was in the area of King City, California at about midnight when I decided to find a place to pull off and call it a day – or two.

There were no gas stations open where I could ask, "Where can I camp around here?"

It had been easy to find a place to sleep up in the redwoods in Northern California, but down in this relatively civilized farmland of the central coast, there were lots of fences with gates and lots of no trespassing and private property signs. In the middle of the night, and with me being dead tired, it didn't seem so simple. There were no public lands, national forests, or campgrounds around. Forget paying for a motel room with the money I didn't have.

I took an offramp at random in the darkness of the farmlands, far from the nearest town. Turning right onto a paved road, I followed it until it turned to dirt and started winding uphill. Before long, I found myself in some oil fields. I was never one to sleep in the open alongside a highway or in a rest stop, as I always felt too vulnerable for that.

Maybe it was just a lack of trust, and I had a lot of that. I was winding my way up into the hills with my headlight being the only light under the cloudy night sky. Finally, coming onto a wide, flat lot near an oil pumper, I pulled in, shut down, threw out the kickstand, and was home for the night. It was dark and quiet. The oil rig was not running. Nobody was around.

I threw down my cotton drug store sleeping bag, pulled off my boots, rolled up my jacket for a pillow, and climbed in.

I was out like a light.

There were no bad dreams this time. After what seemed like minutes later, but had to have been hours, a horn started honking from far away. It got closer until my brain struggled into consciousness. Poking my head out of the bag, I saw that the pitch-black night had changed into a low overcast gray dawn.

A pickup truck parked about thirty feet away. There were markings on the door. The driver was an employee of the surrounding oil fields. He was wearing a hard hat, had the windows down, and looked at me as I tried to clear the cobwebs out of my sleepy head.

Damn, they found me. I expected him to say, "What the fuck are you doing? You can't camp here. This is private property!"

Instead, he said, "You want some coffee?"

Not having to think about it, I said, "Sure!"

He hopped out with a large thermos and a paper sack as I sat up, noticing a damp dew covering my sleeping bag.

He poured hot black coffee into a paper cup. Kneeling next to my motorcycle, he handed it to me and asked, "Would you like a donut?"

I said, "Hell yeah, that sounds great."

Reaching into the paper sack, he said, "Five deer were standing next to your bike when I drove up. They wandered off when I honked the horn."

I drank the coffee and munched on what was probably the best donut I had ever tasted in my life.

He admired my motorcycle and asked about my travels. As we chatted in the surreal twilight, I explained where I had been and where I was going. I noticed he was staring off into the fog with a distant look. Then, with a sad smile on his face, he slowly shook his head and said, "Man, I wish I was you."

I thought, 'No you don't,' but I said, "I can't thank you enough for the coffee and donut. I hope nobody minds my camping here."

Screwing the cap back on his thermos as he stood and walked away, he said, "Stay as long as you want. You won't be in anyone's way up here."

He climbed into his truck and, with a wave, disappeared into the foggy gray morning. I laid back down. Despite the caffeine and sugar injection, I was soon fast asleep again.

It must have been three hours later when another honking horn awakened me. Opening my eyes and pulling the sleeping bag from my face, I realized the clouds had burned off, the sun was shining bright, and I was sweating. Looking around for the source, I saw another pickup truck just like the one from earlier, but with a different guy in it.

I fought to focus my eyes as he said, "The guy from the night crew told me you were up here. Would you like some cold water and a sandwich?"

Nodding my head vigorously, I couldn't believe it. What was this, room service? Being that I was now hot and thirsty, cold water sounded terrific.

Like the other guy, he climbed out with a thermos and a paper sack and knelt nearby as I answered his questions, drank his water, and ate what was possibly the best ham and cheese sandwich I had tasted in my life.

After another pleasant visit with my new oil field host, he also told me to stay as long as I liked. I thanked him for all the hospitality, but since it was now mid-morning, I said it was time I got moving.

I thanked him again for the food and water. He just said, "Anytime, buddy. You're more than welcome. Now you have a safe trip." With that, he was off.

I pulled on my motorcycle boots, rolled up my sleeping bag, and bungee corded it to the sissy bar behind me for a comfy backrest. Then I put on my jacket, sunglasses, and gloves. After a couple of kicks, the trusty old Panhead fired up.

I followed the dirt road back downhill, taking in the view of the golden grass on the rolling hills, dotted with patches of oil rigs, and the lush green crops lining the highway down in the valley.

I saw another oil field worker in a different colored truck. Probably having heard about me, he raised his arm in greeting. I waved back.

Turning southbound again on 101, I would be back in Orange County late that night after another long day of riding.

Chapter 8
The Banshee Debacle

While I was hanging out with the boys one Friday night, the So.Cal. chapter had just had their meeting, and the topic of the Banshees motorcycle club had come up. The Banshees were a little start-up club that wanted to pretend they were bikers, but they were just a bunch of punks with a few motorcycles thinking they were big-time simply because they had designed a patch to wear on their backs. They had named their club after a wailing female spirit of Gaelic folklore. Good thinking, you guys!

We were all in Uncle Tom's living room when Gremlin, who was president at the time, called the Banshee president and told him that they were not to try to start a chapter in Orange County. I couldn't hear the other side of the conversation, but the Banshee president told Gremlin to fuck off. Gremlin's answer was, "Okay then, we're on our way."

Not the best way to attack anyone: to tell them that you're coming. An element of surprise is always nice to keep things in your favor.

About fifteen of us jumped into cars and sped away. Remember, the club tried to never take care of business on bikes, wearing cuts. That was for movies and television. I didn't have a patch then, anyway. It was a long drive – about thirty-five to forty minutes – from Anaheim down to Huntington Beach, where these guys were based. Most of them were living together in an apartment complex.

That was our target. The plan was to park in random locations so we could attack them from different directions.

My mind wandered during the ride. I tried to imagine how it might go. Maybe nothing at all would happen. Or maybe the whole thing would turn to shit. I rode in a car with four other guys. One of them was Mark, my old buddy from high school.

Finally, the wait was over. Sliding to a stop at the curb in front of the apartment complex that was ground zero, we bailed out and ran to the sound of the action. Some of our guys had already arrived. Shouts, curses, and noise in general were emanating from the apartments.

Running to find targets of opportunity, Mark and I raced around a corner to see four Banshees standing in a group. As we hurried toward them, they turned to look at us. As we continued our charge, one of them raised a pistol and fired. We kept coming at them as they turned and ran.

Chasing them through the projects, I thought that the shooter had missed. They should have named their club the Rabbits instead of the Banshees because they could run so fast. Shortly after, Mark slowed down and stopped, then grabbed my arm and said, "Hey, man, they shot me."

I said, "Fuck, where are you hit?"

He said, "In the shoulder."

We could hear shouts and thumps and a gunshot or two echoing around the apartment complex. I said, "C'mon, let's get you to a hospital." We started back toward the street where he had parked the car. However, getting to it didn't work out when we ran into several police officers who had just arrived. The one who walked up to us was a plainclothes detective. He told us, "Stop right there, put your hands up, and don't move; I'd give a dollar and a quarter to shoot a fucking biker."

Because about nine cops were pointing guns at us, we put our hands up. The action was over for the night. But Mark could put only one hand up. When they yelled at him to get the other hand up, he told them, "I can't, they shot me." Mark suddenly went from a bad guy to the victim and was treated as such. They called an ambulance and took him to the hospital.

Of course, the rest of us were still the bad guys. We got handcuffed and bundled into police vans that delivered us to the city jail. These assholes, knowing we were coming, had called the cops to save their asses and then run. What a bunch of punks!

Not all of us got rounded up that night. There were two funny stories about brothers who escaped arrest: Hipster and Art.

Hearing sirens getting closer and police radios echoing off the buildings, Hipster knew that the gig was up. He vaulted a concrete block wall at the apartment complex's back. Landing in a dark alleyway, he came upon a parked semi-truck.

Crawling up into the front wheel well, he laid over the front tire, hidden from sight by the front fender. The black clothing he wore turned out to be the right choice for that night. It was good camouflage, plus when the police came searching for escapees with police dogs, the smell of the diesel truck masked his scent. The dogs bypassed him.

He lay in that position for hours until the cops and helicopters with their searchlights had left. That left him to find his way home. It was a long night of hitchhiking back to Anaheim. At least no police cars offered to give him a ride.

Art, the other wayward Hangman, upon seeing cops converging from every direction, decided to give up the mission and run for it – a wise move. Sirens wailed throughout the neighborhood and police helicopters shined searchlights over the apartment complex.

Art ran around a corner into the backyard of the apartments. He stopped when he heard someone quietly calling out to him. "Pssst, pssst."

Looking around, he saw a young boy about twelve years old beckoning to him through an open ground-floor window. "In here," the boy said.

Art could hear cops shouting just around the corner. They were closing fast. He ran to the window and dove through it, luckily landing right on the kid's bed. The kid slammed the window and drew the curtain. Art had vanished as far as the cops were concerned.

He spent the rest of the evening sitting in the kid's bed with him, watching television and eating popcorn. Instead of going to jail or hitchhiking all night long, he slept peacefully through the night.

In the morning, the kid had cartoons on when his mother opened the door and was shocked to see a grown man with long shoulder-length hair and a beard sitting in her son's bed. She seemed to not know if she should scream at her son, scream at Art, or just scream!

Trying to help her out, the kid said, in his little kid's voice, "It's okay, Mom. This is my friend, Art."

She stood there with her mouth open, not knowing what to do. Already fully dressed, Art pulled on his boots and, after the kid and Art did the new handshake that Art had taught him, Art quickly said goodbye to his new buddy. Then he smiled at the mother as he squeezed past her into the hallway.

He heard the beginning of the lecture behind him as he calmly walked out the front door, leaving the kid to do the explaining.

As for the rest of us, we all got packed off to jail. Some of the Banshees got arrested, and the cops were smart enough to keep the two groups separated. The Huntington Beach Police Department deposited all the Hangmen into a large holding cell.

There were no bunks or chairs, just a concrete floor. It was probably the drunk tank at the HBPD jail. They were nice enough to leave us handcuffed behind our backs.

Not knowing how long they planned to leave us this way, I decided, "The hell with this." Pulling my hands underneath my butt, then my feet,

I got my handcuff key out of its secret hiding place in my belt and took mine off. Naturally, everyone else wanted theirs off too.

Shortly, a pile of handcuffs sat by the door while we lounged in relative comfort. Late in the evening, an officer unlocked the door and came into the room with papers in his hand, expecting to find us all handcuffed. He walked in confident and arrogant until he saw the pile of handcuffs and our hands now free.

He seemed to forget what it was that he was going to say. Looking at us for a couple of seconds, he froze. Then, seemingly in a panic, his face went pale before he dashed out the door and slammed it behind him.

We were all booked at the Huntington Beach City Jail for attempted murder (apparently, for trying to kill our own guy). Somewhere, they were holding the Banshees. I'm not sure how many were caught, as they seemed to be so good at running and probably had apartments in which to hide. We didn't have that option.

The police now accused everyone in both clubs of shooting Mark. The next day, we were transported to the Orange County Jail, where we got booked again on the same charge.

When you look at my arrest record, it shows two arrests or charges for attempted murder for two locations in two days. It makes me look like I was a busy guy.

At the county jail, after processing, we were deposited in a large dorm-type room where we spent the weekend together, hanging out, swapping stories, sleeping, and enjoying the free food.

Everyone else who wasn't with us knew who we were, and there was no trouble with anyone. Monday morning, they took us all to court for our arraignment. One after another, the judge looked at the charges: twelve of us charged with doing the same thing, attempted murder.

He looked at the assistant district attorney, who represented the county, and asked, "How can you charge all of these people with the same crime?"

The D.A. sputtered, "Someone had shot someone, and we don't know who did it, so we charged everyone who was caught at the scene."

He must have been new on the job.

The judge asked, "What evidence do you have?"

The D.A. said, "We have a Hangmen with a bullet in him."

The Judge said, "These men in front of me are Hangmen, are they not?"

The D.A. said, "Correct."

The judge pounded his gavel and said, "Case dismissed!"

Mark was out of the hospital before we got out of jail. The doctors decided it would do more damage to remove the bullet, so they just left it in there. It tended to wander as Mark carried it for the rest of his life.

We never heard another word about Banshees after that.

Hangmen Mark

Chapter 9

Gentleman Jim and the Satan's Slaves

The Satan's Slaves were up in the San Fernando Valley (SFV) or LACO, for Los Angeles County. They were a rough bunch of hardcore, 1% outlaws. But so were we, having been there at the meeting in No.Cal. when the 1% patch was agreed on.

The Slaves had started in the early '60s. Most of them patched over to Red and White in 1978, and their particular patch has not been around since.

Not having been a member at that time, I was not privy to all of the information. I heard some of it at the time and more later when I was a member, as then they could tell me what happened. The year was 1969, and the story was that someone from the Hessians had stolen a motorcycle that belonged to a Satan's Slave.

Gentleman Jim was in a bar drinking and playing pool with four Hessians when in walked about twenty Satan's Slaves, looking for payback for the stolen bike. It was apparent they would turn out the whole bar. Before they did, they recognized Jim and gave him due respect. They paused and asked, "Where do you stand in this, Hangman?"

He had not known about the theft. Jim told me that he was about to say, "This isn't my fight."

However, before he could get the words out, one of the Hessians said, "He's with us."

"What else could I say?" Jim said, pissed off that the guy had spoken for him. However, there was no way he could opt out now without looking like he was backing down.

Gentleman Jim had no reverse. He just looked at the Slaves and said, "I guess you know where I stand."

The bar exploded into violence as the fight got underway, fast and furious. One Hangmen and the four Hessians were outnumbered four to one. Making a brave stand, the Hessians were tough, but so were the Slaves, and being outnumbered was even tougher. Jim would never give up.

After knocking out three or four Slaves who made the mistake of getting too close to him, he was holding his ground, trying to keep his back to the wall as best he could. He was a one-man buzzsaw when it came to cutting through an avalanche of pissed-off bikers, none of whom were his equal.

The outnumbered Hessians were taken down one by one. Jim was the only target left standing. Now they all descended upon him.

Jim never gave up. He had all the moves of a trained fighter, but not the daily conditioning and stamina. However, this was not a boxing ring with rules, one on one. He was like a cat that fights in a burst of fury, putting everything into it with blinding speed. However, he was starting to get tired, not to mention just a little distracted trying to fight in all directions.

When he got pulled away from the wall, the danger came from behind. A Satan's Slave swung a five-foot-long steel tire iron into the back of his head, knocking him out. Jim fell forward onto the bar floor covered with spilled beer, blood, and broken glass. Instinctively, he crossed his arms across his chest to keep the attackers from taking his cut. Unable to pull it off him, someone pulled out a knife and cut through the shoulders, taking it off him that way while the other Slaves put the boots to Jim's face, creating wounds whose scars he would bear for the rest of his life. The Slaves collected the patches of all the guys they had beaten down, and then they left.

Jim was never, ever beaten by one man. Not even two or three. It took twenty. He woke up in the hospital with a severe concussion, not knowing where he was or even who he was. It was weeks before he could function normally. But, then, which of us were ever normal anyway?

As soon as the phone call came in about what had happened, and that the Slaves had taken Jim's patch, a plan was put together to get it back.

Part of the QRF (Quick Reaction Force) was So.Cal. Art was as daring as they come. Plus, there was Jaxon, a super buff Italian Stallion badass who'd grown up in the inferno of Hell's Kitchen in New York City.

Two more Hangmen were part of the team. One was a guy with the appropriate name of Daffy, from Kansas City. Daffy was not named after a duck; he was a little bit crazy, not in a mentally ill way, but in more like a homicidal way. He wasn't very tall, but he didn't need to be. His shoulders looked as wide as his height. He had the face of a boxer.

His buddy, Gates, was also from Kansas City. Both had mysterious pasts. What they used to do in Kansas City was kept pretty quiet. The rumor was enforcement work for the KC mob, but both were smart enough to never talk about it. All we knew was that they were badass motherfuckers and not afraid of anything or anyone. Gates was African American – the only black Hangman ever, at least as of this writing.

Later that same night, at the Satan's Slaves bar in Venice, California, about twenty-five of them were feeling comfortable and confident on their home turf, especially after their one-sided victory. Then the front and back doors opened simultaneously. One biker stayed at the front door while three walked in the back. Nobody noticed them until it was too late.

Four against twenty-five. This time, the Slaves were outnumbered. Daffy had taken control of the front door, while Jaxon and Art walked into the middle of the bar. Gates stood covering the back entrance with a sawed-off twelve-gauge, double-barrel shotgun he had borrowed from Gremlin. Daffy, at the front door, didn't need a gun. He had… himself.

The Slaves were taken by surprise when Art, staring into the face of the Slave's president, produced a hand grenade, pulled the pin, and slammed it down on the bar while holding the spoon to keep the fuse from being lit.

The bar got very quiet until, finally, Jaxon said, in his New York accent, loud enough for the entire bar to hear, "I want that Hangmen patch back here in ten minutes or nobody will leave this bar alive."

Then Art announced to the whole bar that machine guns were covering the front and back doors and advised that nobody try to leave.

The Slave's president asked the bartender for a phone. He made a call, and then they waited.

Unfortunately, a guy from the Question Marks, a hang-around club of the Slaves, made the mistake of walking in the front door where Daffy was waiting. Seeing that shit was going down, the Question Mark made the even bigger mistake of turning around and trying to walk back out.

Daffy didn't like that.

Socking him in the head, Daffy knocked him out. While the guy lay in the bar's entryway, Daffy jumped up and down on his back with all of his weight. He didn't need to, but I think he enjoyed it and probably wanted to get some payback for Jim.

Between the armed hand grenade and the sawed-off shotgun at the back door, none of the Slaves made a move to stop what was happening. The four Hangmen owned the situation.

Eventually, Daffy decided to save the rest of his energy, and the guy was left unconscious on the floor. The bar quieted down again – quiet with tension at a fever pitch. Finally, someone walked in the front door holding out Gentleman Jim's cut as if it was a sacrificial offering. Which it was.

When they handed over the patch, Art and Jaxon politely said, "Thank you," and turned to leave, heading for the back door, holding the hand grenade up in plain sight with the pin still pulled.

Daffy melted back out the front door to head for the car. Under cover of the hand grenade and the shotgun, the other three were allowed to walk out through the back door and disappear.

There was no need to collect the guys with the machine guns. They were never really there.

Sitting in the front seat of the getaway car, Art spent the next five minutes in a dark car trying to force that damn pin back into the grenade to disarm it.

The others in the car held their breaths. If he fucked it up and that spoon popped off, he'd have had to throw it out the window, and they would have had to floor it out of there. But he got the pin in, and everyone breathed a sigh of relief. It was over. They had pulled it off. Kind of a do-or-die suicide mission, but it worked.

Within an hour, some brothers were standing around Jim's bed in his hospital room, with him barely coherent. Art handed his patch back to him, laying it across his chest.

His head bandaged, and through the mind fog of the concussion, Jim realized what they had done. He reached out, misty-eyed. Taking their hands, he embraced his brothers who had risked their lives to get it back. He knew that brotherhood was absolute and that he could always count on them. Always.

It worked both ways. Nobody deserved it more than Gentleman Jim.

Chapter 10
Harleys Don't Lean: July 4, 1970

Mark and I were running late, accelerating, braking, grabbing gears, and leaning hard as we hauled ass up the lovely swerving curves of Highway 74 on our way from Hemet to Idyllwild, California, for a joint run with the So.Cal. Outlaws.

At Mountain Center, we cut north again on Highway 243. As we climbed higher, the twisty roads got tighter – just the way we liked it. There were three of us: Mark leading the way, me right behind him, and Hangmen Billy following me.

Mark and I were having a great time getting it on, blasting around the curves as fast as we could go. We had ridden together for years. Usually, Harleys or choppers are not meant to be canyon carvers, but our bikes sat high enough that we could corner hard without dragging footpegs, primary covers, or exhaust pipes.

Billy's bike, not so much. It was a low rider with a stock-length springer. At first, I wondered what that scraping sound was on every corner. I thought it was something on my bike, but finally I figured out that it was Billy dragging metal through the curves.

He was leaning as hard as he could, still staying right behind us, doing a good job, holding his own, up until the point that we came around a tight hairpin right-hand curve. Gearing down to second and leaning hard, then powering out of that curve, I didn't notice right away that he was no longer back there.

After straightening out, I saw Mark looking in his mirror and seeing that Billy was no longer with us. He braked hard as we came to a straight stretch and made a U-turn. I followed, immediately knowing why we were turning back.

What we saw coming back to that curve was not pleasant. Sitting cock-eyed in the middle of the lane was an old Willys Jeep pickup, listing lopsided with a flat front left tire. In front of the truck, in the middle of the road, was Billy's bike in pieces, with Billy lying face down in the middle of this mess.

Flying in hard, Mark and I skidded sideways into this scene. We parked in the middle of each lane to block traffic, leaped off our bikes, and went to work.

I parked closest to Billy, and Mark stopped right behind the truck as the driver of the Willeys was climbing out of his cab, in a very foul mood.

Not giving a shit about Billy's condition, he was pissed about his truck's damage and freaked out because his wife and daughter were with him. But the bottom line was, they were not hurt, and Billy was.

Throwing out my kickstand and shutting off the key, I headed straight to Billy, who was now sitting up in the road next to the remnants of his motorcycle. They were scattered all over the asphalt.

He was holding his head with both hands, blood running through his fingers and down his arms. The angry driver was now standing over Billy, yelling at the top of his lungs. Mark jumped between them, intercepting the old man, who must have been at least fifty. Mark, with his hand in the man's chest, pushed him back to his truck, overriding the guy's panicked hysteria with some cool-headed common sense like, "Calm the fuck down, or the biggest casualty of this shit will be you."

The guy quickly realized his anger was not as important as not getting his ass kicked right there in front of his family.

Of course, there were no cell phones back then. Some people who stopped to see if they could help were asked to find a phone booth and call for an ambulance, which they did once they got to town.

It was probably at least thirty minutes before the Highway Patrol got there and fifteen more until the ambulance arrived. In the meantime, we took stock. Billy's bike was in four pieces. The biggest piece consisted of most of the frame along with the motor and rear wheel. The whole front end was by itself, slightly bent. The gas and the seat were in the dirt alongside the road.

Astonishingly, Billy was still in one piece. We didn't wear helmets, and the fact that he survived hitting a Jeep head-on at thirty-five to forty miles per hour was, to me, a fucking miracle!

When he'd tried to lean hard to the right, Billy's footpegs and exhaust pipes had dug into the pavement. If you force a lowrider to go hard over, the hard parts will dig into the pavement and lift the tires off the road, causing you to lose traction. Traction, it seems, is kind of important. That is the glue that keeps motorcycling together.

Dragging parts and losing traction caused him to go wide on that right-hand hairpin turn. In other words, Billy's arc was way too shallow, and he went left into the oncoming lane. Sometimes you can get away with that, but not this time.

This time, there was an arrogant asshole with his family, in his Willys Jeep, smack dab in the way. Being properly in his lane, he didn't much like getting smacked in the kisser by some careless, dirty biker who was just out having a good time.

Mark kept the situation under control while we sorted out what happened and what needed to happen next. Amazingly, Billy's worst injury was a deep cut above his right eye, with a large piece of skin hanging from his face. He had contacted some portion of the Willey's front end, which had caused the gash.

We couldn't believe that it wasn't worse as we pushed the loose piece of flesh back into place. Someone handed him a wadded-up T-shirt to hold against the wound until the paramedics put a bandage on it before loading him into the ambulance.

He had significant aches and pains all over his body, as you would expect for someone who had come to an instant stop against a thirty-year-old truck. It was amazing that he was still alive.

We started cleaning up the mess, leaving the police to deal with the angry driver as we picked up the pieces of Billy's bike. I snapped a few photos of it. Somebody with a pickup truck stopped and volunteered to take the motorcycle to our proposed campsite.

Later that evening, we were surprised to see Billy back at the camp. He had a bandage around his head and over his right eye, covering the stitches.

At least he was enjoying copious amounts of drugs for all the aches and pains that he suffered. Unbelievably, he had no broken bones.

We had a good party that night at the Hangmen/Outlaw campsite, celebrating Billy's good fortune (and shitty riding).

But the next day would prove to be more trying than the last.

Mark, Dennis and Hangmen Skip

It will be fine with just a few adjustments.

Chapter 11
Idyllwild and the Outlaw/HA Fight

Gremlin, Indian Dave and Skip. Billy's broken bike is to the left.

It almost starts like a joke: 'A Hangmen, a Hells Angel, and an Outlaw walk into a bar...'

The punch line?

'And then the shit hits the fan.'

In Southern California, the small town of Idyllwild is in the San Jacinto Mountains just east of Hemet and west of Palm Springs. Some of the pictures in Tom McMullen's little "Outlaw Chopper" magazine were from a Hangmen run to Idyllwild in 1967.

Up in the pines and out of the smog, it was still the July 4th run, the day after Billy's meet and greet with the Willies truck. Downtown Idyllwild wasn't far from our campsite, so the next morning, a large pack of Hangmen and So.Cal. Outlaws headed into town for coffee and breakfast.

Just to be clear, the So.Cal. Outlaws were not part of the original Chicago Outlaws, but they were just as tough and they had an uneasy alliance with the club back east.

We didn't intend to 'take over the town.' That's Hollywood bullshit. In addition to breakfast, we needed food and supplies, meaning beer and wine, for the camp.

When we got into the middle of town, we found a bar. It was open, and motorcycles were out front, so we headed in there for refreshments.

Walking into a small market, as I wasn't able to afford a breakfast of bacon and eggs at the cafe, I purchased a pint of chocolate milk for breakfast. Then a can of Heublein Whiskey Sour caught my eye. I thought that might be a good idea too. What was I thinking? Well, I wasn't.

It turned out the bar was occupied by about a dozen Hells Angels, mostly Berdoo. I didn't know any of them, but the Hangmen did. They greeted each other and proceeded to order beers and hang out, swapping stories and laughing, just getting going at 11:30 in the morning.

All was going well, and we were getting along just fine. Jaxon was out on the front porch talking with an Angel when one of the Outlaws, named Fred, came out of the bar and started talking shit about "fucking movie stars" – trying to make fun of all the publicity and movies about the Angels. Just jealousy, I think.

The Angel tried to ignore Fred, but he wouldn't shut up. Finally turning to Fred, the Angel asked, "You talking about Hells Angels?"

To which the Outlaw replied, right in his face and too damn close, "If I meant fucking Hells Angels, I would have said fucking Hells Angels!"

The Angel replied appropriately by socking him.

The fight was on, but wanting to keep a lid on it, several people on both sides shouted, "One on one!"

This is the way it should be, especially between clubs. Let it be man to man. Let the best man win instead of two clubs trying to kill each other. Unfortunately, that never seems to work.

We had a history with the Hells Angels that went back to Richmond in 1960. That history was a whole ten years old, which seemed like forever then. We had partied with them and gone on their runs and to their funerals.

We were never good friends, but we were never enemies either, and we preferred to keep it that way.

I'd been told that some of the original Richmond Hangmen had gone over to the formation of the Richmond Hells Angels charter. The remaining Hangmen who did not want to go Red and White went either No.Cal. or Nomad, Dutch, Willie Lump Lump, and Gremlin moved south and started the So.Cal. chapter.

One of them, probably Rex, headed east and separately started the Oklahoma chapter. Dennis Burns was also one of the Richmond Hangmen. I don't know what happened to him.

Unfortunately, the fight didn't stay one on one. As the two were going at it on the bar's front porch, both Hangmen and Hells Angels gave them room.

When the fight started, it was a universal decision that it wasn't our fight. We respected the Angels, and they respected us. There was no reason for us to go against them just because a loud-mouth Outlaw wanted to prove how tough he was. Besides, we felt the Outlaw was in the wrong on this one.

Suddenly, things got worse. Another Outlaw walked out of the bar and saw a Hells Angel fighting with one of his brothers. He pulled out his Bowie knife and stabbed the Angel in the back so hard, the blade went through him and the point poked out the front of his shirt. The Angel didn't seem to notice; he kept fighting as if nothing had happened.

Everything went to shit. It was chaos as Angels and Outlaws dove at each other. The fight spread into the middle of the street. It was fast and furious, with many wielding knives.

The peaceful atmosphere in the center of little downtown Idyllwild exploded into violence.

Hangmen pulled back into a perimeter, trying to account for our brothers. TK, our president, was yelling orders to stay out of it. I was outside of this melee and running toward the action when DeVinch stopped me and handed me a sawed-off pump shotgun. I was told to cover the crowd.

Not knowing what the hell that meant, I ran up to a pine tree just outside the fight and used it for cover, holding the shotgun down but ready.

Only about fifteen yards from the surging mass, I watched the fight while I checked the chamber to make sure it was loaded. I flicked off the safety, but I didn't know what the hell was in it. Slugs, buckshot, birdshot? How could I use a shotgun to shoot anyone in a crowd like this without hitting the wrong people?

Lurch was there, but was not wearing his patch because his bike was down and he had not ridden. When he got too close to the action, an Angel grabbed him and caught him by his long beard.

They grappled for a couple of seconds before somebody yelled at the Angel, "That's a Hangmen." The Angel immediately let him go, but not before having pulled out the whole chin portion of his beard, which left him with long, strange-looking mutton chops. That must've hurt! When he got home, he just shaved the whole thing off and started over.

Another humorous incident occurred when someone who hadn't heard TK's orders to stay out of it handed prospect Hipster a pistol and told him to get in there and "do something," Not knowing what that meant, the Hipster dutifully charged down the street, firing the gun in the air, yelling, "Stop it!"

Hearing the gunshots, all of the fighters paused for a second, looked around, and saw a skinny Hipster standing there, looking like a teacher with a ruler trying to break up a gang brawl at school.

After a very short pause, everyone went right back to business as usual, swinging and stabbing. There were other sporadic gunshots, but they were not warning shots. The fight was fierce, violent, and bloody, with neither side backing off or giving quarter.

We felt terrible for not helping or backing someone. Being on the sidelines felt strange, like watching two friends fighting.

Finally, the police started showing up – several cars of Riverside County Sheriff's Deputies. When the cops arrived, the fighting ceased. Both sides pulled back and started tending to the wounded.

Hangmen pitched in to help. I was able to withdraw and ditch the shotgun in the trunk of a car before any of the cops spotted me with it. Then I ran back to the scene to see what I could do.

Remember that chocolate milk and whiskey sour that I had bought? I had downed both on an empty stomach just before the action started. There were some severely wounded people from knife and gunshot wounds.

I helped load up two people, one into the back of a pickup truck and the other into an El Camino. Both times, an awful lot of blood was running off the beds and onto the street.

Suddenly, that terrible combination of chocolate milk and whiskey sour decided that it wasn't going to stay down any longer.

When the makeshift ambulances took off down the mountain, I walked quickly to the nearest building, getting around the corner just in time for my poor choice of 'breakfast' to come up. Having just turned nineteen, I was not used to seeing that much blood.

For some perspective, however, consider that, in Vietnam, hundreds of thousands of young men the same age as me were going through much worse violence than this.

There were no arrests. There were not enough cops for that, and they could not prove who had done what. Nobody was going to press charges or testify.

They just told us all to "get the hell out of town," which we were happy to do. We went back to our bikes, saddled up, lined up, and soon were in an orderly pack headed back out of town to our campground.

A couple of brothers, like Lurch, had caged it to town and were available to ride the injured Outlaws' bikes. We found out later that, amazingly, nobody died from those terrible bloody wounds.

No Hangmen were hurt, except for Lurch and his beard. But we did not like our numbers being used to start a fight. It wouldn't be the last time.

The short newspaper article a few days later was comical at best.

It said in part, "Three members of the Hell's Angels were stabbed and another shot and wounded Sunday in a fight between about 100 members of the motorcycle gang and a rival motorcycle group called the Hangmen."

With atrocious spelling, they got almost nothing right, as usual. The reporter never mentioned the Outlaws at all. What they don't know, they make up.

Hell's Angels Hurt

IDYLLWILD, CALIF. (UPI) —Three members of the Hell's Angels were stabbed and another was shot and wounded Sunday in a fight between about 100 members of the motorcycle gang and a rival motorcycle group called The Hangmen. Shefirr's deputies from two neaby communities were called to assist local authorities when the gangs began fighting outside a local cafe.

As usual the news media can't seem to get it right. At least they spelled our name correctly, even though spelling seemed to be a challenge for this reporter.

Lurch.

Chapter 12
Heading North Again

Not long after that Idyllwild run, I was on my way back to Washing-ton State. It seemed my little girlfriend Sheri had a new boyfriend. She called me saying he was giving her trouble and asked if I could help her out.

Always up for somewhere to go, I told her I would be there in a few days. I'm not sure why, as I didn't owe her anything. However, I still liked her, and besides, I didn't have anything better to do. So, after packing my sleeping bag on my bike, off I went for another eleven-hundred-mile trip, one way.

Surprisingly, I have almost no memories of that long ride back to Tacoma, Washington. It's like it was a day ride, although it took longer than that. Maybe it's because I had already done it a few months ago. It just seemed familiar, a hop, skip, and a jump up I-5. So.Cal. to Tacoma is a quick and comfortable three-day ride as long as it isn't raining – and it didn't.

This time, I was able to contact Gentleman Jim in Modesto. We hung out at the Classic Cat strip joint, and he put me up at the place he was renting. It felt good to be connected, even peripherally, to the club. Brotherhood, taking care of each other, was still a new concept to me, but it would eventually become part of my life.

On the second night, I camped in a state park near Rogue River, Oregon. I was on my way early the next morning.

When I got to Tacoma, I met with Sheri. It was nice to see her, but the spark was gone. I found out about the problems that she was having with her new boyfriend. He didn't seem to respect her and was just being a run-of-the-mill asshole.

I asked what she wanted me to do. "Do you want me to run him off?"

"No, could you just talk to him?"

"Sure, no problem."

She called him to come to the apartment, and I met him out front. He was chesty at first until I started shoving my finger into that puffed-up chest, staring him straight in the eye, and telling him that if he didn't treat Sheri right, I would be back and would beat him into a small puddle resembling hairy strawberry jam.

He must have believed I was serious, which I was. After I left, I never heard another complaint from Sheri. Either way, I figured I had done my part. I walked away from that chapter of my life and never heard from her again.

I dropped back down to Larry's house in Olympia. Life was good again. He, Steve, and I rode our bikes to a rock concert in Southern Washington State at Washougal. On the north side of the Columbia River, it was a mini-Woodstock, emulating what had just happened the year before.

The concert featured live bands and crowds of hippies, drugs, LSD, wine, whiskey, and, of course, rain. Yes, it was a lot like Woodstock. We rode in, slipping and sliding in the mud, which is rather tricky with a suicide clutch.

Seeing motorcycles, we headed for their camp. Larry introduced me to Jack, a biker buddy of his from Tacoma, and a couple of other guys.

We hung out together for those two days, having more in common than we did with the rest of that crowd. It was a good time. The bands were pretty good – nothing big, no Jimi Hendrix, Jefferson Airplane, or Carlos Santana. But we felt we were part of the experience, Peace, love, sex, drugs, and rock and roll. And, most importantly, motorcycles.

After three days and two nights of mud and delirium, we were back up in Olympia, just a short ride up Interstate 5. During the week, I relaxed at Larry's house when he had to work.

But when Larry and Steve weren't working, we got back into our old lifestyle of having fun, riding, and drinking. My nights were usually spent trying to sleep while listening to Larry pound his lovely and very vocal wife for what seemed like all night long. It was hard getting to sleep.

I would stay only another week before heading northeast to Spokane, where Gremlin had asked me to investigate something for him. I discovered that a young drug dealer named Bobby was renting the house right next door. While Larry was off at work during the day, I would go over to the house next door and hang out.

Not for the drugs, though. I didn't have the desire or the dollars. Instead, I found that many young teenage girls were hanging out there. Because I was still a teenager myself, having just turned nineteen, it seemed like the place to be. I hung out there part-time for about five days, I never did get lucky, but it was a pleasing diversion until I left.

Other than stopping by Spokane, I didn't have a plan.

The living room in the neighboring house had big windows that looked out into the front yard, which angled sharply up to the road. One afternoon, while I sat there chatting with a couple of very young ladies, half a dozen men in civilian clothes came racing down the hill from the street, carrying a wheel from a car.

I thought that was quite odd and asked the girls if these guys might be their fathers. But just as I was asking that, the front door came crashing in.

They had used that wheel as a battering ram. In came the men with guns drawn, yelling, "Don't move, police!"

Okay, I was a little slow on the uptake, but now I got it. They were local narcotics officers and this was a drug raid.

Bobby, the drug dealer, was in a back bedroom at the time. All but one of the cops ran straight back there to the sound of a toilet flushing. Then came a lot of thumping, crashing, and more yelling as the raiders started beating the shit out of him.

The one remaining cop put a set of handcuffs on me behind my back. Ignoring the two young girls, he pointed at the sofa and told me to sit down. There was a bar stool in the middle of the room, so I sat on that instead.

With the noise coming out of the back bedroom, this cop either thought they needed his help or just didn't want to miss out on the fun. He looked at me, said, "Stay there," and then turned and ran to the back of the house.

Being left alone, with no hesitation, I looked at the girls and said, "See ya!" With that, I was up and out of the still-open front door, running as fast as I could with my hands behind my back. All the while, I was expecting to hear gunshots ring out behind me.

The distance between the two houses was about one hundred yards of mowed grass, and I probably covered it in record time. It seemed like an eternity, but there were no bullets whizzing past or shouts of "Halt."

When I got to Larry's door, I turned my back and opened the doorknob, then burst into the room, and slammed the door behind me. Larry, who had just gotten home from work, was wide-eyed with surprise and asked, "What the hell is going on?"

After a brief explanation, I sat down, pulled my cuffed hands under my feet, took off my belt, and pulled out my handcuff key to remove the cuffs. Meanwhile, Larry went all around the house, pulling down the shades.

The neighborhood suddenly filled with police cars searching for the escaped fugitive. I stayed hidden for three days, waiting for the excitement to die down.

On the local radio station, we heard about the raid. As usual, the police and media had it wrong. They said that the escapee was the drug dealer's supplier from San Francisco. I don't know if they made that up, or perhaps Bobby had told them that to try to take the heat off himself.

I also heard later that it was on the television news in Tacoma and Seattle. More than once, I peeked out through the closed blinds to find a police car sitting on the street, watching the house.

Worrying that they might decide to get a search warrant to come looking for me, we hatched a plan to get me out of town. Larry called Jack, the biker in Tacoma whom we had been hanging out with at the rock concert in Washougal just the week before, and asked him if he could hide me for a while until things blew over.

I had parked my bike in the garage. The yard between there and the house was visible from the street, so on the fourth day, Larry walked back and forth wearing his black leather jacket and a baseball cap.

Steve had parked his car in there also. The door faced toward the lake, away from the street. A little after noon, wearing my black jacket, with my red hair tucked underneath, and Larry's cap, I walked out to the garage and climbed into the trunk of Steve's car.

With Larry driving the car and Steve on my motorcycle, they pulled out of the driveway and headed in different directions. Meeting up on the outside of town, they got on Interstate 5 and headed north.

I had been taking life one day at a time. Staying out of jail seemed like a capital idea while I was at it. Now, riding along in the dark trunk of a car, escaping Olympia, I wondered about my future and where these new developments would take me.

I pondered these things in the dark trunk as we bumped down the interstate. Finally, after several stops and turns, it was gratifying to hear my motorcycle following the car. Eventually, the car stopped, and the motor shut off.

When Larry opened the trunk, I climbed out into a dense, dark evergreen forest. Thick trees blotted out the sky. My faithful, shiny motorcycle was sitting there, leaning on its kickstand, and my friends were standing there, smiling. We were on Nisqually Road, the Old Pacific Highway.

'Aiding and abetting a fugitive,' I think the charges would have been. They had taken a risk to get me out, and they had succeeded. After thanks and hugs, I gave Larry a gift of the handcuffs that I had escaped in. Then, it was time for me to head north.

I climbed on my bike. It felt great to be on the road again, especially considering the bogus charges that awaited me down in Olympia. I cranked on the throttle and grabbed gears as I accelerated up the on-ramp of I-5, feeling as free as I ever had.

I had to check myself so that I didn't go too fast. I didn't need any attention from the law.

Larry had told me that Jack said, "No problem, he can stay with me as long as he needs to." The old house on 38th Street was easy to find. It was getting dark when I backed into the curb next to two other Harleys. Jack met me on the porch with a back-slapping hug and then proceeded to give me shit about not being able to stay out of trouble.

"Yeah, it's a bad habit of mine, but I'm workin' on it."

Walking into the living room, I greeted the two guys who owned the bikes out front. I'd met them at the rock festival in Washougal the previous week. On the couch sat three young ladies.

Not wanting to expose my current legal problem, I wasn't going to say anything about why I was there until Jack announced, "This is the guy everyone is looking for."

I cringed. Damn! I should have told him I wanted to keep it quiet. I hurried to explain, "It's all a big mistake. Yeah, they're looking for me, but the news has it all wrong. I'm not who they say I am."

Fortunately, no reward was being offered, so I figured I could trust these people. I tried to relax. Falling into a soft chair, I gave everybody a brief rundown on what 'really' happened and how it was classified information. Nobody outside that room was to know.

They all got a big laugh that I was not the dangerous criminal that the police and news media had made me out to be. I told them all that I was broke, on the run, and needed to make some money. I also mentioned going to Spokane to see some people there, although it was not immediately necessary.

One of the girls had already caught my eye. She was a pretty brunette with a quick smile, long thick wavy hair, flashing eyes, and an infectious laugh. She also looked great in a pair of tight bell-bottom Levi's. Returning my gaze, she spoke up and said that her name was Kasey. She had seen me at Washougal.

"So, you're that California guy I keep hearing about."

I didn't know people were talking about me, but I suppose that's normal when you have a stranger in town.

I said, "Do you live around here?"

"No, I live in Eastern Washington. I just came to town to visit my friends and go to the concert."

"A country girl, huh?"

"Not really. I live in the town of Prosser. I'm leaving to go home tomorrow. It's apple-picking season. All the local kids do it. It's a great way to make money before school starts."

"You're still in school?"

"No." She giggled. "I'm twenty years old."

I smiled, happy to know that she was legal.

She said, "You said you needed to make some money. I'm sure you could get a job there, as long as you're willing to pick apples."

"Hell yes, I'm willing. That sounds easy, but I would have to find a place to stay."

When she said I could stay with her, I was surprised. It was the best offer I'd had all day. One door closes, another opens.

I wondered if she had an apartment or a house, but I didn't question how or why. I just wanted to get as far from Olympia as possible.

We made a deal that I would see her there the next day. It was a short ride, only two hundred miles. She wrote her address and some directions on a piece of paper.

After a few beers, the conversation drifted to the rock concert and some of the bands that had played. I was happy to have the conversation off of me.

Soon, the girls left. Shortly after that, the other two bikers roared off into the night.

Jack told me to pull my bike into the garage with his.

I was exhausted. He showed me to a guest bedroom, where I passed out, feeling relatively safe for a change.

Chapter 13
Prosser

In the morning, Jack treated me to coffee, bacon, and eggs before I hit the road. Wow, free food again. Maybe I should have been used to it by now, but I was continually amazed by all of the great people I met in my travels.

I was anxious to put some miles between Olympia and me. I thanked Jack profusely for the hospitality and the shelter from the law. "If you're ever in Southern California, look me up. I don't have a place or a phone, but if you can find the Hangmen, you can find me."

After a bro-hug, I was off. It was a pleasant ride that time of year: the middle of August, late summer. Not too hot, not too cold.

Following the instructions Kasey had written down for me, I left Tacoma on Highway 18, holding my breath every time I saw a police car, but they ignored me. The police in Olympia had thought I was a hippy or a drug dealer; they didn't know that I was neither. To us, it was a significant distinction. Often, I have been asked, "What's the difference between a hippy and a biker?"

I always like to answer, "Hippies are non-violent."

After I left town, the scenery turned rural and then became a forest. I climbed into the Cascade Mountains until I hit Interstate 90, which runs from Seattle to Boston. I turned right, heading east, up into the mountains to Snoqualmie Pass, where it got cold. However, that didn't last as I headed down the other side, into the more arid Eastern Washington, full of farmland. At Ellensburg, I turned south on Highway 82. The bike, as usual, purred along.

It sometimes amazed me how dependable it was. I rarely had to work on it, but of course, I made sure I changed the oil at what I thought were the right intervals. Not having a speedometer or odometer, I had to guess at it.

Nor did we run oil filters, as the old ones, even when chromed, didn't look cool. At least we didn't think so. You couldn't ride a Harley back then without knowing how to work on them. Being as we built them from the ground up, we knew every inch of our bikes.

After getting gas in Yakima and cleaning the bugs off my sunglasses (due to all of the farmland), I continued down Highway 82 until, just after crossing the Yakima River, I finally found the tiny town of Prosser.

The instructions were right on, and before long I was pulling up in front of Kasey's house. Neighbors peeked out of their windows as I shut the bike down and leaned it on its kickstand. Looking around the quiet neighborhood, I thought, 'This is about as middle America as I am ever going to find.'

Hearing the bike, Kasey came skipping happily out to greet me. She asked how the ride went and then said, "Come on in, my parents are anxious to meet you."

Parents? I was a little disappointed and started to crush all of the fantasies I'd had in my head since leaving Tacoma while wondering how this was going to work.

They were very nice people and, much to my surprise, they were okay with me staying with them. They even had a place all ready for me… In the garage at the back of the property. Oh well. At least I would get to sleep near my motorcycle. A mattress on the floor and a garage door: Who could ask for more? They invited me to eat with them at dinner time, which is always a good deal, and I could use a bathroom just inside the back door, which they never locked. It was not exactly what I had hoped for, but I was still more than happy with the deal.

The foreman at the apple orchard hired me right away. Just about any warm body that was reasonably mobile could pick apples. Spanish was the predominant language of most of the workers. Kasey had an old Volkswagen Bug, which we took to work in the orchards every morning.

I picked apples for only about an hour. I don't know why, but the foreman came up to me on the morning of the first day and asked if I could drive a tractor. Maybe he had heard who I was and thought that if I could ride a motorcycle, I could also drive a tractor.

I said, "Of course." I had never touched a tractor before, but I had operated forklifts, and driving anything had to be better than picking apples.

After a briefing on the controls, I was off on my new career. Instead of getting paid by the apple, or by the thousand apples, I got paid by the hour. I could relax and drive around at my own pace, picking up bins that were five by five square and three feet high. The tractor had a forklift on the back.

When the containers got filled with apples, I picked them up and took them out to the edge of the orchard by the road, where a larger forklift loaded them onto flatbed semi-trucks. Then I went back and distributed an empty bin to the location where I had picked up the full one. Pretty complicated, but I was up to the task.

Before long, I was practicing wheelies with the tractor, as the weight of a bin of apples on the back made the front end very light.

Kasey and I picked apples five days a week for a month. On the weekends, we partied with her friends. Most of them she had known her whole life in that small town.

Some mornings, already fully dressed, I would wait for her parents to leave for work. Then I would go into the house, sneak up the stairs to her bedroom, and creep in on my tiptoes to surprise her. She would wake up with that pretty smile on her face, framed by tousled curls. The sight of the lovely white skin of her bare shoulders, just visible above the covers, was tantalizing.

The author and Kasey in Prosser, WA. 1970

But, with giggles and laughter, she always resisted my playful attempts to join her in that bed, so I would go back downstairs and make us both coffee before we left for the Apple Kingdom.

Getting ready to take Kasey for a ride one day, I discovered that my rear tire was flat. After popping it off the frame, I had Kasey drop me off at just about the only gas station in town while she went shopping. The bib overall-wearing owner of the station was right out of Mayberry RFD.

"Do you repair motorcycle tires?"

"Nope."

"Do you mind if I fix my tire here?"

"Nope."

Being the nice small-town guy that he was, he allowed me to use his tools, mainly some large screwdrivers to use as substitute tire spoons and then his tube patching material when I got it out. Finally, once the wheel was aired back up and ready to go, I asked Mr. Mayberry what I owed him. He said, "Nothin."

And then he offered me a job at his gas station.

I thanked him and said I wasn't going to be staying in town. A steady job was not something I needed or wanted. If I had taken his offer and started earning an honest living, where would that have led? I was a motorcycle rider, and winter was on its way. Soon it would be time to get moving.

When we weren't working, Kasey and I spent almost all of our free time together, often with her riding on the back of my bike. Blasting up and down Highway 82. Riding through the vast fields or cruising alongside the Columbia River. Parking on a hilltop to watch the sunset, never at a loss for conversation. I relished her smile, her laugh, her flashing eyes. So many times, I longed to kiss her. But I didn't.

By the middle of October, it was turning colder; brown leaves were falling all around. Our breaths would come out in white clouds in the evenings, mingling and hanging in the air.

It was beautiful and calm there, a happy place. Small-town America, the way life used to be. The way it should be and still is for a lot of people. I wondered...

Sometimes I think I could have stayed there forever. But that would have taken commitment, and nothing scared me more. I've never been good at that, then or since. My parents split up when I was ten. When they were together, they seemed to hate each other, and it didn't get any better after the divorce. I could never understand why. Family and home life was not a comfortable place for me. It was something to flee from.

I wanted to stay in Prosser, and I wanted to leave. The apple harvesting season was coming to an end, and I needed the open road. I needed freedom. I needed to head to Spokane to take care of some business for the Hangmen. My default setting was to leave, so that was what I did.

Finally, the morning came. After saying goodbye to Kasey's gracious parents, it was time to leave. My sleeping bag was tied on over the headlight and Kasey was on the back. My left foot eased up on the suicide clutch as we pulled out of the driveway, away from the old house on the quiet street, now covered with autumn leaves blowing across it.

Before leaving town, I dropped Kasey off at the bus station. She had to go to Richland that morning. I got her there just in time. Promising to write, we said a quick goodbye. She gave me a hug and a sweet kiss – our first one.

I watched her dark wavy curls bounce as she turned and hurried onto the bus. She didn't look back.

After getting gas at Mr. Mayberry's gas station, I rearranged my sleeping bag behind me to lean on, then got back on Highway 82. Before long, I caught up with the bus to Richland. Coming up on its left side, I slowed down to match its speed.

Searching down the line of windows, I saw Kasey looking out at me with a hand pressed against the glass, a sad, faraway look on her face. She wiped her cheek with her other hand.

My eyes were watering too. Then I noticed that the other passengers on that side of the bus were staring out at me, as if they were seeing a wild animal that had escaped from its cage.

Getting self-conscious, I gave Kasey one last look and a little wave. Then I reached down, whacked the shifter into third gear, and poured on the coals as I pulled away from the bus and from another chapter in my life.

I had nothing to offer her. I loved her. But what did I know about love? And besides, she never asked me to stay – all the more reason to ride away. The only thing I felt like I knew was riding a motorcycle down the road. So that was what I did. Putting everything behind me, literally and figuratively, I raced to Richland, where I picked up Highway 395 northbound, heading to Spokane. I never saw her again, but I never forgot her.

The Washington interlude.

Chapter 14
Spokane

It was another five hours to Spokane from Prosser, including gas stops. I got there late in the day. Darkness had descended upon the city when I pulled up in front of the bar. Bikes were parked along the sidewalk, so I squeezed my way between them as I backed in and parked.

Some guys were standing in front of the bar. I got a few compliments on the bike and the usual questions: "Where are you from?" "Where are you going?" They seemed to be a little

surprised when they noticed the California license plate. I asked them about some guys calling themselves Hangmen.

Suddenly, I was surrounded by what seemed like the whole lot of them. They became rather hostile, demanding, "Why do you want to know?"

I thought, 'Well, this must be who I am looking for.'

I asked, "Who is your leader?" I felt like I was in an old science fiction movie: 'Take me to your leader.'

A tall guy stepped forward and said that his name was George. He wanted to know why I wanted to know anything about Hangmen and just who the fuck was I anyway?

I handed him a piece of paper with a phone number and told him, "This is Gremlin, president of the So.Cal. chapter of the Hangmen. He sent me here, and you need to give him a call."

"I need to, huh?"

"Yes, you do."

He told me to wait outside while he went in and called. I stood on the curb while some of the guys alternated between trying to check out my bike and trying to stare me down. It wasn't working, but they gave it their best shot.

After about ten minutes, George came out onto the sidewalk and whispered something into someone's ear. Then he went and talked to a couple of others. I thought, 'This doesn't look good. I might have to fight... or should I get on my bike and run for it?'

While I was trying to form a plan, one of their guys came up to me and, with a sly smile, said, "Come with me." He escorted me inside the bar and asked, "What are you drinking?"

"I'll take a beer."

"Hungry? How about a hamburger?"

"Sure, thanks."

He told me I would have a place to stay for the night, and they had assigned a girl to me. At first, I thought it was just a joke, but I found out later that it was not. I would have said, "No thanks," but she was small and cute and had a nice smile.

The way she started hanging on my arm and looking up at me, I thought, 'What the hell.'

I wondered what Gremlin had said to them. I didn't find out until months later.

I gratefully ate the burger and fries, but knowing I would have to ride somewhere, I took it easy on the beer, drinking only a few. Friendlier now, some of the guys asked me about the Hangmen and other clubs down in Southern California.

We talked about motorcycles and they asked about my travels. "Did you ride all the way up here to find us?" They never did explain the hostility when I first showed up, and I didn't ask.

When the bar closed, they told me I needed to get on my bike and follow them. Because I had not made any arrangements, the prospect of a place to stay for the night sounded good. I could take care of myself.

Usually, I found a rest stop or camping area out of town. But I had learned that if someone offered something for free, what the fuck? That was hard to turn down.

Still, sometimes, you had to be careful. Like a brother of mine likes to say, "That awkward moment when you get in the car, and there's no candy."

The house we came to seemed like it was at least one hundred years old. However, the modern music – Led Zeppelin, The Doors, Jimi Hendrix – made those years disappear. Black lights and psychedelic posters set the mood. It had a hippy feel to it, like a sixties drug scene.

It had been a long day. I continued to talk with the guys, who asked more questions about my travels and motorcycle clubs. After a few more beers, I was shown to an upstairs bedroom, along with my date for the night.

Because of the beer, maybe a hit or two of pot, the fatigue, and the thunder and lightning that eventually came, the rest of the night seemed surreal.

The music, the sex, the dark, brooding old room with dim light coming in from the city street, the falling leaves blowing in the street, and the intermittent flashes of lightning that lit up the room like someone using an arch welder outside – it all seemed like a dream.

The whole time I was in Spokane, I had a sense of urgency to leave. Winter was coming, and Spokane was no place to be on a motorcycle. I could get trapped all winter. I had been planning on leaving town the next day, but a chance meeting in the bar that night led to my finding some more work.

This guy was a citizen, not part of the bikers whom I had just met. I told him that I was just passing through, but that I wouldn't mind making a little money while I was in town. I was thinking of something quick and simple, like collecting debts or roughing someone up for a price. But he had something different in mind. He offered me a job helping him paint houses. That was okay too. It took a little longer, but offered less risk with the law.

I even got a place to stay. I slept on the couch in the living room of his single-wide mobile home while he and his wife stayed in the back bedroom. I couldn't complain about anything as long as it was indoors... unless it was a jail.

I worked hard almost every day and was glad to hit the couch in the evenings.

It was well past the middle of October. After two weeks, I had some more money in my pocket, and the mountains around the town started to show more snow every morning.

Before leaving town, on a Sunday afternoon, I stopped back by the bar where I had met the local guys whom I had partied with, but none of them were there. I drank a couple of beers and left. I never saw them again.

It was almost Halloween, which meant that it was almost November. Winter was approaching, so this California boy needed to get his ass heading south to warmer climates.

Chapter 15
Southbound Again

From the money I had made, I spent twenty bucks on a pair of insulated ski gloves at a sporting goods store. I knew that my simple leather work gloves would not be enough in the rapidly dropping temperatures.

After saying my goodbyes to my latest employer and host, I left Spokane on Halloween of 1970. I headed southwest on Interstate 90, hoping to beat the snow. Travel was a lot of guesswork back then. You depended on paper maps, usually pinned to the wall in a gas station, to see where you were and where you were trying to go.

The weather could be iffy. There was no Weather Channel on television, let alone an app on your phone. If you were lucky, you would catch a weather report on the TV news, but televisions were hard to come by when you were camping off the side of a highway.

Cutting farther south on US 395, I didn't stop when passing through the Tri-Cities, where I crossed over the Snake River. Then I picked up the Columbia River and followed it until 395 turned south again. I rode about eight to nine hours a day, as I had nothing better to do anyway – no stopping for sightseeing.

There isn't a lot to talk about when it comes to riding in Eastern Oregon. Barren vistas with nothing but sagebrush, and sometimes not even that. It is nothing like the forested beauty of Western Oregon.

I traveled on narrow two-lane roads, sometimes winding up and down low mountain ranges, vast stretches of flat valleys and straight roads, often without another vehicle in sight for long periods.

I was left to my imagination, thinking things like, 'This must be what it would be like riding across the surface of Mars and I'm the only one on the planet.' Of course, that wouldn't explain who built the road, but it was fun to toy with the idea.

As long as I had some cash, I didn't use the stolen gas cards. They were for emergencies when I had no money. There were just enough small towns for me to put gas in my small tank and little grocery stores for me to buy a can of pork and beans or beef stew to heat up over a fire for dinner.

Gas for the bike was the big priority; food for me was secondary. At least the weather, while getting cold, stayed dry with no rain or snow.

My cold-weather gear consisted of a long-sleeved sweatshirt over my black T-shirt, a leather jacket, a fake fur liner zipped into my tattered black trench coat, the new ski gloves that I had purchased in Spokane, two pairs of Levi's (one clean underneath my outside pair of slicks), and a set of red heavy wool socks under my boots. As long as the temperatures stayed above freezing, I was pretty comfortable.

After sunset, I pulled off the highway onto a dirt road, then found an isolated place to spend the night. Despite my good encounters with strangers earlier in the year, I was still paranoid when sleeping alone. Maybe it was the Easy Rider scene where they got attacked while camping and Jack Nicholson's character was killed. That stuck with me for years.

As I snuggled down into my sleeping bag, lying on my back next to my motorcycle, I looked up at the stars, the Milky Way, our galaxy, and beyond that, the universe.

I couldn't help but think about Kasey and Prosser, the community, and the stability of growing up and living in a small town. The kind of roots I never knew.

The connections, the permanence of having childhood friends, living in the house where you grew up, having family, aunts, uncles, cousins, and grandparents, living in the same small town. It was all very foreign to me, and memories of the family I did have were not encouraging.

I didn't even have a sense of permanence with my own siblings. We had all run away from our family as soon as we could. Our family was never a happy place. It was like a prison – a place from which you wanted to escape. And we did, as soon as we could.

From the time I was a little kid, my family moved from one place to another. No location was ever called a hometown. There were too many rented houses, and we never stayed in one place long enough to consider it home. Being from New York City, my parents thought it was normal to rent from someone else. Neither one of them ever owned a home in their lives.

My only roots were shallow, like those of a tumbleweed, tearing loose early and left far behind as I drifted with the wind.

Then, I drifted off to sleep.

The sun peeked over the horizon and stabbed an accusing finger of light into my closed eyes. I had another day of riding ahead, so I'd best get to it. As I sat up in my sleeping bag, I heard it crackle and crunch with the frost that had formed on it during the night.

Staring at the frost, I realized I was cold and had been for a while. My motorcycle looked like a sugar-coated donut. With a shiver, I wished I had a coffee maker to brew a steaming cup of coffee.

But that was a big wish that was not about to come true anytime soon as I sat on my ass next to my bike in the middle of nowhere. I pulled on my cold, stiff boots and my equally stiff leather jacket and started packing up.

I set off, riding in search of coffee and breakfast. Early on day two, I entered Northeastern California, which, like Eastern Oregon, is very remote country – good ranch land. I'm sure there are more cattle than people. Maybe cattle don't need coffee, but cowboys do.

I stopped at the first hint of civilization I came to, New Pine Creek. It was not much more than a wide spot in the road, but there was a cafe, and it was open.

The town was right on the border of Oregon and California on the eastern side of Goose Lake. Which part of town you lived in, north or south, determined which state you lived in.

I fueled myself on coffee and the cheapest breakfast they had. Then I fueled the bike and set out again. My good luck continued with the weather, as it was cold but dry. Four hours later, I crossed into Nevada and soon found myself riding through the big city of Reno. Civilization again!

It was the first big city I'd been in since Spokane. On the south side, I found Highway 431 and started up the hill. It was a joy sweeping around the twisties and the curves as I climbed high into the mountains of the Sierra Nevada range to Lake Tahoe.

After all those long, straight roads, I was now riding fast, leaning hard, braking, and shifting gears. I love riding in the mountains.

Incline Village was on the Nevada side of the lake. Pulling into a gas station, I found a phone booth where I could call Danny, an acquaintance who lived there, to get final directions and announce my arrival.

He had told me to stop by sometime, so I was stopping by. A free place to stay indoors was always a treat. Unless it was pouring rain, I considered a motel room a waste of money.

I had thought that I would hang out for five days or so in this mountain paradise: clear, crisp air, a log cabin in the tall pines with a view of Lake Tahoe, and a soft, cozy bed in the guest room. However, I had waited too long to get there.

Winter had been dogging me all the way from Spokane, and now it continued to try to trap me into staying in one place. Mother Nature and her spokesperson, the weatherman, changed my plans. The day after I got there, after a late night and numerous beers, Danny and I were sitting around in the late morning, drinking coffee and talking about what to do for the day.

The television in the living room was on, and the top story was that a snowstorm was coming – and it was going to be a big one. It was supposed to hit that afternoon or evening. They were already talking about Interstate 80 being closed to vehicles without chains.

. Well, my motorcycle had a chain, but on second thought, that probably wouldn't be good enough. The weatherman expected the mountain passes to be closed for as long as a week. After that, they predicted that winter weather could have me stuck here for who knew how long. Reluctantly, I decided to hit the road right away.

I was heading for Modesto to visit Gentleman Jim and his buds. Checking the map, I found that Interstate 80 seemed to be the quickest route, but it was farther north, the direction from which the storm was coming. Besides, 80 included Donner Pass, where the infamous Donner party had to invent all kinds of culinary necessities to stay alive. Of course, some didn't stay alive.

Being at Donner Pass in a snowstorm sounded like a terrible idea. The thought of having to eat tourists didn't appeal to me –too much fat! So, I would have to go south to State Highway 50, mostly an old two-lane road that wound through the mountains. Maybe the state authorities didn't think they needed to worry about closing it, at least not yet.

After saying goodbye to Danny, promising I would be back to visit when I could, I strapped my sleeping bag onto my bike and hustled off to find Highway 50.

I filled up the gas tank (we're talking, at most, about three gallons with a fill-up), I headed south out of town. Riding through the maze of communities on the lake's eastern shore, I wound through the town of State Line and passed back into California.

Riding through more small towns like South Lake Tahoe, I finally found myself back on remote mountain roads as I negotiated curves and hairpin turns. Light snow was starting to fall as I tried to put enough miles behind me to get to lower ground and warmer air.

After an hour, the snow flurries had stopped. I saw a sign that said GAS, so I hit the brakes and clutch while getting the jockey shift into neutral as I pulled in and stopped. The little old building appeared to have been there since the 1849 gold rush.

Out front, the only gas pump looked like something you would see in a museum, with a big glass container on the top. An old guy walked out and looked at me like someone in West Virginia would look at a city slicker from New York.

"Need gas?" he said.

"Yup."

"How much?"

"Fill 'er up," I said.

He looked at me like I was wasting his time, then repeated, a little louder, "How much?"

Trying to figure out how to play this game, I thought, 'Let's see, how far and how long have I been riding? How much do I need?' Remember, no gas gauge, no odometer.

"Two gallons," I finally said, hoping that I had passed the math test.

Without another word, he worked a lever on the side of the antique gas pump. Suddenly, the big glass tank on the top of the pump started filling with pinkish-colored gasoline until it reached the two-gallon mark on the side of the glass.

When it got there, he took the hose with the spout off the pump's side, put it in my open gas tank, and pulled the lever. The gas drained from the glass tank on top of the pump into my tank. I cringed and held my breath.

This antique gas pump fascinated me, but I was sure the gas would overflow all over my bike if my calculations were wrong.

I got lucky, breathing a sigh of relief as the gas stopped just short of the gas tank's filler cap. You would have thought I had known what I was doing all along. He didn't take credit cards, so I had to use cash. Snow started to fall again.

The gas station and store looked like an interesting tourist spot, but I couldn't dally because of the weather. Soon, I was heading downhill to warmer weather and back to civilization as the light snow turned to light rain.

Highway 50 took me to Sacramento. It was getting dark as I turned south on Highway 99, familiar territory. Motoring through Lodi and then Stockton, I finally arrived at Gentleman Jim's house in Modesto at about ten o'clock at night.

When I parked my bike in his garage, he came out to greet me. It was one of those rare quiet nights. Jim drank whiskey as he watched John Wayne Westerns on the television.

He didn't have a guest room, so I shared his whiskey. After watching a couple of movies, we laughed because we both knew the dialog by heart.

Finally, I was done. After another long day of riding, and some whiskey, I threw my sleeping bag in the corner of the living room and went to sleep.

I stayed there for five days, resting up and hanging out with the Modesto crew. However, getting rest was elusive. Going to bars every evening was mandatory, though we got into only one bar fight during the time I was there

The most memorable thing that happened (when I say memorable, I don't mean in a good way), was when somebody spiked a pint of peppermint schnapps with liquid LSD and passed it around.

I hate when that happens.

It was not my first experience with LSD, but I never liked it. Everyone kept saying how terrific it was, so I tried it a couple of times, but I never thought it was that great. After that, I would avoid it, but still, there were times when it snuck up on me when I wasn't paying attention.

About a year prior, in 1969, Mark, Lurch, and I had ridden our bikes about an hour from Anaheim to the Elsinore area, where we camped out and took acid. After we spaced out all night, which seemed like one Twilight Zone episode after another, the eastern sky began to turn pink and then pale blue, gradually getting lighter.

We were still stoned, or at least I was. The others decided that we needed to head home, so we fired up the bikes, and off we went.

I don't want to try too hard to describe what it felt like riding a motorcycle on LSD except to say, "Don't do it." All the hard metal parts like handlebars and front ends start feeling like rubber or elastic. And time gets distorted, going either too slow or too fast.

Also, you can never tell which one is which. It's just weird. At about six o'clock, the sky had turned into one of those soft grey dawns with a low overcast. I was following the others through the city of Corona when they both went through a yellow light, which then turned red.

Stopped at the intersection was a police car that I saw very clearly. However, instead of slamming on the brakes, I motored on through the red light right in front of the cop.

My decision-making process was totally out to lunch at that moment, and I was not surprised when the cop swung in behind me with his red lights on.

Pulling over, I now had to deal with the cop while being heavily under the influence of the Twilight Zone. Fortunately, I was able to act normal enough that he did not become suspicious. Instead, he happily wrote me a ticket.

The funny part was that I was using a false driver's license, which claimed that I was older than I was. The name on the I.D. was Jack Casady. He was the bass player for Jefferson Airplane, which I had seen in concert a couple of times.

When the cop handed me the ticket book to sign the citation, I signed my real name.

Finishing the signature, I tried to hide my shock when I realized what I had done. Nonchalantly handing his ticket book back to him, I exhaled a sigh of relief when he didn't check the signature and just tore off the copy, telling me to be more careful as he handed it to me.

I did not pay the ticket and I quickly got rid of that driver's license. I never heard another word about it.

Fast forward back to Modesto. I started feeling the LSD coming on as the other guys laughed about getting everyone stoned, or spaced out, or whatever.

I planted my butt on the front lawn with my back to a tree and stayed there the whole night.

Somebody got the bright idea to jump on the bikes and head into town to party at some bar.

I said, "Absolutely not." I wasn't moving, and I didn't move all night until it wore off.

I watched the guys on five bikes roar off into the night. The chrome and colors flashed, leaving tracers that lingered in their wake as the thunder slowly subsided.

I was entertained as I watched the trees and the grass grow to extraordinary lengths and change colors. The lawn ornaments, rabbits, and squirrels came to life, chasing each other around the yard.

A couple of hours later, the boys returned. I was in the same spot, still unable to feel my body as my head hovered above the lawn.

Chapter 16
Prospecting

I was back in So.Cal. again with the club. It seemed they were my only friends nowadays. When I was in high school, I had wanted to join the Marine Corps, but my separated parents would not sign for me to join.

They said that if I wanted to get myself killed, I would have to wait until I turned eighteen and sign up on my own. They would not help me. I wanted to go to Vietnam because I thought that was where the action was. But that motorcycle accident and the two fractured vertebrae in January of 1969 put a crimp in those plans, and I had no plan B.

I would have to figure out other ways to try to get myself killed.

I had been hanging around the Hangmen off and on for over two years. Some of the guys asked me why I wasn't prospecting to become a member. I didn't really want to. It seemed like the club was for grown-ups, which I wasn't. It required responsibility, and I preferred being responsible only for myself.

I liked being around the club. but I also enjoyed my new lifestyle, going where I wanted, when I wanted. After my travels and freedom that year, becoming a member seemed like too much commitment.

I always had excuses as to why I couldn't sign up. Being a prospect didn't appeal to me either. Though I had long hair and a full beard, looking more like I was twenty-five, and I never, ever got carded when I went into bars, I was still only nineteen. That was a good enough excuse by itself, as the bylaws said you had to be twenty-one.

Somewhere along the way, I picked up another phony driver's license that said I was twenty-three. Well, there went that excuse. I had inadvertently proven myself to the club many times, including holding my own in bar fights.

I'd been roaming around the country by myself for most of the year, as well as looking into club business in Spokane, and had gone to jail with them more than once. Plus, I was riding a bike that fit right in.

Finally, Gremlin cornered me and wanted to know why I didn't become a prospect. I pulled the nineteen-year-old excuse, but he said my age was not an issue to the club anymore. The fake I.D. was all I needed. My last reason was that I could not afford the twenty-five-dollar fee required for the patch, which had to be paid upfront.

Gremlin said, "I'll sponsor you and front you the money. You can pay me back when you get a chance."

Damn! I had run out of escape routes. What else could I say but… "Okay."

I reluctantly bid my life of freedom goodbye.

It was December 1970 and suddenly I was a prospect for the already legendary ten-year-old Hangmen Motorcycle Club.

Oh well, here we go. Life started getting even more interesting… and dangerous.

One of the first things I did was pay Gremlin back. I knew a guy who had borrowed a leather jacket from me, and it was worth at least fifty bucks. He'd never returned it. He lived in a small travel trailer not far from where I occasionally stayed at my mother's apartment.

I asked him several times to give it back or pay me what it was worth, but he kept ignoring me. So, one night, I went over to his trailer and shoved him around a bit, telling him I was tired of waiting.

He swore he didn't have the money, so I collected his stereo, turntable, and speakers, telling him that he could have them back when I got my money. I didn't wait to hear back from him. I took the stereo setup to Gremlin and asked if this was adequate to pay back the twenty-five dollars I owed him. He said, "Sure, no problem." So, I paid my way into the Hangmen with a confiscated stereo.

Someone had given me a small leather motorcycle jacket, the kind with all the zippers. It was probably a woman's size. I had never worn a cut before, but now I needed one. I went to work on it with a knife and a pair of scissors. I pulled out the liner, cut off the collar and front zipper, and then all the zippers on the pockets, which I sewed shut.

After cutting the sleeves in half, I cut the upper half into a long fringe, reversed the lower part, and sewed them onto the ski gloves I had bought in Spokane to make elbow-length gauntlets.

I used the snapped belt loops to make snaps across the front so that it wouldn't flap in the wind.

In Long Beach, the Jungleland Bar was a favorite hangout for the Hessians. I had been there with the club several times. Shiny choppers were always lining the curb, with long front ends, lots of chrome, and colorful paint jobs.

Most of the Hessian bikes were as pretty as ours were. More parking was around the back, and because it was a Hessian bar, that was where most of their bikes were. We liked it in front, on the street, for a quicker getaway.

One of the times I was there, Gremlin had stopped by on his way home from whatever ironworker job he was on. He was in his pickup truck and was not wearing his cut. He managed to get himself arrested when out in front of the bar. A cop asked him how much he'd had to drink. Gremlin's answer was, "Fuck off."

The cop didn't appreciate that and promptly slapped the cuffs on him. Seeing this going on, about a dozen Hangmen headed to the scene. Distracted by the crowd of bikers approaching, the police officer quickly shoved Gremlin into the back of his cruiser before taking the time to get his identification.

Without a patch on, the cop didn't know who Gremlin was or that he was one of us. Seeing what was happening, Hangman Skip immediately came up with a plan. To create a diversion, he walked up to the cop and started asking him questions about something unrelated.

When the cop's back was turned, Gremlin seized the opportunity that Skip was providing. You're not supposed to be able to open the back door of a police car from the inside. I don't remember how he did it, but somehow Gremlin slipped out of the back of the patrol car, handcuffs and all, and took off.

I watched him running quietly in his soft-soled work boots, going as fast as he could with long strides. He leaned forward with his arms behind him as he crossed the wide and busy Long Beach Boulevard, dodging traffic with his hands cuffed.

The cop didn't realize his captive was gone until Gremlin was across the street and out of sight. It was comical to watch the cop look into the back seat and do a double-take. He looked again with his flashlight, then turned and scanned all around, even looking under the cruiser, trying to figure out where his prisoner had gone.

Skip and the rest of us calmly and innocently walked away and back into the bar, pretending not to notice as the cop barked into his radio microphone. He got more and more agitated, trying to find his handcuffed suspect.

Within minutes, more police cars started arriving with red lights flashing. A helicopter showed up overhead with its blinding spotlight as they began the frantic search for the extremely dangerous fugitive.

We said our goodbyes to the Hessians, fired up our bikes, and roared out of town. Later that night, as soon as he could, Uncle Tom went back in his car, tying back his long blond hair and wearing a baseball cap, trying to not look like a biker. He became just another hippy in his big black hearse. Not exactly commonplace, but it was the only car he had at the time.

With Gremlin still missing, the police presence had died down. They appeared to have given up. It was past two AM when Tom, driving slowly around the neighborhoods and up and down alleyways, somehow found Gremlin hiding in some hedges on a side street. This was quite a feat in the time before cell phones. Gremlin carried a handcuff key and had already taken them off and put them in his back pocket.

With Gremlin lying in the back of the hearse, Tom drove several blocks to where Grem's Chevrolet pickup truck was parked. Afraid the cops were watching it, they made several passes. It looked like the coast was clear. After Gremlin had been dropped off at his truck, they planned to make a quick exit for the freeway and head back to Anaheim.

As soon as the two vehicles pulled out onto Long Beach Boulevard, a police car appeared behind the Chevy truck. Uncle Tom and Gremlin held their breaths as the cop followed them for about four blocks, waiting for the red lights to come on.

When they came to the entrance to the 405 freeway, both vehicles calmly put on their turn signals and took the freeway entrance. The police car kept going straight.

Finally, letting their breaths out with huge sighs of relief, they hit the freeway, both flooring it. The Great Escape! The cop's name and badge number were on the handcuffs, so Gremlin sent him a Christmas card at the police station every year.

About a month later, we had shown up again at the Jungleland, and for some reason, there was friction. Still being a prospect, I was not privy to what the issues were.

The Hessians were a big club and our relationship could be tenuous at times. We had mutual respect. Sometimes we were a bit adversarial, but we were never quite enemies.

That night, however, when our buddies, the So.Cal. Outlaws showed up, the Hessians seemed to be upset about something. They started loading weapons, preparing for some shit.

I knew that because I was standing outside watching the bikes, and there was a small private room off to the side of the bar. It had an open window. I could hear the racking and clacking of shotgun slides. Magazines slapped into pistols, and slides, snapping into battery. Something was going down and I had no idea what.

Nothing ever came of it that night. After being at the bar for about two hours, we saddled up and split. I was never told what all the tension was about.

Chapter 17
Hostage Situation

A couple of weeks later, we were back at the Jungleland for another casual visit. There were about eighteen Hangmen that night and at least sixty Hessians. Earlier in the evening, some of our boys had gotten a head start on the party. Hangman Art had a bit of a run-in with someone he said he didn't get along with.

It was a guy named Peppermint Schnapps. Well, not a guy exactly; more like a full bottle of it, and he said they just didn't get along. It seemed Mr. Schnapps had a nasty habit of making Art do the most unusual things. Crazy things. And Art was no stranger to crazy things, even without the schnapps.

We had been there for about an hour and the evening was going smoothly. Instead of my usual station outside watching the bikes, I was inside the bar, and so was Art. He was walking around through the crowd, limping as he went.

Looking back, I think stalking might be a better description. I didn't think it was odd that he was limping, as I knew he had broken his leg in a motorcycle accident. I thought maybe it was bothering him.

TK, our So.Cal. president, was sitting at a table with a Hessian named Ropeman. They seemed to be arguing about something. It was getting a little loud. Though I was paying attention, nobody else in the room seemed to care much.

That kind of behavior among bikers is not unusual and the Hangmen and Hessians were generally on good terms.

Without saying anything to anyone, Art calmly limped over to where TK and Ropeman were sitting. Then he reached into his waistband and pulled out a short-barreled Mossberg 12-gauge pump shotgun. It was a long draw to get it out. I was amazed. How the hell did he hide that in his pants?

But Art was tall and skinny, and his black chinos were loose, so he did. Only now, the shotgun wasn't hidden. He loudly racked the slide, which seemed to make the whole room freeze and go very quiet.

Art grabbed the Hessian by the collar, put the shotgun against his head, jerked him up out of his chair, and took him hostage. Right there in the middle of a bar full of Hessians. I was pretty sure this was not a good idea.

I stood there dumbfounded, probably with my mouth open, trying to figure out what was going on and what to do next. That was when Hangman Mark, my old high school buddy, came up to me and said, "Prospect, go get behind Art and watch his back."

It seemed that all of the Hessians in the room were pulling out guns and pointing them at Art, so anywhere near him was the last place I wanted to be.

However, failing my brothers was not an option. What the hell... I never expected to live to be twenty-five anyway. That was only another six years, so I immediately crossed the room to take my place. Art was now the center of attention, so nobody tried to stop me.

I was able to get back to back with Art as he held their brother hostage. It appeared to me that every Hessian in the room who had a gun was pointing it straight at me. Of course, they were aiming at Art, but I was also in their line of fire. I am sure they would be happy to go through me to get to him.

The silence was unbearable. It was so quiet, I could hear that eerie sound of hammers clicking back and Buck knives snapping open all around the room.

Once again, faintly in that back room of the bar, I could hear the sound of more guns being loaded and cocked.

Other Hangmen were quietly taking up strategic positions around the room so that they would be close enough to deal with anyone who pulled a trigger. If any of our guys had guns, I wasn't aware of it. It looked like all of us Hangmen – except Art, of course – had brought knives to a gunfight. I wish he had given us a heads-up, but Mr. Schnapps was up to his old tricks again.

Had this been a bar full of civilians, they would have been running over each other, probably screaming, trying to get to the exits and safety, but not this crowd. Everyone in that room was ready to stand their ground no matter what.

The ones without guns had taken out their knives. All it would take was a shouted order or a shot fired.

Art was cool and calm, with no shouting or demands. He was quietly talking into Ropeman's ear. The Hessian, for his part, was cool as a cucumber. He did not appear angry, scared, or even upset at what was going on – kind of like another fun night down at the bar, nothing unusual.

TK was standing with his arms stretched to his sides, palms out, signaling for calm, trying to quell what had instantly become a timebomb about to explode.

TK wanted to tell Art to put the shotgun down, but he knew that now that this ball was rolling, it would have to play out one way or another. Besides, Art wouldn't be listening anyway; he was busy at the moment. After what seemed like an hour, but was probably only about thirty seconds, I heard Art tell Ropeman, "We're leaving!"

He started pulling Ropeman toward the front door as I did my best to maintain my position at Art's back, trying to anticipate his moves and still cover his back with my body. The Jungleland was not a small place, and it was crowded. It seemed to take forever to get to the front door. Fortunately, this hardcore bunch let us through. They parted like a grubby, long-haired, well-armed version of the Red Sea as we slowly and carefully made our way outside.

I tried to make eye contact with many of the people pointing guns at us, partly to see if they looked mad enough or crazy enough to start popping caps, but also hoping that maybe, if they looked into my eyes, they would be a little less likely to shoot me. That may sound desperate, and right then, it was.

One gunshot would have turned that place into a bloodbath, and hardly anyone would have gotten out alive. I think everyone understood that. It would have been like the Wild Bunch's final shootout, only we were all a lot closer together than in the movie.

Once outside, the well-armed crowd continued to part and then follow us. Art and I made our way to the street as the crowd waited to pounce. Slowly, we moved up the sidewalk, past the parked bikes. Farther down, several cars were parallel parked at the sidewalk.

Art's car was one of them. His bike was down, so he had driven. Besides, it would have been difficult for him and Mr. Schnapps to bring the shotgun on a motorcycle.

The three of us turned and moved slowly and awkwardly down the sidewalk, like a six-legged insect that hadn't yet learned how to use its legs. Art kept his back to me and the direction we were moving, walking backward, holding Ropeman in front, between him and all the Hessians who were following us.

Along the sidewalk, a chain-link fence guarded the property next to the Jungleland Bar. Then there was a narrow sidewalk and the cars parked at the curb. It was no longer possible for the Hessians to surround us without moving into the street. This would have been difficult because of the passing traffic on a four-lane city street.

Not having anticipated which direction we would move, the Hessians did not position themselves to block our exit up the sidewalk. We were now on point and free to move toward Art's car.

I led the way as we moved away from the bar with the mob following us. We were out in public in front of the bar with cars passing on the street. Art's body hid his shotgun so that the people in the cars couldn't see it.

The Hessians had to keep their guns down and out of plain sight, but they were still ready. Being on high alert, I noticed a young man, a biker, moving down the sidewalk toward us from the direction we were trying to go.

I don't know where he had come from, but by his demeanor and movements, it was evident that he was looking to get behind Art. He had probably left the bar when the shit went down and had gone to a vehicle to arm himself. I had no doubt about this after I saw a flash of light reflecting off the metal in his hand.

It was reasonably dark on this part of the street, so I took a gamble. The guy was still about thirty yards away when I left Art's back and slipped between two parked cars to the street. Crouching, I went up the road between the parked cars and the traffic whizzing by a few feet away until I passed the guy moving to intercept Art.

Maybe he had tunnel vision as he focused on his target, but I was able to sneak back to the sidewalk behind him. When he was five yards from Art, I grabbed him by the collar, stuck two fingers in his back, and said, "Don't move or I'll shoot you. Give me the gun."

Fortunately for me, that was just what he did. It was a revolver with a four-inch barrel. After he handed it over, I told him to walk out to the street and join his buddies. I didn't want him behind us.

Returning to my position at Art's back, I suddenly felt full of confidence. Finally, in this crazy situation, I was armed. That feeling didn't last long when my buddy Mark appeared. He had seen what I did and said, "Give me the gun, Prospect." I handed it to him with a deflated sigh, and he returned to the group of Hangmen in their blocking position between the Hessians and us.

I continued my guard duty behind Art, once again unarmed. I was carrying a Buck knife in a sheath on my belt, but there seemed no reason to take it out. Art and I were now in a relatively safe place. Fortunately, about that time, we had reached his car.

I don't think Art had much of a plan this whole time. Being drunk, he was not in a planning mood. That takes too much... well, planning. He had just tried to stop what he thought was going to go down, feeling the shit was going to hit the fan because of the argument between Ropeman and our president.

Now, with the Hangmen's protective screen between him and the angry Hessians, Art released his hostage and slipped into the passenger door of his car.

Moving the shotgun to his left hand, he started the car and threw it into gear. Then he made a U-turn in the middle of Long Beach Boulevard and disappeared into the night. We all breathed sighs of relief, but now we realized that we had to get ourselves out of there.

We were pretty good friends with most of the Hessians down in Orange County, but many of these guys were from L.A. County. We didn't know them as well, and they were pissed! For the last five or six minutes, which was about how long that whole event lasted, Art had been the main target of the Hessians. Now, the rest of us needed to follow Art's lead and get out of there.

It turned out that the "argument" that TK and Ropeman were having was nothing more than a good-natured back and forth. Ropeman was fuckin' around, raising his voice, trying to make a point about something, not pissed off or anything. Art was just too drunk to see it that way.

I don't know what kind of truce TK made with whatever Hessian leadership was there, but even though they outnumbered us about five to one and were still not happy with us, they seemed content to let these crazy Hangmen leave before something else happened. Any further partying was out of the question by now anyway.

The crowd of pissed-off Hessians parted again as we went back up the sidewalk to where our bikes were parked and started kicking them over. Soon, we were sitting at the curb with the satisfying rumble of Harley motors loping at idle. As the large group of Hessians glared at us, I realized that someone's bike would not start at the other end of the line of motorcycles.

It was Gremlin's Sportster, which had a magneto. They were notorious for being hard to start. Alas, a graceful exit was not to be had. What a time for this to happen! It seemed like the Hessians were debating whether or not to let us go. Being way outnumbered, we preferred to not have to fight our way out. We wanted to leave before they changed their minds. Leaving my bike running, I put it on the kickstand and, with several others, ran over to start pushing Gremlin down the street for a jump-start.

No luck. We tried it several times, and it still wouldn't start. After much sweating, panting, and cussing, finally Gremlin said, "Wait a minute, I think we've got it primed now. Let me give it a try." With that, he kicked the starter again, and it immediately fired to life. The rest of us climbed on our bikes, pulled into formation, and roared out of there.

In a short time, we were cruising east on the 405 Freeway with the wind on our faces, happy to be out of there, to be on our bikes, to be alive.

It had been a close one. I have been in many situations involving guns, but never one in which so many guns were out, aiming at people, ready to go, without being fired.

Years later, I asked Art why he had decided to put all of us into a life-or-death situation. He just said, "It seemed like the right thing to do at the time, but… if it hadn't been for my evil twin Mr. Schnapps, I'm pretty sure it wouldn't have happened that way."

Eventually, Gremlin told me the story about his bike not starting that night. He said that for years he was too embarrassed to tell anyone what really happened. As we went to leave, he had forgotten to turn the ignition switch on.

With the magneto ignition, the headlight did not come on until the engine started.

After all the kicking and pushing, he saw the problem, reached down, and quickly switched on the ignition. He gave us that enlightened explanation, then kicked the bike, which started. He said he really felt like an ass, but we can laugh about it now. All ended well.

Hangmen Art

Chapter 18
Yuma Prison Run

The author on Highway 8 heading to Yuma. Taken by Gremlin's wife Jan.

It was the first week in April and time for the Yuma Prison Run, still being held today. While the rest of the So.Cal. guys went straight to Yuma, Gremlin (packing his wife, Jan) and I rode to San Diego to meet up with some of the Dago chapter of the So.Cal. Outlaws.

We stayed overnight at Gator's house. He was their VP at the time. The next day, Saturday, April 3, we saddled up – Gremlin and me with

Gator, Seymour, and an Outlaw prospect named Rich or, to some, Richie. He was twenty-three years old and I was nineteen.

I was wearing a beret, trying to keep the sun off my head out there in the desert. Richie kept calling me Bronson because of the television show where Michael Parks rode a Harley and wore a watch cap. I suppose the beret looked like that, so he had to give me shit about it. He was a good guy. Both of us being prospects, we had a lot in common and got along well.

Leaving the city's perfect temperatures, we headed east on Highway 8, climbing into Eastern San Diego's hills. After getting gas in Alpine, we passed through Pine Valley, then descended into the hot, arid desert.

It was decorated by sand, cactus, and not much else as we rode through small, ancient desert towns like Jucumba and Ocotillo and the big agricultural city of El Centro.

On Highway 8, we finally came to a wide spot in the road, called Winterhaven. The California side of the border had two bars, a gas station, and a liquor store. We found the rest of the Hangmen, Outlaws, and Hessians already there, holed up in the bars.

At that time, Arizona had a helmet law, and California did not. None of us had brought any, so we stayed on the California side.

It was the middle of the afternoon when we pulled in, and the drinking and partying were already well underway at two bars that were on the main road, about one hundred yards apart.

The Hangmen and Outlaw contingents were parked at the Red's bar back to the west, while the majority of the bikers, mostly Hessians, were at the bar farther east toward the Arizona border. I don't remember that bar's name. Today, neither one of them is standing.

Not long after we got there, TK assigned me to go with some Hessians to scout out a place where we could camp in the desert near the Colorado River. There were four of us. TK sent me so that I could lead our group there if we decided to cut out on our own.

With two Hessians and an Outlaw leading, we rode out and checked out the camping spot for the evening. It was somewhere out in the desert. I am sure that if I had had to lead everyone there, especially in the dark, I would never have found it.

Everyone knows that Yuma is a real desert. It gets hot, but this was the first week of April; while temperatures were warm, they were relatively mild compared to what they would be later in the summer. It certainly was not like Blythe on the 4th of July! We had pleasant, dry daytime temps in the ninety-degree range.

An interesting thing happened as we headed back to town. One of the Hessians was packing a lady with him. I assumed that she was his Ol' Lady or girlfriend, but it turned out that she was a Mama, meaning that she didn't belong to anyone.

Our little pack suddenly pulled off to the side of the road and stopped. The guy packing the girl unstrapped the sleeping bag from his bike and the two of them walked off over a little rise and into the desert.

I asked the Outlaw what was going on. He told me that she wanted to show us all a good time. That wasn't exactly how they put it, but I laughed and said, "Yeah, right."

This kind of thing was not unusual in the biker world. The sun was getting low in the western sky as we sat on our bikes alongside the road, waiting. The other two guys smoked; I didn't. Sure enough, one guy would come back, and another one would go out.

Being a prospect, I was quite sure I was not going to be participating. That was okay with me. I wasn't sure how to handle it anyway. What would I do? Make funny conversation? Buy her a drink? Finally, the third guy came back, and the three of them looked at me expectantly.

I stared back until one of them said, "Get going. We haven't got all day."

It sounded like an order.

As a prospect, you need to step up to challenges, so you can't wimp out when it comes to, well, acting like a biker. So off I went, walking over the low hill to find our host.

She was fully clothed, sitting on the sleeping bag with a smile on her face. Looking at her as if for the first time, I realized she was pretty, with long dark hair. She was probably about thirty-five or a bit older.

I briefly wondered why she was doing this, but just as quickly I decided not to ask any questions. This arrangement was obviously of her own free will, if not her idea.

She motioned for me to lie down on the sleeping bag and surprised me by saying, "You're the one I've been waiting for."

Surprised, I asked, "What do you mean?"

I figured she probably told the other guys that too.

But she said, "I really wanted to be with you, but I knew that wouldn't be possible unless I did the other guys first."

I didn't believe her, but I did appreciate the compliment, whether she meant it or not. It helped to settle my nerves. I never even got her name.

When we got back to the bikes, the sun was sliding into the distant hills, turning the sky from bright white to pale blue, then pink. The guy who was packing her strapped his sleeping bag back onto his bike.

No one said a word as we saddled up, pulled out onto the highway, got into formation, and headed back to town.

Getting back to Red's Bar, we parked our bikes and went inside. There were only a few Hangmen and Outlaws inside. Most of our group was at the other bar up the street.

I hung out at Red's and reported to TK, our So.Cal. chapter president, the information on the camping spot for the evening. I hoped he wouldn't ask me exactly where it was.

I ordered a glass of beer with tomato juice. It kind of tasted like food that way. Then one of our guys came in and said that some shit was going down at the other bar. I took a big gulp from my beer and hustled to catch up with TK as he hit the front door with long strides.

When we arrived, we found out that a club called the Huns, who had been around a long time, had shown up and were hanging out, having a few beers. However, trouble started brewing because the So.Cal. Outlaws' colors were black and gold, the Hangmen's colors were black and gold, and the Huns' colors were black and gold.

Bikers have more in common with each other than the rest of the whole fucking world. You wouldn't think a small thing like that would cause friction, but... When a bunch of bikers gets drunk and on who knows what kind of drugs, sometimes they don't need much of an excuse to get some action going.

Unfortunately, somebody – I never did find out who, whether it was a Hangman or an Outlaw – had the dumb idea to start pulling the Huns' patches. They were not a lightweight club, but they were outnumbered, surprised, and confronted individually at gunpoint and knifepoint. Even though no patch holder should ever do this, they handed over their patches, as they had no choice.

Your patch or a bullet to the head? Hmmm, let me think about this... Except there was no time to think.

What would I have done? We don't know until we're there. The 'live to fight another day' strategy made sense. Taking an ass whooping is one thing; getting shot or stabbed can be very final and directly affect your retirement.

I wasn't there when it went down, but I think they took only about three Hun patches. One would have been enough. Bad vibes were in the air. At least one hundred or more bikers in various degrees of drunkenness were milling around inside and outside the bar among the bikes. Here and there were some very pissed-off Huns.

We were about to find out that they were nobody to be fucked around with. It was dark now, but still hot. I was wearing my leather cut with no shirt under it.

Showing good leadership, TK, hoping to diffuse the situation or at least the part under his control, started calling for all Hangmen to get back to Red's Bar.

I hung out until it looked like all our guys had left. As I turned to head back up the street, I saw that Uncle Tom and Sportster Jack were still there outside the bar. Figuring that they had gotten the word and would be on their way, I continued up the street to Red's Bar.

The Outlaws who were at the other bar, where the patch pulling started, had stayed there.

When I got to Red's, TK came up to me and asked, "Are all of our people back?"

"No, Uncle Tom and Sportster Jack are still there. I thought they were coming."

"Go get 'em. I want everybody back here now."

Immediately, I turned and trotted back down the street to the other bar.

The sides of the road were dirt. Some commercial buildings had sidewalks in front of them, but old Highway 8, which ran through town, was just a narrow two-lane road with no shoulders or sidewalks. I walked down the side of the road in the dirt.

As I approached the other bar, still thirty or so yards from the group of bikers and bikes in front of it, I saw that, connected to the bar on the west side, was a commercial building of some kind. It stood to the right and had enough room to park several cars in front of it.

This building had stucco walls, no windows, and recessed doorways just a couple of feet deep. There was a sidewalk in front, and the cars were parked facing in against that sidewalk.

Walking along the edge of the road just behind the parked cars, I passed a guy sitting on a motorcycle. He had no patch on his back. The bike was idling. Not thinking anything of it, I walked around the guy and his bike, still heading for the bar to look for Uncle Tom and Sportster Jack.

I probably hadn't taken five steps when I passed three Outlaws walking in the opposite direction. It was Bill, Seymour, and prospect Richie. They ignored me as I passed, but I could hear them talking.

Seymour asked Richie, "Which one has the gun?"

Richie pointed past me to the guy on the bike and said, "This one right here."

I probably hadn't taken more than three steps after that when loud, rapid gunfire started thundering behind me. The shots came fast, some louder than others, with more than one gun firing.

I could see that everyone in the direction I was facing was diving for cover. Thinking that seemed like a good idea, I did the same.

Turning toward the parked car on my right, I ran down its left side. Then, with a little help from a dose of adrenaline, I dove headfirst over the hood, landing on my hands and feet like a cat on the sidewalk.

In a crouch, I made my way to one of those recessed doorways only to find Sportster Jack and Uncle Tom already huddled in there and no room for a third.

Well, at least I found them.

The initial shooting lasted only a few seconds. But now more gunfire started up, and it was getting louder and more intense. It appeared that everyone who had a gun, which seemed to me like literally everyone, was now using it. Feeling rather exposed on that sidewalk, I turned around and jumped into the dirt between two parked cars only to find myself face to face with Bill, who was laying there with Seymour and Richie. Richie was not moving.

Bill held his gun up to me and said, "I'm hurt. Here, get that guy."

I thought, 'What guy?' I didn't even know what he looked like! But I supposed he would be the guy with the gun, so I took Bill's revolver, which turned out to be a Smith & Wesson Model 29 .44 magnum with a four-inch barrel, and raised up from between the cars to see where 'that guy' had gone. Big mistake! As soon as I stuck my head up, the car windows that I was between exploded with bullet impacts. I could hear bullets hitting the doors and see puffs of dirt as the projectiles kicked up the ground around us. Damn! I ducked back down.

The guy on the bike had disappeared, leaving it lying on its side next to the road. Meanwhile, at the bar to the right, all of the Hessians, Outlaws, and who knows who were shooting at who knows what. I sure didn't know, but it seemed to be mostly in my direction. A lot of lead was flying my way.

Probably some of the Huns were returning fire, but I could not see from where. That covering fire may have been the reason why the guy on the bike was able to escape.

I found out later that, not to be left out, in the other direction, the Hangmen and some of the Outlaws back at Red's Bar were also popping caps at my location.

It seemed to me that everyone was shooting at me, or maybe that was just because I was a little focused at the time. When I talked to people later, I learned that not one person admitted to having a target in their sights. They were shooting where they thought the threat was, which was where it started, which was where I was.

Every time I stuck my head up to find the initial shooter, the incoming rounds increased. They must have thought I was the shooter. After the third volley of incoming, I learned to stay down. I can be a slow learner sometimes.

Now with some extra time on my hands, I could see that Bill had been shot in the shoulder, Seymour was hit in the hip, and Richie had taken a round in the throat.

I tried to decide what to do. Keep trying to find a target? First aid? Then I realized that the gunfire had subsided; I thought that everyone was reloading. I could hear Uncle Tom calling me from the doorway.

I turned to see what he wanted. He told me to throw the gun under the car next to me. I thought, 'Well, that's a dumb idea. What if I need it? Besides, I don't want to get it dirty.' Then I heard the word "cops."

Instead of throwing the gun under the car, while still in a crouch, I started tucking it into the back of my pants. As I was doing that, I became aware of a spit-shined pair of shoes on the other side of where Richie was lying.

My eyes followed the legs of a khaki uniform, up to the badge he was wearing and the pump shotgun he was holding, and then, finally, the face of the Imperial County Sheriff's Deputy who was not even looking at the Outlaws laying on the ground or at me.

He was looking side to side, scanning for threats. Then, another deputy appeared, armed with an M1 carbine and doing the same threat scan all around, but not at me.

Not a good situation! I had three wounded people in front of me and I was holding a loaded gun (which, I found out later, Bill had fired four times) after a gunfight with two very nervous cops right in front of me.

I have to say, it took a lot of nerve for them to run into that melee in the dark of night.

It didn't look like they'd noticed me, so with the revolver now tucked safely into the back of my pants, I put my hands out to my sides and watched them closely. Slowly standing, I waited for them to start shouting orders and pointing their guns at me, but they never did. Thankfully, their presence had silenced all of the gunfire, and now it was all over but the shouting. And there was a lot of that.

Other Outlaws showed up. There was a lot of confusion about what to do with the wounded. Not wanting to turn around, I backed over to the sidewalk, expecting the deputies to tell me not to move and to come and search me. That didn't happen. Too many people were converging on the scene.

Tom was now standing in that same doorway. Because he was a patch holder, I walked up to him and quietly said, "Let me give you Bill's gun."

He looked at me like I was from Mars and whispered, all too loudly, "Are you fuckin' crazy? I don't want it. Take it back to the bar."

I glanced nervously at the cops to see if they'd heard. They hadn't. They were busy.

I said okay and turned to my right, then headed down the sidewalk toward Red's Bar.

Getting to the end of the building, I crossed a small side street and walked onto another lot. As I passed a small building, I saw Gator, the So.Cal. Outlaw VP, running up to me and asking what had happened.

"Seymour, Bill, and Richie have been shot. Here, I've got Bill's gun."

I was reaching back to pull it out when two more deputies appeared with shotguns. I pulled my hand away from the revolver as they leveled their shotguns right at Gator.

They shouted for him to get up against the wall of that small building, which he promptly did. Then they started searching him, completely ignoring me. Again!

It was bizarre, like I was invisible. Guardian angels, perhaps? Or maybe it was just that I was younger and smaller than Gator, with no patch on my back. Perhaps I didn't appear to be as much of a threat.

One cop held his shotgun on Gator while the other searched him. I slowly turned away and again started strolling toward Red's Bar. After passing out of sight beyond another building, I ran as fast as I could. I wanted to get rid of that gun as soon as possible. It never occurred to me to just toss it. It belonged to a patch holder, so I had to take care of it.

Back at Red's, TK, Skip, Gremlin, and others bombarded me with questions. I was trying to answer them and at the same time find someone to take Bill's gun, but nobody would. Somebody told me to hide it, so I found a large flowerpot in front of the bar and stashed the gun underneath it. Later, another one of the Outlaw officers came up and asked me for it. I finally turned it over to him.

Gremlin asked me to go back up the street and show him what happened, so I accompanied him and his wife Jan back to the scene with the crowds and confusion. When we got there, bikers were milling around, some arguing about whose fault it was.

An ambulance was there, and more cops were arriving. It was an eerie scene, with red lights flashing, reflecting off the buildings, the cars, and the bikes.

Paramedics were loading Bill and Seymour into the ambulance. We found out that Richie was dead. He had been shot in the throat and was still lying there in the dirt. Someone had put a jacket over his upper body and face.

The cars parked at the sidewalk where I was hiding were riddled with bullet holes, and the windows were shot out. The front walls of the commercial building where Tom and Jack took cover had also taken many rounds.

Later, the newspapers said that the liquor store across the street, which is still there as of this writing, had taken quite a few shots through the front window, smashing numerous liquor bottles. All sides had expended a lot of ammo in that short time.

Bill and Seymour's wounds were severe, but they would survive. It turns out they had walked up to the guy on the bike and grabbed him. Seymour put his .45 auto to his head, Bill stuck his .44 into his chest, and Richie put a knife to his throat.

Despite that, the guy came up shooting. No doubt, he had watched them coming and was ready. His weapon of choice that night was a .380 auto, and he took out all three of them. Someone else wounded him, but the newspaper reports didn't clarify his injuries.

There was a bullet hole in the seat of the motorcycle that was impounded at the scene. According to the newspaper article, a wounded man, the owner of the bike, was treated and released at a hospital in Tucson.

No charges were filed. I never asked them why they thought it was so important to try to take his gun after he had already given up his patch. Maybe they thought he would open up on them anyway, and they were trying to prevent that.

We all know people who like to carry big guns: .44s, .45s. But here was a situation in which the big guns didn't get the job done, and the little one did. Of course, it would have been different if they had gotten any significant hits, but they didn't. Only hits count.

John Wayne said it best in his last movie, The Shootist. Talking to Ron Howard while teaching him to shoot, he says, "It's not always being fast or accurate that counts... It's being willing!"

By now the dust had settled. The wounded had been taken away to the hospital and poor Richie to the morgue. The police now outnumbered us, with more showing up every minute. We later heard that every law enforcement agency within one hundred miles had responded. They told us we were leaving. Someone informed them there was a place we had scouted in the desert, and fortunately, someone remembered how to get there.

The police had all of the bikes line up in a massive pack on the street. Then, they escorted us – with a long line of police cars ahead and behind, their red lights flashing – to our overnight camping location. They guarded the entrance and told us that nobody was to leave until morning. Then, they expected us to leave town.

Somehow, plenty of beer and drugs accompanied us to the campsite. They kept everyone entertained, and the party continued long into the night. It was almost as if nothing had happened. I wished that I at least had a picture of Richie.

Gremlin and Seymour center. This was not taken at Winterhaven.

Chapter 19
Patching In

The following Friday was April 9, and the chapter had its weekly meeting. It was in the garage at Gremlin's house. I was outside, watching the bikes with the other prospects, when someone came out and called me into the meeting

Wondering what I had done wrong, I walked into the smoke-filled garage to hear Uncle Tom speaking. "Last week, in the middle of all of that shit where Richie was killed, I watched Dale stand his ground with a gun while bullets were hitting all around him, I've never seen anything like that before. I think he should be brought up for a vote right now."

I was surprised. He wasn't even my sponsor. TK called for a vote and it was a unanimous YES!

Suddenly, just like that, I was voted in as a member of the Hangmen Motorcycle Club!

I was stunned and delighted. I had expected to be a prospect for a lot longer, but now I was one of them. My head was in the clouds as Gremlin handed me a brand-new patch, glowing yellow on the black background, even though we called it gold. The club headed to a bar to party. On my way there, I raced to my mother's apartment because she had a sewing machine.

After breaking three needles on the tough leather of my vest, she told me to sew it on by hand, which I did in record time. Then I hauled ass to the bar where the guys were so that I could enjoy my new elevated status. I was no longer a hang-around or a prospect. I was now an equal, one of them. In the parking lot, they initiated my new patch with beer and piss. Fortunately, I was not required to be wearing it at the time.

Just a week prior, Richie and I had been hanging out at Winterhaven, both proud to be with our respective clubs. Little did I know that within that week, we would both get patched in.

The next day, we rode to Long Beach for his funeral. I was proudly wearing my newly sewn-on and mostly dried-out back patch. Richie was wearing an Outlaw patch. They buried him in it. He was no longer a prospect. He had earned it.

He paid the ultimate price. I did not.

His mother couldn't stop crying. Many of us were shedding tears as well. It seems like I have been to way too many funerals. This one seemed sadder than most because he was so young.

Over one hundred motorcycles rode in the funeral procession – Outlaws, Hangmen, Hessians, Galloping Gooses, Misfits, Chosen Few, Mescaleros, Iron Horsemen, and many more, plus, of course, a variety of loners who hung out with just about all the clubs.

One moment that remains in my mind from that day was Gremlin having brought an 8mm movie camera with him. He got there ahead of us. As we pulled into the large parking lot of the cemetery, Gremlin stood there, filming us.

Feeling good about my new patch, and seeing the camera, I decided that I needed to put on a show. As the rest of the pack made a right turn, I continued straight at Gremlin. Popping the foot clutch, I raised the front end of my bike toward the sky.

Heading straight for him as he filmed, I suddenly found myself out of control. Balancing precariously on the rear wheel, you need momentum to keep from falling over, and steering from that position is almost impossible. Fortunately, Gremlin stepped aside while still filming, letting me pass by him. Then I got the front wheel back on the ground again without hitting anything or anyone.

Later, Gremlin said, "Wow, that looked so cool! I can't believe your riding skill."

I said, "That skill was a complete illusion. I was totally out of control. If you had not stepped aside, I probably would have hit you."

It would have been bad form to start as a new patch holder by killing your sponsor. I never did see the footage that he took that day. He said it got damaged when he sent it to get developed.

DUI? What's that?

In East Anaheim, there was a bar named the Galloping Goose. I am sure there was no connection to the well-known club that started in 1942. We knew the Galloping Goose and had good relations with them. This place was a frequent watering hole for us around 1971.

One night, a bunch of us were there, and I'd had a lot to drink – mostly beer, but maybe a shot of tequila. Or two. It was rather unusual back then for me to drink much, but I must have been celebrating something, or perhaps someone else was buying and I was happily drinking. It was late in the evening and we were feeling pretty good. We had been there for hours, with the bikes parked safely in the back behind the bar. Gremlin's wife, Jan, enjoyed letting some of the guys put their hands inside her blouse and feel her breasts and hard nipples. We were enjoying it too.

At some point, I decided that I needed to leave. Saying goodbye to everyone, I walked out the back door to where the bikes were parked only to do an immediate U-turn and go back into the bar. I'd found two police cars sitting there: Orange County Sheriff's Deputies.

I knew I was too drunk to try to kick-start that bike without wobbling all over the place in front of two cops. Going back inside, I went up to Barry, who also had long, red hair, only lighter than mine. I gave him my key and told him to go out and start my bike, then act like he had forgotten something, leave it running, and come back inside.

He did as I asked. After he came back in, I calmly walked out, got on the bike, pushed the suicide clutch in with my left foot, whacked it into gear, and rode off. We thought we had fooled the cops. All bikers look alike, and they couldn't tell the difference. It seemed like a good plan at the time, but probably didn't fool anyone.

Whether they really didn't notice or just couldn't be bothered, I'll never know. Or maybe they knew I was drunk and might kill myself, which would mean one less Hangman for them to worry about.

Back then, that area of East Anaheim was mostly industrial. I pulled out onto the late-night deserted streets and made my way to the 91 Freeway. Accelerating up the onramp while cranking on the throttle, my left hand reaching down to shift gears, I found myself cruising along the 91 when it started to rain.

I don't even remember where I was going, but I do remember leaning back on my sleeping bag, enjoying the feel of the rain on my face.

I could feel the headache even before I forced myself to open my bleary eyes to unfamiliar surroundings. It was someone's living room and I was on a couch, but I couldn't figure out who's. Lifting my head to look around, I saw Hipster in the kitchen, making coffee. He had been at the bar the night before and greeted me with a derisive, "Good morning, Sunshine!"

Confused, I asked, "How did I get here?"

He said, "Damned if I know. When I pulled up, your bike was sitting in the driveway on the kickstand, in front of the garage, and you were lying in the front yard, on your back, in the rain! I brought you in here and put your bike in the garage. Other than that, I don't have a fucking clue."

I said, "Do you have some aspirin to go with that coffee?"

Just another day in the life.

Hipster

Chapter 20
Gladiator School

The author in Anaheim, California

I liked to ride up to Modesto and party with Jim and the boys. I was drifting from one place to another, staying with my brothers or maybe a temporary girlfriend. It didn't matter whether I was down south or up north. I lost track of how many trips I made up there; it was just a short six-hour motorcycle ride up Highway 99 in the San Joaquin Valley. It would have been my home away from home if I'd had one.

My home was on my bike. After Gentleman Jim moved up there, he collected a crew of hardcore bikers. Jim liked to drink and fight, probably because he was so good at both. All of the hang-arounds were the same way. They were a tough crowd, and it was never a dull moment.

Oddly, for as much as we used to drink and ride our motorcycles, I don't remember any crashes or DUIs because of drinking.

It's like the police didn't care that much about it back then, maybe because this was before Mothers Against Drunk Driving got the laws changed.

Back in Modesto again, I left a bar one night and rode along a dark country road, heading to an old farmhouse that Jim was renting.

I was going pretty fast – how fast, I didn't know because we didn't run speedometers. Suddenly, red lights lit up behind me. The local constabulary!

I pulled over, put down my kickstand, and got off the bike. Only then did I realize how drunk I was.

It was going to be impossible to stand without swaying back and forth or stumbling, so while I was getting my wallet out, trying to look casual, I leaned against my sissy bar to steady myself. There I stayed the whole time I was talking to the cop.

"Do you know how fast you were going?"

I said no and pointed to the front of the bike so he could see for himself.

He said, "This is a forty-five-mile-an-hour zone, and you were doing seventy."

I was relieved. At least I wasn't going really fast! As he wrote the ticket, he went on and on, talking about how sometimes cows would get out on the road at night, and some of them were black, and you would never see them until you hit one.

He also said he did not want to be the one to have to come and clean up the mess. I had to admit, he had a good point.

This was something I had not thought of – but then, being drunk, I had not thought of much, which was kind of a bad habit of mine. I did appreciate his concern for my safety, though. As we parted, I thanked him. And I never paid the ticket.

We didn't get into fights in every bar, every night, but it seemed like we did, and sometimes more than one a night. The big clubs in the area were the Bar Hoppers and the Mofomen. Plus, there were a lot of independent bikers and plenty of cowboys. That part of the country contained many ranches, and Modesto was a cowboy town.

What do cowboys like to do? Ride horses, drink, and fight. What do bikers like to do? Ride motorcycles, drink, and fight. And maybe, occasionally, play a game of pool.

It seemed there were always plenty of good-looking women, on both sides, to cheer us on – or, at least, to cause a fight.

It was like a sport. The shit could hit the fan for the smallest reason, or sometimes no reason at all. Cowboys and bikers didn't like each other. We were too much alike. It was kind of like the situation with motorcycle clubs. We're too much alike, so we hate each other.

A good movie analogy is Tombstone, with the characters Johnny Ringo and Doc Holiday. They find they are so much alike, that they hate each other. This boils down to hating... themselves? So they hate anybody like them? Not judging here, just posing a question.

So, it was no surprise that we all used to go at it a lot. If nobody pulled a knife or a gun, it could be fun, like the brawls in the saloons you used to see in old cowboy movies. It really was just like that at times.

Most of the time, nobody held a grudge after it was over. And most of the time, nobody really 'won' anyway. We often fought to a draw when everybody got too tired. We were happy to leave before the police got there, and our opponents were glad to see us go.

Being outnumbered was normal. You might have six or ten bikers, but when you went into a cowboy bar, which would tend to resent it, you could end up fighting the whole bar.

At times, the fights involved some of the women. Guess they wanted to get in on their share of the fun. Back then, we got

away with a lot, when there weren't cameras everywhere. Now, there would be too much evidence.

I think it was Hipster who appropriately dubbed Modesto "Gladiator School." To us So.Cal. guys, that was what it came to be known. Not that we didn't have our share of fights down south, but it really seemed like the wild west in Modesto.

The melee in Oakdale.

Sometime in the summer of 1971, there was a disagreement with the locals. Although I was in town, I was not at the bar that night in Oakdale. Fifteen miles east of Motown, Oakdale is another cowboy town right on the outskirts of the ranch lands and cattle country of the foothills of the Sierra Nevada range.

I never heard how the fight started (not that it mattered), but it sounded like a whopper: Five of our guys – Chuck, Kanaka, Huey, Crazy Jack, and a guy named Tramp – against a whole bar full of cowboys, about twenty of them.

I've put descriptions of some of these guys in the back of the book. They were a hardcore bunch.

Our boys walked out of there standing up, but just barely. Chuck wasn't hurt badly, but Kanaka left the bar with a broken jaw and spent the next six weeks with it wired shut. Baby Huey was slammed in the head so hard with a piece of firewood that it crushed part of his skull. He was conscious and walking, but in a daze.

When he was taken to the hospital, they operated and removed the shattered bone, which was about the size of a waffle. His brain was left unprotected for months before they could put in a plate to protect it.

Crazy Jack was unhurt, but somewhere during the fight, he had slammed his Buck knife into the side of a guy's head, at a bit of an angle. The blade pierced the guy's skull and then snapped off, leaving Jack holding the handle. He just stuck it in his pocket and went back to swinging. Later, on the way back to Modesto, he stopped along Highway 108 and tossed the handle into the Stanislaus River.

The knife blade's new owner got into his pickup truck and drove himself to the hospital, where they removed about two inches of razor-sharp steel from his head. No charges were ever filed against anyone.

Bar Hoppers President Manuel Victor.

About a week later, the Bar Hoppers held a bike night event at a drive-in movie theater in Ceres, just south of Modesto. Jim and I showed up with some of his crew. None were patch holders yet.

It would be four more years before he felt he had enough dependable guys to start a new No.Cal. chapter. Along with us were Kanaka, with his jaw wired shut, and Huey, wearing a chrome German steel helmet, as he was still recovering from the fight and his brain was unprotected. Chuck and Crazy Jack were there too.

Manuel Victor was not only the Bar Hoppers' president, but also the founder of the club. The Bar Hoppers were a big club then and they're even bigger now. Manuel had been a Hells Angel for a while, but was unhappy with the club's structure, so he decided to start his own.

In addition to the Bar Hoppers MC legacy, there is now a Manuel Victor Memorial MC. How cool is that, to have a whole club named after you? Talk about respect! I know of no other club named after a person. Back in the '50s, he was known as the toughest man in Stanislaus County. Manuel Victor was a legend in his own time.

Gentleman Jim and Manuel had a good relationship, with mutual respect. It was late afternoon and the sun had set, but there was still a bit of daylight at the event at the drive-in. Jim and I heard a commotion nearby: shouting, pushing, shoving.

Making our way to the action, we saw that some of our guys were involved, and we dove into the middle of it. Crazy Jack had a bloody knife in his hand, a new one after last week's fight. Jim grabbed him and pulled him back. The pushing and shoving were still going on.

When we got everyone separated and a little bit calmed down, we were surprised to find that his target was none other than Manuel Victor.

I always wondered why some of these guys, like Jack, who was strong enough and tough enough, were so quick to use a knife when most of the time their fists were more than adequate. If you don't NEED a knife, don't use one.

I saw it many times. I have to think they just liked to stab or slice someone.

Jim asked Crazy Jack what the fuck he was doing. Jack said that Manuel and Kanaka were having a disagreement about something, and he was afraid that Manuel was going to hit Kanaka, whose jaw was wired shut from the fight last week.

While we were trying to sort out the problem, Manuel Victor walked up to us, holding his T-shirt up and saying, "Jim, I'm hurt. I need to go to the hospital." When I looked at him, I hope my eyes didn't bug out.

He had about five or six stab wounds in his stomach with intestines protruding from each one of them. It looked just like pink bubbles from bubble gum.

Oh shit. It's bad enough to stab someone from another club when you're at their event and way outnumbered. But stabbing their president and founder? Not good judgment!

It was just as bad as when, several years later, another Hangman stabbed the president and founder of our friends, the El Forasteros, in Kansas. I wished they wouldn't keep doing that! That one was a case of mistaken identity because Tom Fugle was not wearing a patch at the time. But I wasn't there when it happened. It got handled, and I will let someone else tell that story.

Manuel was loaded into a car and shipped off to the nearest hospital to get the wounds sewn up. I was surprised at how calm he was. He was no stranger to a life of action and violence; Manuel had been there before. That left Jim and me to try to calm down a bunch of really pissed-off Bar Hoppers.

Eventually, after Manuel got out of the hospital, all was forgiven and forgotten, as it turned out that Manuel Victor was Crazy Jack's uncle! I guess he decided to keep it all in the family.

Ironically, thirty-five years later, his grandson, also named Manuel Victor, who for a time wore a Hangmen patch, was also stabbed in the abdomen during an altercation in Oregon.

Baby-Sitting Baby Huey.

After getting part of his head crushed and, for a time, not having the proper amount of bone to protect his brain, six-foot-six Baby Huey was starting to get a little paranoid. I couldn't blame him. Probably still suffering from a severe concussion, he was getting very erratic and unstable.

When you have someone his size, it is not as if you can take control of the situation without shooting him. He took to wearing a chrome World War II German helmet to protect his head. He was getting very unpredictable, like his buddy Crazy Jack.

But Jack didn't need an excuse. With Huey, it was like having the Incredible Hulk as a friend and trying to keep him from hurting anyone for no reason.

That was what happened one night a short time later. I rode down to Ceres one evening to visit with Huey, but he was not at home. He was down at the local tavern having a few brews.

This was probably not a good idea, not only because of the head injury, but also because of the medications he was on at the time. It was going okay; we were hanging out and having a few beers. I was about to call it a night, get on my bike, and head out. I put on my jacket and walked out to the parking lot.

Huey and I were standing outside the bar when a guy came out and, seeing my patch, started talking about the Hangmen. He was friendly and complimentary, saying something like, "Hangmen, you guys are fuckin' cool, Hangmen rock, you're the best."

But somehow Huey didn't hear it that way. He exploded at the guy, shouting, "You don't ever talk about the Hangmen like that!" Huey socked him and the guy flew back against the bar, probably hitting his head against the stucco wall, in case the punch wasn't enough. He slid down the wall, unconscious.

I turned away, looking for witnesses, thinking, 'Oh shit, here we go again.' Only that, too, was a mistake. When I looked back, Huey had taken out his knife and was slashing back and forth across the guy's chest and stomach, still ranting and raving about how the guy should not talk about the Hangmen.

I was horrified and jumped forward to grab his arm, trying to haul him off the guy. Fortunately, he listened to me. He was literally twice my size, at least in weight, but I was a patch holder and demanded his respect.

Thank goodness that, even in this situation, it worked. It was like having an unruly elephant on a leash. I finally succeeded in dragging Huey by the arm over to his pickup truck. Then I told him to get the hell out of there and go home. He reluctantly started it up and left.

Running back to the guy slumped down against the wall, I checked his pulse, which was still strong. He seemed to be breathing steadily. When I pulled up his shirt, I saw that the knife wounds were just light superficial cuts, with no deep punctures, protruding intestines, or heavy bleeding. The knife must have been dull.

I hoped he would be okay and I felt terrible that the guy got hurt for no reason. Worrying about patrons of the bar coming out, especially after possibly hearing "Hangmen this and Hangmen that," I wanted to get out of there too.

I switched on my key and jumped on the kick-starter. My trusty bike roared to life, causing me to wish, for once, that the pipes weren't so loud. As soon as it fired up, I whacked it into gear and was gone. Just a couple of blocks away, I made a right turn and headed back up Highway 99 to Modesto.

Huey smoothed out after a while, but in the meantime, I felt like a lion tamer, trying to keep the beasts under control while hoping they don't turn on you and eat you too.

Saturday night's alright for fighting

~ Elton John

We were riding down to Turlock on Saturday night, as one of the local clubs was putting on a dance, and a lot of bikers were there: Hangmen, Bar Hoppers, Mofomen, and the usual loners. Despite what the '60s biker movies convey, most bikers don't dance. Just making an appearance was good enough: hang out, have a few beers, and then hit the road to another bar.

I never found out what started it. What difference did it make anyway? It was always something. I think the girls were there to dance at a dance, and the guys were there to drink and fight. So, it was no surprise when, suddenly, there was that familiar sound of stomping feet, cursing, thumping, chairs hitting the floor, glass breaking, and girls screaming. Looks like it was party time again! I had been standing near the front door with Jim's girlfriend, Guy, when it started. She glanced at me. Then, without saying a word, she darted out the door and into the night while I headed toward the sound of the commotion. Some were pulling back while others, like me, were pushing toward it. When I got there, Chuck, with one hand, had ripped a pistol away from some guy while slugging him to the floor with the other.

As I got behind him to guard his back, it looked like the guy he had hit had friends. They were rushing us from all directions, but they came to a skidding halt when the thundering explosion of a pistol shot went off right behind me. Indoors, that's always loud.

Thinking someone might have shot Chuck, I glanced back to see him holding the gun up. He had just fired a shot into the air, or, I should say, through the roof of the dance hall, trying to get people's attention and telling them to calm the fuck down. He then leveled the gun toward the people in front of him as if to say, "Okay, we're ready to rock and roll if you still want to." It seemed to work, as the crowd suddenly got quiet.

I had pulled out my knife, but kept it still closed in my hand. Glancing around, I waited for what was going to happen next. A movement at the front door caught my eye. I saw Guy calmly walk back in, holding a blue blanket with something about three feet long underneath it. I knew what it was. Jim walked up to her, casually reached under the blanket, and pulled out his M1 .30 caliber carbine. He had loaded it with a thirty-round magazine, racking the bolt to chamber a round. It sounded loud in that suddenly quiet room. Heads turned to look at him.

Guy had driven a car and brought the backup artillery, and Jim now took tactical control of the situation with superior firepower. Fortunately, we didn't need it. Any opposition melted away as people started leaving. The guy whom Chuck had knocked out was still lying there at his feet. He could hit hard!

It appeared that the dance was over as the room emptied. Not wanting to be around when the police showed up, with shots fired and all, we decided that would be a good plan for us too.

Chuck flicked on the safety and stuck the gun in his belt, while Jim put the hardware away and handed it back to Guy. We made our way to where the bikes were parked and fired them up to ride back to Jim's place.

Later, we got back to the house and Chuck pulled out his new prize. It was a Colt 1911 in .38 Super caliber – quite a nice piece. But the funny thing was, there was no magazine, and it was empty of ammo.

We reconstructed the mystery and figured out what had happened. When Chuck saw the guy pull the gun to try to shoot him, he jumped toward him and got control of it, but had to struggle for possession of it for a few seconds. In that time, one of them must have accidentally hit the magazine release.

The full magazine of ammo had popped out and fallen to the floor. With one round left in the chamber, Chuck fired his warning shot to get people's attention. That was the last round in the gun. When he fired, the slide functioned normally, not locking back because there was no empty magazine. He was now holding off a dance hall full of bikers with an empty weapon.

We laughed and laughed. Good thing Guy had produced the artillery and we had Jim on overwatch. We could've had a problem.

Chuck Chapman

Chapter 21
Meeting OKLA

In early 1971 we got a phone call from somebody in Oklahoma who claimed they were Hangmen and wanted to know who the fuck we were. Well, of course, we wanted to know who the fuck they were. After a couple of phone conversations between our presidents, both sides decided that we needed to meet and talk this out.

The plan was to send some of us So.Cal. boys on a trip out to Oklahoma to meet with these guys. If they were punks, we would pull their patches, and that would be it. Of course, they felt the same way. Little did we both know.

We set a date for the meeting in Oklahoma City. This was May of 1971. I was a new patch holder and gung-ho as you can get. Two factions from So.Cal. would go east. One was Charlie, Uncle Tom, and Curt, who would fly to OKC in Curt's airplane, a tiny four-seat Piper Tri-Pacer. The other was a ground operation involving Skip's 1964 Lincoln Continental. Black, of course. I don't know where he got it, but it was a nice car. In it were Skip, TK (who was So.Cal. President at the time), and me, the kid. I was still nineteen.

The trip both ways was an experience of a lifetime all by itself. 'Road trip!' We drove straight through, with no hotel rooms, as we couldn't afford them. We took turns driving, and the back seat was big enough for one of us to curl up on and sleep.

When we stopped to eat, it was usually at little mom-and-pop diners. That was mostly what was available back then. But there were Denny's as well, and sometimes we stopped there.

Skip would always order a hamburger with cottage cheese and coffee. After he ate the hamburger, he would take out a little matchbox that he carried.

Covertly opening it, he would produce a dead fly and mash it into the cottage cheese. He knowingly advised that you had to order cottage cheese because you could not make a fly look cooked in french fries.

He would call the waitress over, looking kind of sick, and show her the fly in his cottage cheese. Oh, the horror! He always got his meal for free. The first time, TK and I got a big laugh out of it, but after that, we would help him out by trying to look repulsed by the icky fly in the cottage cheese. It got to be routine.

After getting to Oklahoma, we soon linked up with the OKLA boys. After one look at each other, the party was on.

Unfortunately, Curt, Tom, and Charlie were delayed because they'd accidentally landed at the wrong airport. It was the U.S. Army base at Fort Sill. The Army started shooting up flares to try to warn them off because they weren't on the proper radio frequency and didn't belong there. Curt and the boys thought, 'Isn't that cool? The guys here are setting off fireworks to welcome us.'

They landed, but when they got the airplane stopped, Jeeps full of military police greeted them, aiming M-16s at their heads. After being escorted to separate rooms, they underwent a third-degree interrogation for several hours.

They were finally allowed to leave with a warning to be more careful in the future. After flying into the right airport, they called us, and we sent a car to pick them up. They joined the party.

OKLA was started by Rex in 1969. He had been a charter member of the Richmond Hangmen. After leaving Northern California, he did not know about the So.Cal. chapter.

It didn't take long before both sides knew, "These guys are righteous Hangmen." No two ways about it: They were just like us, and we were just like them. There was no discussion; it was a no-brainer. It was weird, having never met each other, but we were suddenly one club.

We partied it up, filled each other in on backgrounds, and started making plans to get all of the chapters together and make it official. It was decided that all chapters would meet at the Grand Canyon on July 4, 1971. It was to be the first National Run.

You know how parties are. If it's a good one, there is not a lot to re-member. We were there for three days. The visit was over too quickly, and suddenly it was time for us to leave.

We had cemented the relationship, which continues to this day. OKLA is one of the strongest chapters we have, and they have a history and reputation in that state that is second to none.

We also learned that the boys in Oklahoma had another Wild West atmosphere. They had not only bikers and cowboys, but also Indians.

Before it was a state, Oklahoma was known as "Indian Territory." In the nineteenth century, the U.S. government forcibly relocated many of the tribes around the country.

So, there are a lot of them there. Like bikers and cowboys, they like to drink and fight. They aren't so good at the drinking part, but they're good at the fighting part. The warrior spirit is still strong.

On average, the OKLA boys had been shot or stabbed, or both, more than the So.Cal. and No.Cal. boys put together.

Besides lots of driving, sleeping in the back seat, and dead flies, I don't remember a lot about the trip back. However, an interesting thing happened one night while we were driving in a monsoon season thunder-storm.

We were east of Flagstaff, on Interstate 40, although lots of it was still the old Route 66 back then. We stopped for gas at a Shell station right alongside the road in Winona, Arizona. Lightning was flashing all over the sky and had been for quite a while.

I was driving and had the left window down when I pulled up to the pumps. Before I could get out, the whole gas station filled with incredibly white light. Then two crashes of thunder sounded, like someone firing off both barrels of a shotgun, one right after the other, right next to your head, only a lot louder. Then, immediately, the whole gas station went dark.

We didn't see where the bolts hit, but it was very close. We sat there in the dark, smelling the pungent ozone. For a few seconds, the air seemed to crackle. We waited for the gas station to explode, but it didn't. If it were going to, it would have done so by now.

With the power out, we weren't going to be getting gas there. Feeling as if we'd had a very close call, we got a good laugh about almost getting killed by a bolt of lightning after the life we lived.

I started the car and we headed down the road a little bit to Flagstaff to find a station in working order.

Who'll Stop the Rain?

June 1971 found me hurrying back to Modesto again. I'd been sitting in So.Cal. with not much going on when the phone rang. It was Hipster.

He was at the No.Cal. clubhouse, which meant Jim's rented farmhouse out in the countryside.

Hipster had just had an altercation with a Hells Angel from San Francisco. Jim physically picked up Hipster and hauled him away after he had gotten in the guy's face and threatened to kill him. Enraged, the Hells Angel left, saying, "I'll be back tomorrow with a hundred Hells Angels, and we'll level this place."

So, Hipster and the Modesto Boys needed some backup. Two more Hangmen ought to do it. Curt had a Chevy panel truck with a Corvette engine. It hauled ass and had a lot of room in the back, so Curt and I loaded it up with all the guns we had and a few that we borrowed from some brothers before we left town.

Soon, we hit Interstate 5, then Highway 99, speeding to Modesto to arrive before all of those Hells Angels did. We didn't want to miss the fun.

We arrived at the 'clubhouse' in the late afternoon. It was just an old farmhouse, but someone cultivated a crop of corn on three sides of the place.

Sitting about one hundred yards off the rural farm road, it had one way in and one way out, with a two-story pumphouse, which made for a perfect sniper position. There were cornfields all around as far as you could see, and a big, old, red barn next to the house.

Gentleman Jim was there, of course, as was his crew: Baby Huey, Kanaka, Tramp, Mexican Bob, Jimmy Joyce, and Crazy Jack, to name a few. Jim always had a hardcore bunch of guys backing him up, even if they weren't patch holders. Although, later on, some would be.

Curt and I arrived with the arsenal in the late afternoon. After passing out guns and ammo for the defense of the Alamo, we started drinking. Before long, someone offered us peyote. Or was it LSD? Either way, the effect was pretty much the same.

We were in the living room, talking strategy for the night, when a gunshot rang out in the kitchen. Without a word, we all charged for the kitchen, bursting through two different doors at the same time with guns drawn to take down the threat, only to find one of the local Modesto boys laughing and apologizing for accidentally putting a round into the refrigerator.

The evening and night devolved into a party. So much for defending the Alamo. At one point, someone called us into a bedroom where some girls were screaming. Upon arriving, one squealed, "It's in his mouth!"

Jim and I pushed the door open and found Tramp sucking some guy's dick, apparently trying to show the girls how it was done. Tramp was a good man to have at your side in a fight, but I guess he had spent a little too much time in prison, probably thinking that kind of thing was okay, but it wasn't. He got sent down the road and I never saw him again.

I'm not sure what drugs they gave us, but neither Hipster nor I were able to sleep. We were wide awake and blazing on some kind of trip.

When Hipster disappeared, I assumed he had gone to sleep like the others. I spent most of the night sitting on the front porch of this old farmhouse out in the countryside, with cornfields all around.

I sat in a rocking chair and whittled on a stick with my knife, weapons ready, my feet propped up on the old, paint-chipped railing around the porch facing that long driveway, which was the only way in.

I don't know if there was a record that was sticking or what. It seemed to me that the only song that played that night, over and over, was "Who'll Stop the Rain" by Credence Clearwater.

In my spaced-out, drug-distorted mind, the "rain" was the onslaught of Hells Angels that was supposed to arrive to attack us, probably at sunrise. And the "Who'll stop" part was us. But since nobody else was up or awake, it seemed that it would be just me.

Over and over, I checked my weapons to make sure they were loaded and ready. I had a short-barreled Mossberg 12-gauge pump shotgun loaded with double aught buck and a .38 revolver. Boxes of extra ammo were nearby.

Throughout the long night, with an almost full moon, hearing the same damn song over and over, I watched that long driveway, expecting an invading army. The moon sailed across the sky and set in the west. The night got very dark.

Eventually, the eastern sky began to lighten. The morning was on its way. It surprised me because I had no sense of time. It was like one of those dreams that just goes on and on forever.

When it was light enough to see, I noticed someone walking up that long driveway. I sat and watched, knowing that an invading army would not send one person on foot. I kept carving on my stick.

Soon, as he got closer, I could see that it was Hipster, walking back to the house. As he came within range, he just kept marching toward the front door of the farmhouse.

Covered in mud, he looked like the Swamp Creature. It was in his hair; it was everywhere. Limping as he walked, he was carrying one boot, which was full of mud. He didn't seem disposed to talk, and I didn't think it was important in the overall scheme of things. I was still on duty.

"Mornin', Hipster."

"G'mornin," he mumbled back as he stomped up the steps of the wooden porch and into the house.

I didn't find out until later that he had somehow gotten lost in the cornfield, which had just been irrigated and was full of mud. It's easy to do even if you are sober, as when you're inside a cornfield, you can't see any direction but up.

Not being able to get his bearings in the tall corn, Hipster had been there in the dark for hours, just about all night, still on a psychedelic trip that he had not planned on.

He was floundering around, lost, feeling like he would never get out. He had visions of dying in there, with no one ever finding his body. It would get plowed under by massive farm equipment after the corn was harvested.

He said that he kept seeing people in the cornfield and would chase after them, begging them to help him, but they would disappear into thin air. Nobody was there.

He was probably going in circles much of the night. When he finally burst through a wall of corn stalks into the open, it felt like a reprieve from a death sentence.

What a fucking ordeal, a real nightmare. Certainly, worse than shooting it out with a hundred Hells Angels.

After Hipster went inside, the purple sky slowly turned to red, then pink, and then pretty soon faded into blue. The sun broke from the horizon and started blasting me with unbearable shafts of light.

The porch faced the eastern sky, which left me at the mercy of the sun's angry glare. But it showed no mercy.

Everyone was sleeping and no one seemed to care if the invading army was about to arrive.

Suddenly, I didn't care either.

As fatigue crept into my brain, I decided to call it quits too. In case I have not already explained it, getting caught crashing was usually not a good thing, depending on where you were or who you were around. I always made it a habit to disappear if I needed to sleep.

Rather than going inside the house and searching for a bed of some kind, I headed out to that big old red barn that was probably at least one hundred years old. In it, I found a nice pile of straw that would do for a little shuteye.

Before giving it up, I stretched my muscles, which were cramped from sitting all night. Then, in the slanting morning light of the open barn door, I practiced some of the karate moves that I had learned from the Ed Parker Black Belts whom I had trained with in Anaheim when I was a prospect.

Finally, lying on the soft hay, I took off my leather jacket, put it over me, stretched out, and closed my eyes. After what seemed like just a few minutes, I woke up, still lying on the straw, burning hot. The sun was shining in through the open barn doors and I was sweating.

It must have been ten o'clock in the morning, so I figured I had gotten enough sleep. Guess I'd go in and see what was happening.

When I walked into the kitchen, it seemed everyone was sitting in there, eating cereal, bacon, and eggs or drinking beer.

Surprised to see me, they asked, "Where the hell have you been?"

"Sleeping."

"Where?"

"In the barn."

Shocked and amazed, they said, "What the fuck?"

"Yeah, why? So what?"

Jim said, "We've been using the fucking barn for target practice all morning."

They looked at me like I was crazy for sleeping there, but I shrugged and said, "I wasn't the one who was shooting guns."

As I was lying there, snoozing away on the hay, my buds were popping rounds through the thin wooden barn walls, right over my snoring head, and I never knew it. I'm glad nobody shot low.

Another funny aside to this story is that when Hipster got home to So.Cal, he went straight into the bedroom and crashed for about twenty-four hours.

Lovie, his Ol' Lady, saw that his clothes, along with his cut and back-patch, were a mess. She decided to do him a favor and put them in the washing machine.

We might spend years cultivating a set of jeans, collecting oil and dirt, turning them into what we called "slicks." They were like imitation leather.

At least part of the excuse for wearing them was that if you found yourself traveling across the asphalt without the benefit of a motorcycle under you, the slicks would slide rather than tear. Frequently, we wore a clean set of jeans underneath them, but not when it was hot.

We used to joke that you could stand them in a corner when you took them off. Of course, our slicks didn't really stand up by themselves (although I did have a pair of thick wool socks for wintertime that I could stand up next to my boots).

When Hipster woke up, he was horrified to find that his Levi's, cut, and patch were now immaculate. Only motorcycles are allowed to be immaculate.

Back then, nobody wanted to have a clean patch. It took years to earn it, and once you got it, nobody wanted to look like an FNG, a 'Fucking New Guy.'

He read her the riot act for making him look like a newbie all over again. It was his fault, of course, for not giving her the briefing.

When we saw it, we got a good laugh, knowing that we would have to initiate it all over again.

The first National Run at the Grand Canyon was coming up in a couple of weeks. We decided to save it until then.

Hipster and the author in Modesto, the day before the cornfield story.

Chapter 22
Arrested for CCW

O ne of our associates in Modesto was called Karate Rich, and he was a
real badass. He had invented his very own style of karate by training
for years in his basement. He had gotten so good at it that the American
Karate Foundation had sanctioned him with his own specific style.

He was another guy who was good to have beside you if the shit hit
the fan. As you've seen, in Modesto, there was a lot of shit and a lot of fans.
He used to show us drills on things like how to take a knife from someone.

I never actually saw him fight. It seemed he never had to. He was pretty well known, and everyone was afraid of him. But he was a Hangmen
hang-around, so we didn't have to worry about Rich. He was on our side.

We were expecting trouble for some reason, I don't remember why,
but that was standard in Gladiator School. I was carrying a .38 Smith &
Wesson revolver in a shoulder holster and vbv I had it loaded with the best
ammo at the time: Super Vel brand hollow points.

Rich and I headed out from Jim's place on our bikes to go somewhere,
but I didn't know he had some arrest warrants. All the cops knew who he was
and were probably scared to death of him and his abilities. So, when he was
spotted, it wasn't one or two cops who stopped us; it was about ten of them.

He had warrants, so Rich was going to jail. That was guaranteed. He knew it and the cops knew it.

I was just there, and once they ran a records check, there was no reason to fuck with me. However, one cop didn't see it that way. He came over to me and said, "Get up against the car!" Then he grabbed me, threw me against his patrol car, and started searching me.

Back then, the police in California did not like it when you carried a gun. Although they take an oath to defend the constitution, somehow, they didn't believe in the Second Amendment. How do they justify that? I'm sure it is even worse now.

When he found the .38 in my shoulder holster, he acted like it was a personal insult to him. With me leaning against the car, he ripped it out of the holster, cocked it, and put it to the back of my head, shoving it over and over against my skull and yelling in my ear, "Is this going to go off if I pull the trigger? Huh? Is this loaded? Shall I pull the trigger and find out?"

Trying to stay calm I said, "Yes, it's loaded." I didn't want to excite him any more than he already was.

Smith & Wesson revolvers, when cocked, have a very light hair trigger. It wouldn't have taken much to make the gun go off. I started to sweat. The situation was somewhat stressful, as there didn't seem to be much I could do about it.

Not content to do it once to make a point, and probably showing off for his buddies, this idiot cop couldn't get enough. He kept at it for a good thirty seconds or more as I tried to talk to him and calm him down. Finally, a couple of the other cops came over and told him to knock it off.

I let out a deep sigh of relief when he uncocked the gun, put me in handcuffs, stuffed me into the back of his car, and took me to jail for Carrying a Concealed Weapon – such a no-no in California.

When I went to the arraignment for the charges, my public defender made a motion to dismiss the case, saying that the cop had no reason or probable cause to search me. Fourth Amendment, ya know. Remember, that pesky Constitution?

The judge asked the cop what probable cause or justification he had for searching me. The cop said that I was with a dangerous wanted criminal. The judge felt that wasn't good enough.

Slamming his gavel down, he said, "Case dismissed. Illegal search and seizure."

I even got the gun back.

We had a lot of contact with the Modesto P.D. The kicker to all this came about three weeks later.

Late one afternoon, while speeding up 9th Street on my well-known red chopper, I was greeted with red lights and a siren from behind.

Throwing out the kickstand and stepping off the bike, I reached for my wallet, but the cop said, "I don't need that."

Hesitantly, I said, "Okay… What's up?"

He said, "You might find this interesting. Remember when you got busted for carrying that gun last month?"

"Yeah, of course, that cop was a jerk. The charges got dropped."

"I know, but have you heard what happened to him?"

"No, what happened?"

"He got fired. Last week he called in sick, then got picked up down in Merced driving drunk with a woman in the car, but it just so happens he is married."

"No shit? Well, that's good news."

"I thought you'd be happy to hear that. He's been a problem for a while. When the chief found out about it, he canned him immediately. Nobody liked the guy and we're glad to be rid of him."

"Thanks for letting me know. You made my day."

He turned back to his car and said over his shoulder, "And slow it down, would ya? Next time, I'll write you up."

Angels Camp, California.

It was May of 1971 and I was still in Modesto. The Calaveras County Frog Jump was going on. Having been written about by Mark Twain, it had been held continuously since 1928. Leading his Motown Gladiator School Crew, Jim and I decided to ride up there because it was a popular biker run.

In the foothills of the Sierra Nevada mountains, it was an easy hour and fifteen-minute ride up to Jamestown and north on Highway 49 through rolling hills and the beautiful goldrush country, with oak trees lining the highway.

The weather was great, springtime in California. About ten of us rode in tight formation, cruising up into the hills and rumbling through small towns. We arrived at Angels Camp at about noon on Saturday and picked an open field of dry grass in a clearing as a space for camping.

We broke out the beer and started having fun, walking around and greeting some of the other clubs. There were Bar Hoppers, Mofomen, Chosen Few, and Booze Fighters.

Jim seemed to know everyone. It was now about a year after the fight in the bar with the Satan's Slaves and the situation to get his patch back.

It turned out that Hells Angels came here every year, as the name 'Angels Camp' made it sound like the place belonged to them. It did not, but they had been a constant presence since about 1957, so it was expected that they would show up. This year, there were some Satan's Slaves from way down in Los Angeles.

Not only was this the same club that Jim had fought and that had taken his patch after outnumbering and overwhelming him, but these were some of the very same people, including a guy on crutches whom

Jim pointed out to me, standing with a group of Hells Angels. They all scowled at us, looking our way from about fifty yards. They did not look happy to see us there.

The guy on crutches was the one on whose back Daffy had jumped up and down at the front door of the bar. Daffy just liked doing things like that. It could be hard to stop him from doing what he wanted to do. Besides, at the time, the other three Hangmen in the bar had been busy.

It seemed that this guy, still on crutches a year later, held a grudge, and maybe the rest of them did too. No doubt they also recognized Gentleman Jim. The way they were looking at us, it seemed they were plotting some payback for this guy's injuries.

Instead of being sociable with the vibes that were going on, Jim decided it was best to stay away from this group and not poke the bear. Our relations with the Hells Angels had always been respectful, but tenuous.

We set up a defensive perimeter around our campsite, put our Motown crew on security alert, and waited for the fireworks to start. It got dark. We had a backup car full of guns if needed.

Despite the tension, I was having a good time, drinking beer, wine, whiskey, or what anyone handed me. Wearing my leather cut with fringed sleeves, and with my long red hair and beard, I somehow ended up with a girl on my arm. I was not even sure where she came from.

She followed me around, hanging on my arm, telling me how cool I was. She said her name was Sally and she was also very drunk or stoned. I dragged her along as I walked from camp to camp. It seemed everyone wanted to give you something, either booze or drugs.

As the night wound down and the crowds thinned, I ended up in a little encampment with this girl's friends, whom they had driven up with from San Jose. A campfire was going between the two cars they had come in.

With a beer in my hand, I sat on a log next to the fire. Sally sat nearby with her back to the front wheel of one of the cars.

All was peaceful and mellow. Another girl was sitting across from the fire from me. She was very pretty – small and thin with long dark hair. She looked like a young version of Jennifer Connelly and caught my attention right away. We started a conversation.

Soon, I found out she was the younger sister of the one who had been following me around – the one who was now passed out, leaning against the front wheel of the car.

The little sister seemed very sweet and intelligent. The more we talked, the more I liked her. Realizing that her big sis was not going to wake up anytime soon, I asked the little sister, "Would you like to go for a walk?"

She said, "I would love to."

So, we got up, I took her hand, and she followed me a short distance to where I had parked my bike. Taking my ever-present sleeping bag off the sissy bar, I tucked it under my arm, and we walked off into the dark, down the hill through the tall, golden grass. We ended up in a shallow valley about one hundred yards from the encampments and parties.

Spreading out the sleeping bag on the long grass, we laid down and proceeded to, well, uh, get to know each other. Enjoying her sweet mouth and tongue quickly led to more joys and treats.

Pretty soon, we were naked, and she was attacking me with a vengeance. I was almost twenty years old, but had never been with a girl who was as hungry and aggressive as she was.

It was terrific. The sensations, the feel of her skin, the sounds she made, her aggressiveness – it was all heightened to a degree I had never felt before. She was beautiful and she was perfect. She was too much. She was trying to kill me.

Well, not really, but after several hours, I was crying uncle and asking for a break. I had to beg her to stop and let me get my breath.

When she finally let me rest, I promptly fell asleep. I needed it. At dawn, before the sun was up, I awoke with her on me again. God, this girl was insatiable. Had I known, I would have gone into training.

With the sun now up, we were still making love down in the open field. People cheered. They were a small crowd that had been watching from up the hill.

Only a little embarrassed, we waved at them, then finished what we were doing, got dressed, rolled up the sleeping bag, and headed back up to the camp.

All around, people were waking up and packing up. My pretty young partner of the night said she and her friends had to leave to get home.

I asked, "What's the rush?"

"We have a long drive back to San Jose, and I've got to be back in school tomorrow morning."

I asked, "College?"

Smiling, she said, "High school."

Shocked, I didn't know what to say. I didn't ask how old she was or what grade she was in. Suddenly, I didn't want to know. I started having nasty visions of a very pissed-off mother tracking me down with the police in tow.

After one more lovely kiss, she climbed into the car with her now-conscious sister, smiling and waving as they drove away. Damn, she was pretty, and what a hungry heart.

As I watched her go, Jim said to me, "Hey, Romeo, let's get this bunch saddled up and go find some breakfast." The tension was still there with some of the other clubs, but because there had been no action yet, we figured if it hadn't happened by then, it wasn't going to.

I put my sleeping bag on the sissy bar and pulled on my leather jacket, cut, gloves, and sunglasses. I was ready to ride. After jumping on our kick-starters, we were back on our way down Highway 49, riding in a tight pack within minutes.

Jim was leading on his red bike with the springer front end. I was next to him with my long wide glide. I was zoning out, living in the moment, leaning through the curves, riding in the pack, enjoying living life as we knew it.

Still, I was a little distracted. I was remembering the lovely face, the soft skin, and the incredible, wonderful smell of that girl. Only then I realized, I didn't even know her name.

Chapter 23
The First National Run: July 1971

Run time! Thursday, July 1. The tires were aired up. The bikes were polished, full of gas, and packed with sleeping bags, tools, and extra cans of motor oil. There would be no stopping at a gas station because of one straggler who didn't fill up. Everyone knew what was needed to be ready.

A marine layer had come in overnight; now there was a misty blue-gray light in the overcast morning in Orange County as we lined up outside Uncle Tom's house on Vine Street in Anaheim.

Some of us had struggled out of bed after a late night. A few of the Ol' Ladies came to see their men off with a kiss. I didn't have one, so no goodbye for me. I was with my brothers, riding together. Who needed goodbyes?

Before long, the fog lifted and twenty-two So.Cal. Hangmen thundered out of the quiet residential neighborhood. Jockeying a bit in the pack, doing a few wheelies in the soft early morning light, we were excited, and our blood was up. We were going on a run. This was what it was all about.

This wasn't just any run. We were off to meet our counterparts from Oklahoma, people whom we did not know existed until about three months ago. Some of us had not even met them. We made our way to palm tree-lined Lincoln Avenue, then found Highway 91 eastbound and out of town.

We drove Riverside and then San Bernardino and up, through the sweeping curves to the Cajon Pass. We leveled out into the heat of the high desert, through Victorville and then Barstow before turning east on Interstate 40, stopping only for gas and a cigarette.

It got hotter and hotter, but we were young and tough, and it didn't bother us. We rode through miles of desert in the hot, dry wind with sunburned faces and arms. Eventually, we passed through the middle of Needles, California on Route 66 and then Kingman, Arizona. When we headed into higher country, it started cooling off a bit.

We rumbled through the middle of the old town of Williams, also on Old 66. Most towns and cities had not yet been bypassed by Interstate 40, and we frequently traveled on original sections of Route 66.

In the mountains of Northern Arizona, we left the interstate, turning north at Williams on Highway 64, and pointed toward the Grand Canyon, our designated meeting place. It was one of the worst roads we had ever ridden.

The road had a seam every twenty feet or so, producing a constant th-thump, th-thump, about once per second. We rode on and on, enduring the pain on our rigid frame bikes, feeling the constant pounding in our butts and kidneys. It seemed to go on forever.

We were miserable, and everyone bitched about it when we stopped for any reason. Did I say you had to be tough to ride these bikes the way we did? So, when the guys complained like this, you knew it was pretty bad. After an hour, we finally came to the entrance of Grand Canyon National Park.

Most of us had never been to a national park before. After pulling up to the gate, two by two in formation, we shut down our bikes. We leaned them on their kickstands, got off and stretched, and then said hello to the park rangers, who flatly told us, "You're not coming in here."

"What the hell? Why not?"

"We know who you are, and you're not coming into the park."

Gentleman Jim and the Modesto crew had gotten there just ahead of us and had already tried to enter. Although they were riding, they had a backup vehicle that just happened to be full of guns, which we didn't know, back then, were not allowed in a national park.

The car got searched and the guns were temporarily confiscated. After checking the numbers, the rangers gave them back. Jim and the boys got turned away. When we arrived about an hour later, the rangers were expecting us. They didn't try to search us or our bikes, but they repeated, "You're not coming into the park."

We had to turn the pack around and follow a park ranger in a green pickup truck, who was designated to lead us back down the road to a camping area they set aside for us not far from the park entrance. Riding back south, we turned right off US 64 into Kaibab National Forest, about one hundred yards down a little-used dirt road leading to a large clearing among the tall pine trees that would serve as a primitive campground. There was water, no picnic tables – just trees, pine needles, and dirt. Jim and the Motown boys were already there.

We took up collections for beer, wine, and food. Prospects and hang-arounds were put into Jim's backup car and sent to a store in the nearby town of Tusayan to stock up.

We'd placed another prospect out on the highway. He soon flagged down the OKLA pack, and we were treated to that exciting rumble of an inbound group of Harleys. They were riding up the dirt road, bouncing on their rigid frames, into our new home for the next few days. The party was on.

There were greetings among those who had already met in Oklahoma and introductions all around for those who had not.

We did get to go into the park as long as it was no more than two bikes at a time. We were able to get the obligatory photos of standing on the edge of the Grand Canyon, but no more than a few of us at a time.

I went into a gift shop with Gremlin and bought a tiny silver skull with a hinged jaw and a flag on it that said Grand Canyon, Ariz. I fastened it into the leather on my cut. After thousands of miles of riding and untold numbers of fights, surprisingly, it is still there.

The party for the next three days was good. We would stand around the fire late into the night, with both sides getting to know each other. We told stories and listened to others, laughing so hard our stomachs hurt. We drank beer or took pulls from a bottle of whiskey or tequila or hits off a joint as they were passed around.

Finally, we would fall asleep by the fire or stagger off into the dark forest, hopefully remembering to take our sleeping bags with us. The nights were cool at that altitude, even in the middle of summer.

We woke up in the pine forest with the sun in our eyes and, often, a headache. Alone or in small groups, we rode into the little town just down the road for coffee and breakfast, did a little sightseeing, or just hung out around the camp.

We visited with long-time brothers or got to know new ones – guys with names like Muther, Greg, Zero, Wezil, Papa Joe, Squatty, Mike, Davey, and Spence, to name a few. As the sun went down, the drinking and smoking would increase, and we would do it all over again.

When the run was over, we went our separate ways, but we were now solidly one club, and that has never changed.

The last morning, I slept late. As I lay inside my sleeping bag, which was pulled over my head to keep the sun out, I heard, as if from a great distance, Skip's voice slowly invading my dreams. He was yelling my name over and over. When I came back to reality, I stuck my head out of the bag and said, "What?"

"We're getting ready to go. Everybody is looking for you."

I said, "Why are you standing way over there, yelling?"

He pointed to the empty pistol holster next to my sleeping bag and said, "I'm not stupid."

Unbeknownst to us, law enforcement and the park rangers had been freaking out the whole time we were there. Bizarre rumors of a planned invasion had them calling in reinforcements of police and highway patrol along with more park rangers from four other states.

After the run, the Arizona Republic in Phoenix published an article by the Associated Press, talking about hordes of several hundred Hangmen expected from four states. The highway patrol was doing aerial reconnaissance for two days, looking for the rest of the invaders.

They had 'advanced reports' that several hundred cyclists from California, Arizona, Oklahoma, and Texas were coming. In the article, the park rangers bragged about how they had us outnumbered and how our 'invasion' was a fizzle. Somebody should have told us it was an invasion; we might have tried harder.

As usual, they got very little right. What they don't know, they make up. And they wonder why people call them Fake News.

Hangman invasion bust at Grand Canyon

Associated Press

GRAND CANYON—The last of a small group of motorcyclists left a camp outside Grand Canyon National Park yesterday, their rumored "invasion" a fizzle.

Anticipating many more than the 35 "Hangmen" who arrived by motorcycle and car Saturday, park officials had mobilized park rangers from Texas, Oklahoma, Utah and Nevada.

Bars were asked to be prepared to close and aerial reconnaissance f l i g h t s were made of highways for two days.

Their firearms confiscated as they reached the park, the California cyclists were well-behaved over the Labor Day weekend, a park spokesman said.

"We had them outnumbered," he added.

"All the hotels, bars and restaurants are o p e n and everything is normal because we were prepared," he said.

The advance reports were that several hundred cyclists from California, Arizona, Oklahoma and Texas were coming.

A civil disturbance unit and highway patrolmen, in addition to rangers, brought the police force to 44 men.

The spokesmen said the "Hangmen" were allowed to camp on Forest Service land outside the park boundaries and were kept under close surveillance.

He said another 60 cyclists camped at Zion National Park and a smaller group in the Mormon Lake area near Flagstaff. These had been expected at the Grand Canyon, but they never arrived.

The Arizona Republic

Chapter 24
One Step Beyond

On the east side of Modesto, we frequented a place called the One Step Beyond Pizza Parlor on Oakdale Road. Of course, we'd had several altercations there in the past, but for some reason, they still allowed us in there.

One memorable (for me) but fortunately brief fight was when some of our guys got into a disagreement with a huge guy. I didn't see how it started, but I heard the familiar sounds of thumping, stomping, chairs falling, girls screaming, and glass breaking.

I charged across the bar, aiming at the gathering of Hangmen patches and the action. Just when I got there, not on purpose but only by chance, the brothers who had their backs to me parted. I went sailing right into the middle of the fight to find the protagonist in the middle of the crowd. He was at least six-foot-six – the type of guy who didn't back down from anyone, even a bunch of bikers.

The floor was wet with spilled beer from a broken pitcher. When I burst into the middle of the action and saw the size of this guy, I tried to put on the brakes, but just slid forward on the wet linoleum floor as if I were on ice.

He was turning toward me when I slammed into his chest. To keep from bouncing off and falling, I grabbed his shirt as he looked down at me as if I owed him money. He locked his left hand onto my shoulder and cocked back his right. He was about to let me have it when someone popped him on the back of the head with the heavy end of a pool cue. Down he went, unconscious.

I don't know who swung that pool cue, but somebody really saved my ass that night. We immediately walked out, got on our bikes, and left before the police could stop by for a visit.

Another night, in December 1971, at about 10:30 or so, the bar was full of Hangmen and Modesto Crew. I had maybe a beer or two. I usually didn't drink much back then, partly because I couldn't afford it, but mostly because I wanted to stay alert in case the shit hit the fan, which it often did.

Stepping out the front doors to check on the bikes, which by now was a habit, I saw a fight going on in the parking lot, about fifty yards away. Three people were going at it. To be more accurate, two large cowboy-type men were beating the crap out of a smaller guy.

Interested in what was going on, I walked closer, farther away from the backup inside the bar. As I approached the fight, I recognized the seventeen-year-old little brother of one of our Modesto members named Mexican Bob. These two guys had him down on the ground and were doing their best imitation of a kicker in football trying over and over to make a field goal.

The smart thing to do would have been to run back to the bar, open the door, and yell "HANGMEN!", then get out of the way as the stampede came charging out.

But that didn't occur to me, plus it would have taken too long. I would later regret that. Running toward the action, I yelled at the two men to back off. They were so focused on the fun they were having that they didn't hear me.

When I got close enough, I dove into the middle of them. I body-slammed one guy out of the way and started swinging at the other one. I figured two against two was much better odds. The little brother immediately got to his feet and put them to work, running in the other direction.

He could have run to the bar and notified the cavalry, but for some reason, he just disappeared.

That left me as the center of attention for these two rather large and very angry cowboys, with no help in sight. I was twenty years old, five-foot ten-inches, and weighed about one hundred and sixty pounds. I was used to fighting, but I never considered myself a tough guy.

I had too many examples of club brothers and other friends who really were tough, and I was under no illusion that I was anywhere near as good as them. Still, I had grown up fighting with my older brothers and was not intimidated by guys larger than me. It had always been that way.

I held my own for quite a while. At least, it seemed like quite a long while, but was probably more like a minute, which during an all-out fight can seem like forever.

Two against one is very tiring. At one point, while I was slugging it out with cowboy number one, cowboy number two tackled me from the side, taking me to the ground.

Jumping onto my chest, he grabbed my long red hair and started beating my head against the asphalt while his friend went back to field goal practice wherever he had an opening.

I'm not sure how I did it. Probably, it was pure desperation. I was able to get him off me and get back up. That took every ounce of my strength and now I was exhausted.

I remember glancing toward the door of the pizza parlor, hoping to see some of the boys coming to the rescue. However, except for my two new friends and me, the parking lot was empty.

There was no way I was going to win this fight with maybe the exception of pulling the folding Buck knife in the scabbard on my belt. The truth is, it never occurred to me.

I tried to stay on my feet and didn't give up. It wasn't allowed.

These two guys were a good four inches taller and twenty to thirty pounds heavier than me. I had my hands full.

Completely worn out by now, I was on defense as they continued their attack. In a repeat of the last move, either cowboy number one or cowboy number two (I get them confused) tackled me again, taking me to the ground.

Once more, he was on my chest, his legs pinning my arms to my sides.

I suppose he enjoyed it so much the first time that he wanted to continue. He proceeded to thoughtfully try to pound a hole in the pavement with my head. Of course, his buddy was busy with the boots again too. He was carefully trying to kick me in the head without hitting the other guy's hands or arms.

My vision started to get blurry. I knew I was on the verge of going unconscious when, suddenly, I remembered the knife on my belt.

Somehow, I was able to twist my arm around enough to get my hand on the knife and pull it out. Opening it with one hand, I poked him in the back as hard as I could.

Oddly, for someone who was known to have a hot temper, up until that point, I was not even angry at these two guys, but suddenly that changed. Now I was mad!

I was not just defending myself anymore; I felt that I was fighting for my life. These guys, especially the one on top of me, gave every indication of wanting to kill me, so I responded in kind.

I was ready to start sticking and slashing, but the effect of that one poke was magical. I heard a grunt when the knife went in. Then I was lying on my back in the parking lot all by myself.

I struggled to my feet and looked around to see the two guys running away as if they were late for an appointment.

All this time, not a word had been said by either side. There had been no swearing or threatening. The whole altercation had been eerily silent.

Now I found myself chasing them, yelling in a very hoarse voice that I was going to kill them. In an odd, detached way, it sounded like someone else was saying it.

Hearing someone yell at me from behind, I stopped and turned to see Gentleman Jim running from the bar with the cavalry behind him. Finally! I think I even heard bugles.

I stopped and turned back, folding my knife and putting it in its sheath. Then I started walking back in his direction, gasping for air, trying to catch my breath. Before Jim could get to me, he pointed past me and yelled, "Look out!"

Standing in the middle of the lane between rows of parked cars, I turned around to see a yellow Camaro bearing down on me. The rear tires started squealing and smoking as the driver floored it.

Inside, of course, were my two playmates, cowboy number one and cowboy number two. The looks on their faces seemed to indicate that they weren't having fun anymore.

They were coming fast, and there was no time and no room for me to get out of the way. When they were within a couple yards of running me down, I jumped as high as I could and planted both feet into their windshield.

My lightweight ass wasn't enough to break it, so I just bounced off, landed on the roof, and rolled over the top of their car and back onto the asphalt. I was getting to know the asphalt in that parking lot awfully well.

After that little maneuver, the Camaro swerved a hard right turn and raced out of the parking lot at top speed, turning left on Oakdale Road, tires still smoking.

The whole incident probably lasted only a couple of minutes.

Self-defense or not, our M.O. back then was to get the hell outta Dodge and deny everything. I was dizzy and out of breath. My head hurt. Hell, everything hurt.

Jim started telling me that I had to get out of there because I had cut the guy and the police were on their way. I thought the fun was over for the night, but I was wrong.

In a daze, I nodded in agreement and started walking toward my bike parked in front of the Outer Limits bar. But Jim grabbed me and said, "No, we'll have someone ride your bike. Get in Dave's truck. He'll get you home."

In my condition, I felt it might be nice to have a chauffeur. Handing Jim the key to my bike, I climbed into the passenger seat of the 1955 Chevy pickup.

The guys were heading for the bikes as Dave and I were pulling out of the parking lot. As we turned right onto Oakdale Road, I was beginning to get my breath back. Dave was a hang-around, but never a member. He asked what the hell had happened.

I started searching my mind for an answer when he yelled, "Oh fuck!" I could see that he was looking in his rear-view mirror, so I turned and looked out the back window. My new friends, in their yellow Camaro, were right on our bumper, and behind them were at least six police cars with their red lights going. Then they were nice enough to put their sirens on too.

Yeah... Oh fuck!

Dave floored it. I knew that old truck couldn't outrun itself, let alone the police, so I yelled at him to take the next right. He did. We turned into a residential neighborhood, almost going up on two wheels in the process.

Everybody – the Camaro and the cops – stayed right behind us. We had suddenly become very popular. Immediately, there was another right turn, so Dave took it. Coming out of the turn, he floored it and then slammed on the brakes. It was a cul-de-sac!

There was no conversation – not even a goodbye, thank you, or bro-hug – as the pickup slid to a halt while turning to the left. I bailed out.

I ran in a crouch into a front yard. Because the truck was sideways, I don't think the police saw me come out on the far side. Situations like this can be somewhat confusing for everyone.

I went straight across the front yard of the nearest house, over the front fence, through the back yard, and over the back fence. I found myself in a small half-acre field right next to the One Step Beyond Pizza Parlor.

The parking lot was filled with more police cars, their red lights and radio traffic filling the air.

Expecting police officers to come over the fence behind me, or maybe them calling it in and having the cops in the parking lot come heading my way, I figured that I was fucked.

But apparently, nobody had seen me, so I pressed on. Fortunately for me, the cops in the cul de sac were busy with Dave and the two guys in the Camaro.

There was wood fencing behind the residential homes on one side and the very open, empty field between me and the pizza parlor and all the cops.

Along the fence were small, scrubby bushes. Not wanting to wait around, I used those bushes for cover and headed away from the parking lot.

I am sure they could have easily seen me there, even at night, because of the well-lit parking lot, not to mention the headlights of the police cars. But I guess nobody was looking in that direction.

Most of the next few hours were a blur of running through the night, through apple groves, peach orchards, and whatever else those crops were.

I climbed over electrified fences, with pants wet from the dew-soaked grass, and crossed irrigation ditches. It was a thrill, but I don't recommend it.

I was heading to the place that Jim was renting on Ricky Street, on the other side of town, over near Highway 99. He was no longer at the old farmhouse. I didn't know where else to go.

As usual, I was staying with him while I was in town. It was only about four miles away, but that night it seemed like the Bataan Death March. I was exhausted and hurting from the long fight.

Having spent a fair amount of time in Modesto, I knew where it was direction-wise, but the route through farmlands at night was not very clear. I hadn't had to do cross-country navigation at night. Today this area is full of houses and businesses, but it was pretty rural fifty years ago.

Probably about two o'clock in the morning, it was quiet, and hardly anyone was on the roads. I was making my way down one of the large concrete irrigation culverts with slanting sides that are everywhere in the San Joaquin Valley.

Fortunately, this time of year, they were mostly empty of water. This one paralleled Briggsmore Avenue. I knew I was heading west toward Jim's house when my ears perked up at the sound of a Harley coming down Briggsmore. I ran up the side of the embankment and peeked over the top.

As he passed me, I recognized the rider as VP of the Modesto chapter of the Mofomen. Fortunately for me, the light at the nearby intersection had just changed to red.

He started gearing down and braking as I jumped over the side of the canal and ran for the traffic light. My feet hit the pavement of the road as he slowed to a stop.

Knowing I didn't have much time, my tired, bruised body ran for all it was worth as he patiently sat at the light, obeying the law in the middle of the night with nobody around.

When I was fifty yards behind him, I saw the cross-traffic light turn yellow. I ran faster.

When his light changed to green, he reached down and whacked his suicide shifter into first gear. I came sliding up beside him, slapped my hand on his shoulder, and said, "Hey, can I get a ride?"

He stalled his bike and almost fell over. As he fought to get control of the heavy chopper, he looked like he'd seen a ghost.

He yelled, "What the fuck! You scared the shit out of me! Where have you been? Everybody's looking for you!"

"I got delayed a bit. I just need a ride to Jim's place."

The bike fired back up as he kicked the starter and said, "That's where I'm going. Get on.'"

Off we went. Ahhh, motoring down a smooth highway! It felt great to not be walking through wet fields, fruit trees, and canals in the dark.

When we got to Jim's place, it seemed everybody was there. Someone had ridden my bike back, and it was parked safely in the garage. Everybody wanted to know how the fight had started and where the hell I had been for the last several hours.

I filled them in on the scuffle and gave a brief explanation of my cross-country journey. I found out that Dave, who had driven the getaway pickup, had not even been arrested. He told the police he didn't know what happened and was just giving me a ride. He said that he didn't know who I was. Good man!

I was tired and sore; it had been a long night. I retired to Jim's guest room. My girlfriend, Sue, nursed my wounds, which included a broken right collarbone. I never went to a doctor, so it didn't heal right

I felt fortunate to still have all of my teeth, and my nose was not broken. My head hurt like crazy and was bleeding from a large knot on the back. Sue cleaned it with antiseptic.

It had been a Friday night, and by now, it was Saturday morning. I felt lucky to have gotten away from the whole thing. However, feeling like my luck was running out, I decided to head back to So.Cal. the following Monday.

If I had been smart, I would have hit the road the next morning. But being smart always seemed to elude me.

Spy vs. Spy.

I was still in Modesto two days after the Outer Limits Pizza parlor fight. I decided to recuperate a bit before hitting the road. The house was empty except for Jim's pretty stripper girlfriend Judy, nicknamed 'Guy.'

She said she was going to the store to buy groceries for the house. When she asked if I wanted to go with her, I said sure. It would be nice to get out.

After getting supplies at the supermarket, we drove home to the house on Ricky Way. Pulling into the driveway, I noticed two cars sitting just across the street, parked on the wrong side of the road so that they could face our house. It looked odd right away – no serious powers of observation here on my part.

There were two illegally parked carloads of large men on a residential street at a time when normal people should either be at work or home watching soap operas. Or in Modesto, sitting in a bar.

Guy and I unloaded the bags from the store. We made several trips, and I always made sure to walk behind her so that I could watch her nice ass in those tight jeans. That's not part of the story; I just thought I'd throw it in.

Also, I could look past her and check out the guys in the cars without making it appear that I was looking at them. When we got back inside, I pointed out the two cars to her through the kitchen window, which faced the driveway and down the street.

Watching them from inside the kitchen, we could see that each of these two cars had four or five guys packed into them. Cops maybe? They didn't look like cops, and the cars didn't look like police cars.

We went back out for another load of brown paper grocery bags, pretending not to look in their direction, then came back in and watched to see what they would do.

After about ten minutes, the cars pulled away from the curb together. When they were out of sight, Guy and I ran to her car, jumped in, and followed them.

Because we hung well back, they never picked up the tail. After about thirty minutes of following them across town, we came to the airport district, which, because of its noise, was a 'low-rent' area, a rough part of town with a lot of drugs.

The cars finally pulled over to the side of the road in an old, run-down residential neighborhood with no sidewalks or streetlights – just dirt on the side of the road, dirt driveways, and dirt front yards. The houses had probably been built in the '30s or '40s.

Guy and I quietly pulled to the side of the road about five houses down and watched. We were surprised when nine guys got out of those two cars and strolled across the street.

Each of them was carrying either a long gun (rifle or shotgun) or a pistol in his hands. I think we both felt a chill run up our spines as we realized these assholes were staking out our house with enough firepower to hold off a Viet Cong assault on a Marine Corps firebase in Vietnam.

When they were out of sight, we took note of which house it was and wrote down the street's name. Then we slowly drove away, heading back to the house on Ricky Street.

When Jim and the rest of the crew got in, we told them about our fun day. We decided that we needed to be ready for these guys... whoever they were. Me leaving for So.Cal. was now out of the question.

We pulled out every gun we had (and we had a lot), then loaded them and positioned them all over the house. There was not a window or door that didn't have at least one loaded weapon ready to return fire when the assault started.

The only exception was the personal guns we always carried with us. Mine just happened to be a Smith & Wesson model 36 Chief Special in .38 Special caliber. It was a small, light, and handy revolver, and of course, I had loaded it with hollow points.

The next day, our local intelligence network found out who these guys were. It seemed one of our brothers, named Billy, who had also been up from So.Cal., had supposedly raped a girl who was the sister of one of these 'cowboys.'

Billy had already left town and headed back down south. But in a phone call, he said the sex was consensual. "He said, she said" – not the first time that's happened.

Modesto had a lot of cowboys! It also had a lot of drugs. But whether cowboys or druggies, at least we knew what we were up against. We were on a war footing again, but going against a bunch of locals seemed a lot easier than going up against some other bike club.

We spent several days and nights on high alert, waiting for the airport district thugs to attack. What happened next kind of changed my priorities for a while. Big time.

The house on Ricky Way was mainly a crash pad/party house, like all of the places that Jim rented in those days. They weren't just 'his' place. It was for the club and his brothers.

Patch holders like Jim and I got our own bedrooms. If you were a prospect or hang-around, you were lucky to get the couch next to the rattlesnake cage or on the floor somewhere.

But on the night of December 21, at least a week after I should have headed back to So.Cal., Jim, my girlfriend Sue, Kanaka, a few others, and I were relaxing in the living room, watching television, when we heard dogs barking outside. Jim and I looked at each other, knowing something was up.

I jumped up, said, "I'll check it out," and headed to the kitchen while drawing my .38 revolver from my back pocket.

Coming around the corner of the refrigerator to the kitchen sink in front of the window that looked out over the driveway, I saw two men on the dark front porch. They were dressed in Pendleton shirts and had short hair, and they were getting ready to kick in our front door.

The distance to the two intruders was about three feet at the most. Easy targets! Thinking that these guys were the stalking cowboys, I raised my revolver and tried to pick up the front sight while aligning it with the nearest guy's ear.

My aim followed them as they moved back. As they kicked in our front door, a glint in the darkness caught my eye.

Diverting my attention from sighting on the intruders, I looked to the left, into the darkness of the night. My eyes focused on a line of police officers holding shotguns and pistols.

They were lined up in the flowerbed along the front of the house. It was one of the cop's badges that had caught my eye.

I suddenly realized this was not a retaliatory cowboy attack. It was a police raid.

It all depends on who you are fighting against, and none of us wanted to shoot it out with the cops. There was no reason for that.

Immediately shifting gears from do-or-die defense to surrender, I uncocked my pistol and threw it up onto the refrigerator, at the same time yelling to Jim and the others, "They're cops! Don't shoot! They're cops!"

The front door burst in.

There is no need to go into detail about what happened next. There was lots of noise and cops were pouring into the house, shouting and pointing guns. If you've seen one police raid, you've seen them all.

We were all arrested and charged with one thing or another. Imagine my disappointment when I found out they were specifically looking for me – armed with a warrant for the 'attempted murder' of the guy I had stabbed in the fight in the pizza parlor's parking lot.

My cut, which I had fashioned from a leather motorcycle jacket, had strips of fringe cut from the sleeves. I did not find this out until later in court, but one of the guys I had fought with pulled out several strands of that fringe. They had that as evidence and were looking for the owner of that cut.

Of course, they found guns all over the house. The next day, the Modesto Bee's front page showed all the weapons found in the raid. In the foreground of the picture is my patch, front and center.

The Club's Arsenal

The Modesto Bee the next morning.

Police Arrest 5, Find Arms Cache In Cycle Club Raid

A raid by Modesto police detectives on the headquarters of the Hangmen motorcycle club last night netted officers a small arsenal of firearms and some exotic weapons, including a crossbow and a spiked ball attached to a chain.

Five persons were arrested by the eight detectives who burst into the home at 1924 Ricky Ave. about 10 p.m. All were charged with possessing stolen property — property detectives said included tools stolen in recent Modesto home burglaries.

The three men jailed on charges of possessing stolen property, possession of illegal weapons and burglary were James Tavarez, 22, James Harvey Bass, 29, and Tommy Dale Wilson, 23, who was also charged with attempted murder stemming from a stabbing at the One Step Beyond pizza parlor in east Modesto Dec. 10.

The two women arrested were Glenda Sue Trolinger, 1,

lodged in jail, and Pamela Lynn Polock, 17, lodged in juvenile hall.

The detectives had search warrants when they entered the home. They were working today to identify owners of the property.

Three shotguns, five rifles, nine pistols and curved knives were found in addition to swords, the crossbow and the spiked device. Several hundred

Turn to page A-3, col. 6

Tommy Dale Wilson was the alias and fake I.D. I was running at the time.

The author in Modesto shortly before the police raid.

Chapter 25
1972: A Guest of the County

At the Modesto city police station, the detectives interviewed me about stabbing the guy in the parking lot. Sticking to the plan, I denied having been there. I thought that, with long hair and beards, we all looked alike to 'citizens.'

Maybe I should have considered that we didn't all have red hair and red beards. But at the time, it seemed that denial was my best bet. 'Never cop to nothing.' At least until I talked to a lawyer. I was still unaware that they had the pieces of fringe from my cut as evidence.

Perhaps it would have been different if I had told them the truth, that it was self-defense, two against one. I thought those two fuckers were trying to kill me. But that's not the way it went.

Partly trying to change the subject, I did tell the arresting detectives, Kenny Reid and his partner, whom I knew from past encounters, that I had almost killed them.

"What do you mean?" they scoffed.

I said, "Aren't you supposed to announce your presence, something like, 'Police... Search warrant?'"

I told them about the stalkers we had seen. We were expecting trouble. That was why the guns were all over the house. I went into detail about how I was in the kitchen, just a couple of feet away from them, and how close it had been when I realized the situation. By the time I got done with the story, they were both looking a bit pale, realizing how close they had come to at least one of them getting killed.

They actually thanked me for my awareness of the situation and for not shooting. I said, "You're welcome. But we'd have paid a high price as well."

They still booked me for attempted murder for stabbing the guy in the parking lot. Plus, everybody in the house was charged with burglary and receiving stolen property because the police had found stolen tools in the garage.

It turns out that some kid, sixteen years old or so, who lived down the street and hung around us, was breaking into houses and garages in the same neighborhood. He would bring tools and I don't know what else over, and Jim or some other guys would buy them, not knowing that they'd been stolen.

He told us they were his dad's, and he didn't want them anymore. Anyway, DAs like to pile on all of the charges they can think of and use them as bargaining chips later on.

When I got my phone call, I called Jim, who had already bailed out on the lesser charges. He wanted to know if I wanted the club to pay my bail and get me out. I said no.

I didn't want to be on the hook to him or the club for the ten percent charge to the bail bondsman. I had no money and didn't want to put my bike in hock, so I said I would wait and hang out and see what happened at the arraignment. "Just take care of my motorcycle," I said.

After the police station interview, it was off to the Stanislaus County Jail on the corner of 12th and H Streets. I had already been there a couple of times. When I got my jail-issued clothes, a blanket, and a pillow, they put me in a four-man cell. It had three concrete walls, bars, and a cell door on the front, four metal bunks on the walls, two on each side, and a combination toilet/sink at the back.

Then your new roommates would welcome you. They would eye you suspiciously as they made introductions. The question that always got asked was "What are you in for?" Most of the time, the answers were drugs, traffic warrants, drunk driving, not paying child support, etc. So, when you responded with attempted murder, in this environment, you got instant respect.

Of course, the long hair and beard, along with the Hangmen tattoo on my arm, told the story of who I was. With the club's reputation in Modesto, I had no problems, but I was careful to not tell anyone that I was only twenty years old.

I got to spend Christmas, then bring in the new year of 1972, sitting in jail. If you weren't bail out, they held you for arraignment on the charges. Then there were preliminary hearings and pre-trial hearings. Later, if you're held over for trial, there is no end date, and you don't know if you are going to be there for a few days, a few weeks, or a few months. For me, it turned out to be two months.

Time goes by slowly when you're locked up. Someone gave me a paperback copy of The Godfather, which I quickly read. They had not made the movie yet. Back then, in that jail, there was no television, no day rooms. Inmates on kitchen duty would slide trays of food through a slot in the door, one for each occupant, three times a day. Usually, it was bologna sandwiches on stale bread for lunch. Breakfast and dinner were not bad. At least it was something to look forward to.

Modesto's motto is 'Water, Wealth, Contentment and Health.' It's written on a big sign over the intersection of 9th and I Streets. While I enjoyed the city's hospitality in the form of free room and board, a couple of memorable things happened in the Stanislaus County Jail.

One was the occasional plaintive screams of pain and fear in the darkness when the lights were off – someone getting raped and probably beaten into submission. I felt sorry for them as the screams echoed off the concrete walls throughout the complex. The other inmates would be silent, but sometimes there were comments of encouragement, laughter, and jokes.

It happened several times. I don't know if it was the same guy again and again or if it was someone new each time. It surprised me, the cavalier way the other guys in my cell reacted to it. Or, more to the point, didn't react to it, like it was business as usual.

Maybe there'd be a snide comment – "Sounds like Luke has a new girlfriend" or "Looks like the new guy is learning the ropes" – accompanied by laughter.

For some reason, the guards never seemed to hear the screams at night. Maybe they were behind soundproof doors with the TV turned up. Or perhaps they just couldn't be bothered. I had already spent a fair amount of time behind bars at my young age, but I was still not exactly worldly, especially when it came to the world of prisons. This was not juvenile hall or even the Orange County lockup. This was more like the big time compared to what I was used to.

The Stanislaus County Jail seemed to be more hardcore. Maybe it is the proximity to all the heavyweight places like Folsom, San Quentin, and Vacaville, but still, even this was nothing like the big house. Real prison! In other words, long-time felony shit, which might be where I was heading if I got convicted of attempted murder.

Once a week, the guards marched everyone in my cell and some other cells down to get cleaned up. We stripped and tossed our dirty clothes in a pile, then walked into the showers. The hot water and soap felt great. Nothing ever happened in the showers; I never saw anyone get out of line, as the guards were watching. The water was shut off too soon. We dried and collected fresh, clean clothes and then were marched back to our cells.

Despite my being a skinny kid, I looked older because of my beard, and everyone knew I was a Hangmen. That meant a lot in that town.

The reputation that Jim and his crew had made was well-known and well-respected.

Of course, the clientele in jail was well aware of that reputation, so I was granted immediate acceptance into the community. That meant I was always respected, not for who I was, but for what I was part of.

I wasn't tough. I was average at best. My brothers were the superheroes whom I looked up to. They never lost fights. They were tougher than anyone I knew, and my goal was to be like them. I would do whatever it took.

They were the ones building the reputation of the Hangmen Motorcycle Club. The patch didn't make you; you made the patch. I'm sure they never thought about building a reputation as opposed to just being who they were. And it was a time when we could do that. The club already had a history. In 1971, we had been around for eleven years!

That seemed like a big deal at the time. Having started in the Bay Area in 1960, right alongside the Hells Angels, we believed we were second to none. And when I looked around me, I believed it too. I always felt that we were just as good as, or better than, anyone out there.

We had proven ourselves time after time. And we would continue to do so in the future.

I kept thinking. Someday, when I grew up, I would be as tough as them. All I had to do was keep fighting and just, well, grow up. I never felt like I was a badass, but somehow I made it through.

Maybe I was tougher than I thought. One advantage I had in any fight was that I had learned to never give up. Stay on your feet, try not to let yourself go down, and if you do go down, get back up, no matter what. Don't ever quit. You might die fighting, and that's okay. We're all going to die of something. But you can never run away from what you didn't do. You can't run away from yourself.

Nobody was afraid of me personally, but the club had an enormous amount of respect, and some of that rubbed off on me. Nobody ever fucked with me while I was in Stanislaus County Jail.

Other than meals and showers, the only thing I had to look forward to was my next court appearance, and then the next. The other thing that happened while I was in jail in Modesto was a very ferocious toothache.

One of my molars started hurting. I had not had much dental work when I was young. With four kids, my parents couldn't afford it. That wasn't unusual back then. So, when the tooth started hurting, I asked one of the guards for some aspirin.

Then I asked for more and more. Finally, he got tired of me asking and brought me a large five-hundred-pill jar that had about one hundred left in it. With nothing better to do than feel the pain of that toothache, I kept taking more and more aspirin.

It wasn't long before I was dry heaving and sick as a dog. It got so bad that my newfound buddies in the cell were afraid I would die. They called the guard, and I was carted off to the infirmary for a couple of days, still with the toothache.

It just so happened that this was a Friday night, and they could not, or would not, get me to a dentist until the following week. At least it was a change of scenery for a couple of days.

Finally, after four long days of pain, they transported me to a dentist, who pulled the tooth. That was all the dental work that prisoners received, but I was happy to get it done. Soon, I was back to the joys of life in a cell.

The next six weeks.

At an arraignment, one of the things they ask you is, "Do you waive your right to a speedy trial?" The public defender said, "Say yes," so I said, "Yes." This was probably not a good idea.

Now they can take their sweet time with all the following hearings, which seems to be job security for everyone involved, except for the person being charged.

If you are out on bail, it's not a big deal, but when you are spending your days sitting on a metal bunk with a mattress thinner than your motorcycle seat, trying to keep from going crazy, it seems like a big deal.

Oh well, that was my choice, as I didn't want to pay a bail bondsman.

Finally, I had a preliminary trial, which is when the prosecution presents its evidence. Then the court decides whether to hold you over for trial or drop the charges and let you go.

I had shaved off my beard ahead of time, thinking that I would look different and that now nobody would recognize me.

This was when I first found out about the evidence of the fringe from my cut. My heart sank, knowing that was going to be hard to deny.

Oddly, the "victims" were not present in the courtroom, but one of their girlfriends was. I had never seen any women in the parking lot during the fight, nor did I see them in the Camaro that tried to run me down.

But here she was, saying that she saw the whole thing. Being as I 'wasn't there,' what could I say? Looking back, it was a dumb defense. She stated that the vicious biker had run out of the bar and stabbed her boyfriend in the back for no reason.

"Do you see that person here in the courtroom?"

"That's him, sitting right there," she said as she pointed straight at me.

That was all that was needed to hold me over for trial, which was what they did. The state would try me for attempted murder, a felony. It sounded ominous!

But the big surprise came when my public defender told the judge that I could not afford bail and had already done two months. He asked that the court release me on my 'own recognizance' and the judge granted it!

Wow, just like that! I was free to go! For now, anyway. Back at the jail, they processed me out, and I called Jim to come and get me. Life was good! Party time!

Chapter 26
Death on the Freeway

As soon as the word got around that I was out, the boys in So.Cal. called and said they needed me because they had an ongoing situation with another club, and I belonged down south.

So, two days after getting out of jail, and after one good party, I was back on my bike, heading south, this time with my current girlfriend, Sue, on the back. Got to have something to lean on, you know.

I was happy, back in the groove, back in the saddle, on the road, heading south on Highway 99. The wind was in my face and hair and I was living in the moment. It was great. I was enjoying life again.

The Seekers, who were a big club back east, were looking to start up in California. While at first we had gotten along with them well, riding and partying together, things started to sour when Hangmen Billy's Ol' Lady Sherri began seeing one of the Seekers, named Calvin.

As mentioned at the beginning of this book, Sherri was a stripper. Pretty and charming, she had come on to me when I was a prospect. Fortunately, I had enough sense (for once) to not accept her advances.

Sherri had a nice body, thin, except for tits that were too big and not enhanced. She could have been a candidate for breast reduction surgery.

She was also the sister of Mark's Ol' Lady, Linda, which was how I had first met her.

Billy, instead of cutting her loose because she wasn't faithful, was very jealous and felt that Calvin was stealing her from him. It was as if she didn't have anything to do with it. We tried to tell him to get over it, but he wouldn't. Meanwhile, we said to ourselves that this was not over a girl. It was about disrespect.

Back then, we didn't own much. For me, it was my motorcycle and the clothes on my back. A biker's motorcycle is his prized possession, but right behind that is his Ol' Lady, which, of course, he saw as his possession as well. That doesn't work today, but it's the way it was back then.

Because I was distracted and out of touch while in jail in Modesto, I wasn't there for most of the drama that led up to the problems with the Seekers. By the time I got back to So.Cal., it had already heated up to the boiling point.

The night I showed up down south, the incident that opened this book went down. Three Seekers, including their president, went to the hospital with multiple gunshot wounds. None were life-threatening.

Unfortunately, along with them was a thirteen-year-old boy who had been sitting in the back seat of a car at the gas station. His family had just left Disneyland, and they had stopped for gas on the trip home.

A bullet had come through the door and hit him in the leg. I never found out the extent of the wound; the newspapers didn't elaborate. That shouldn't have happened. Hell, none of it should have happened. But there we were.

Not only were we on the verge of war, but we were also now 'PFNG,' which means Persona Fucking Non-Grata! The Seekers hated us. We had shot a kid. The police hated us. The newspapers hated us. Hell, all of Southern California hated us. I can't say I blamed them.

The week after the shooting, the headlines eventually died down as we waited to see what would happen. There were no search or arrest warrants served. No doors were kicked in. We had been here before, meaning on a war footing with another club.

The club officers and older guys told us what we needed to do or not do. Don't ride alone. Don't wear your patch alone. Don't go out to bars, especially ones that we frequented, while wearing your patch. Understand that both the other club and the police will be out to get us. It was just common sense.

You might think that Pooch would have been reprimanded for opening fire as he did, but he swore that he had seen a gun in one of the Seeker's hands and was afraid the rest of us would get shot, so he was trying to protect us. He remained a patch holder for many years after, until he went back to prison for bank robbery... again.

A week after the shooting in the gas station, some members started getting lax and bored. One night, Curt, Hipster, and his prospect, named Terry, decided to go out for a few beers and a game or two of pool.

They were at a bar on Beach Boulevard in Huntington Beach for several hours, and nothing happened other than them having a good time.

At about one o'clock in the morning, they decided to head out. Curt and Hipster headed north on Beach Boulevard, while Terry got on the Garden Grove Freeway, heading east.

They broke all the rules: going to a bar where we were known and Terry riding alone. Of course, it wasn't really a war yet. So far, it was only a one-sided shooting.

Curt and Hipster went on their merry way with the night air and cool ocean breeze in their faces, slamming gears with their jockey shifters and suicide clutches. With a few beers under their belts, they raced from one traffic light to the next, living the life.

Equally enjoying life and the cool night air as he motored down the freeway on his chopper, Terry was swerving onto the offramp at Harbor Boulevard. As he rolled off the throttle and put his left foot on the clutch, there was a thunderous explosion to his left.

A car had pulled up alongside him and let him have it with both barrels of a twelve-gauge shotgun.

The car continued straight on the freeway. Instead of being knocked down (Terry was a big, stout guy), unbelievably, he rode the bike down the offramp, almost to the traffic light, where he pulled over onto the shoulder and stopped. Only then did he and the bike fall over. There, he died.

Hipster awoke the next morning with President Charlie swearing and throwing a copy of the Orange County Register at him. In red letters, the headline said, "Orange County Cycle War." On the front page was the story about Terry's murder.

Terry Chuck Powell

Chapter 27
Terry's Funeral

Westminster Memorial Park Cemetery is on Beach Boulevard, just a few blocks from where Terry had been hanging out the night of the shooting. It was a big funeral, biker-style. With us were Devil's Disciples, Nuggets, Misfits, Hessians, So.Cal. Outlaws, Iron Horsemen, Mescaleros, and several smaller clubs, plus loners and hang-arounds. There were at least two hundred bikes.

Terry Chuck Powell got patched in. We buried him with a patch sewn onto his cut. It still had holes in it from the shotgun pellets. It was a shitty way to make the grade, but he gave his life wanting to be one of us. He was a brother now. Hell, he always was. We hated to lose him, and we would make the Seekers pay.

Of course, the police were there, as usual, taking photos of everyone with telescopic lenses. The news media was there, too. They had been following the whole 'Cycle War,' as they kept calling it. It also made the news on Los Angeles television.

Back then, we had six TV stations and there was no such thing as cable. Our options were the big three national network stations (ABC, CBS, and NBC) and three local L.A. stations (channel 5, KTLA; channel

11, KTTV; and channel 13, KCOP). Sensationalism and violence sell, so they were all keeping track of us.

The ceremony went well. Then about a hundred motorcycles followed the hearse from the chapel to the gravesite. We had never buried one of our own before; the sense of sadness and anger was almost overwhelming.

Afterward, people saddled up on their bikes, and most went their separate ways. About fifty bikes, made up mostly of Hangmen and Hessians, formed up in a big pack and headed back to Anaheim for a memorial party, of course with a police escort. Well, not exactly an escort; they were running alongside us like a pack of wolves chasing a herd of buffalo.

Anytime you have a large pack, it is difficult, if not impossible, to stay together because of traffic lights. Plus, we weren't doing any traffic breaks, as is frequently done for funeral processions, but that was over anyway.

As we headed north on Beach Boulevard, things stayed somewhat organized until Garden Grove Boulevard. The people in the back of the pack started running through red lights to stay together. That was just the excuse the police needed to come after us. They started trying to pull us over, but nobody would stop.

We were no longer an organized pack. The whole thing devolved into a melee of speeding, swerving choppers with motors roaring and police cars and motorcycles with red lights flashing and sirens wailing.

It turned into a crazy high-speed chase involving about fifty defiant bikers and thirty or so pissed-off cops in cars and on bikes, with more joining in with every city we passed through. Now we were a wild melee as we speeded and weaved through traffic. It began to look more like a stampede.

Racing up Beach Boulevard, Charlie and Uncle Tom started leading us off the main drag of Highway 39, heading for Anaheim, then east on Chapman Avenue, north on Brookhurst, east on Katella, and north on Euclid. All the while, the whole mess was getting crazier and more dangerous, and the number of cops kept increasing.

It was like a bad dream that you couldn't wake up from. If you stopped or tried to pull away down a side street, just like the wolves and the buffalo, if caught alone, you were going to get taken down. So, you just stayed with the herd, or in this case, the pack.

Sue, whom I had brought down from Modesto, was on the back of my bike. I was just a week out of jail for an attempted murder charge, and now here we were in a crazy police chase. It lasted all the way from the town of Westminster to Anaheim, only about twelve miles, but all through the middle of the cities of Southern California.

Some guys cried uncle and stopped. When that happened, we saw the cops push them off their bikes and throw them to the ground while knocking their bikes over. The rest of us decided, "Fuck it, we're not stopping."

The crazy, dangerous, thundering herd kept up the stampede all the way to Uncle Tom's house in Anaheim. The cops got madder and more aggressive while we went faster and became more disorganized, with every man for himself.

The newspaper and television reporters were following along too. The city of Disneyland has probably never seen anything like it, before or since.

The Great Escape.

My motorcycle always had a fifteen-inch over stock front end and, at that time, a nineteen-inch front wheel. With a little rake on the frame, but not much, it sat up at an angle with higher ground clearance than most bikes.

It made for good cornering on the tight turns in the mountains, but being that it was already up at an angle, especially with a passenger, it was easy to do wheelies. If I got on it hard, it would come up whether I wanted it to or not. Today was one of those days.

We were within a block of Uncle Tom's house. DeVinch lived right next to him on the corner of Broadway and Vine. Charlie and Uncle Tom were leading this madhouse.

We were on Santa Ana Street, and the front of the pack was making the left onto Vine Street. I was about twenty bikes back. The cops seemed to know where we were going. Two police cars partially blocked Santa Ana Street, just past the intersection with Vine.

Cops were in the middle of the road, swinging nightsticks. Others were trying to grab guys to pull them off their bikes. They did just that to someone near the front of the pack, making him crash and then descending upon him, nightsticks glittering in the sun as they swung through the air. This was getting worse and worse.

I was not in the mood for an ass-whipping from the cops and I didn't want to go to jail again while I was out on an O.R. I thought that would not look good to the court in Modesto, so I made a split-second decision: 'Fuck this shit, I'm outta here!'

I decided to run for it.

I was on the right side of the pack as it was making the left turn onto Vine Street. Without saying a word to Sue, instead of making the turn, I swerved around a cop standing in the street. He swung his nightstick at us and missed.

I slammed my jockey shifter into first gear, grabbed a handful of throttle, and popped the foot clutch. The front end came up about four feet as I passed between the two police cars and fled from the rest of the herd and the wolves.

I eased off enough for the front wheel to get back on the pavement, then slammed it into second gear and then third, fighting each time to keep some rubber on the road so I could steer.

Looking in my rear-view mirror to see if any of the brothers had followed me, I could see I had company, only it was red lights and sirens.

So much for trying to lead a movement.

In three short blocks, I came to East Street with a motorcycle cop right on my tail and a police car right behind him.

The light at East Street was green, but as I came up to the intersection, I slammed on the rear brake and with my left hand knocking the hand shifter down into first gear, sliding sideways past the crosswalk, with the front of the bike pointed to the right. That was the way I went.

Now facing south on East Street, I popped the clutch and, once again, stood the bike almost straight up. Damn! For a change, I wasn't trying to show off.

I just needed to accelerate as fast as possible, and the wheel stands were slowing me down. In this rather stressful situation, I was grabbing more throttle than I should have.

Racing south on East Street with the two cops right behind me, I went one long block, probably hitting about sixty or seventy miles per hour. I couldn't know for sure because I didn't have a speedometer.

Now approaching South Street, I saw in front of me, coming in the opposite direction, another pack of about twenty bikes with DeVinch in the lead. They had broken away from the herd – I mean pack – and taken a different route. There were no cops behind them.

The light was green, and we were going to hit the intersection simultaneously. I could see a gap in the middle of their pack. The guys in the back half weren't following very close.

I saw an opportunity. If the split-second timing came together, it just might work. I once again locked up the rear brake, skidding and sliding into the intersection, this time with the rear wheel coming out to my right so that I was now facing left.

I rode this bike every day, at least when I wasn't sitting in jail. I was one with it. I practically lived on it for years. Braking might have involved less skidding if I had a front brake, but I didn't.

With my heart in my throat and my pulse pounding, and probably while holding my breath, I pounded the shifter handle down into first gear again while steering with one hand as I skidded sideways. The gap in their formation became available.

In the skid, now facing east on South Street, I once again popped the clutch and took off right through the middle of their pack with my front wheel rising high in the air. I was trying to go as fast as I could.

I found out what happened next several days later, from the guys in the back of that pack, once they got out of jail. Hangmen Phil from Modesto was one of them.

They said that the motorcycle cop right behind me was also sliding sideways to keep from hitting me. If I hadn't made that sudden ninety-degree turn through their pack, he would have.

Right behind him, the police car swerved so hard to the right, trying to keep from hitting his buddy the motorcycle cop, that his car went up on two wheels. Then he almost crashed into parked cars on the side of the road.

It must have been quite a sight: blue tire smoke in the air, red police lights flashing, and vehicles going in all directions. Squealing tires and sirens, all with the rumble of Harleys. Mayhem!

Where was GoPro when you needed it?

Hauling ass as fast as that Panhead/Shovelhead would go, I finally got the front wheel back on the pavement and tried to keep it down every time I shifted.

Looking in my rear-view mirror, to my surprise, I found myself alone. I guess those cops had had enough and decided to look for easier prey.

Time to choose... one lone and very crazy buffalo, or a small herd that might make for easier pickings. Or they may have had to go back to the station to change their underwear.

They made U-turns and went after DeVinch's pack.

Finding myself alone, I noticed that I was gasping for air, as I had probably been holding my breath for the last few minutes. Now, with no cops behind me, I backed off a little and looked up for a helicopter. No, nothing there either.

They were busy with most of the other motorcycles, which by now had to be arriving at Tom and DeVinch's house, where the fun was just starting.

After five long blocks up South Street, I came to State College Boulevard. Once again, the light was green, and I casually made a left, obeying the speed limit.

I went north a few blocks, then turned right on East Virginia Street. I made another quick right into the alley and, about a hundred yards later, came to the back of Charlie's house. Sue hopped off and opened the gate as I pulled my bike into the backyard and shut it down.

I just sat there, still a bit numb, trying to comprehend what had just happened. I could not have pulled off a stunt like that again if I tried. I had been incredibly lucky.

Sue had kept silent the whole time; she later said that she thought it was fun. I knew it was one of the scariest things I had ever done, but at the same time, it was exciting and, well, fun.

The previous five minutes cemented my reputation in the club as an incredible rider – and as thoroughly crazy.

I do not recommend running from the police. I normally didn't do it. But I felt this situation was not normal.

Being as I had recently been staying in Modesto, care of Stanislaus County, and as far as I knew, with all of the brothers in jail, I didn't have a place to stay in So.Cal, I worried that the police knew where Charlie lived. Therefore, I didn't want to stay there any longer than I had to. I let myself in and used his phone to call my sister Christine, who lived with her husband in Garden Grove.

"Hello?"

"Hi, it's me."

"Oh, hi, are you in town?"

"Yeah, I need a place to stay for a couple of nights. I have a friend with me."

"Does this have anything to do with what is on the news?"

"I'll tell you about it when we get there."

"C'mon over."

In situations like this, it was always important to de-identify from the club and pretend you weren't who you were. That happened a lot – trying to sneak away unnoticed.

Not only were the police looking for Hangmen, but the Seekers were too, just like we were looking for them. As we had already seen, riding alone at a time like this was an excellent way to get shot.

I put my patch underneath my leather jacket, trying to look incognito, just a guy and a girl on a chopper. We had a nice, quiet ride across town.

As I spent the next couple of days at my sister's house, we watched some of the television coverage of the funeral and the wild melee of the chase between bikers and cops on the L.A. news stations. The Orange County Register had front-page pictures of cops with shotguns and my brothers and some Hessians lying in the front yard of DeVinch's house, face down and flex-cuffed behind their backs.

It was very nice to not have been part of that. I had risked our lives, mine and Sue's, and who knows who else's, to get away. Was it worth it?

What the hell... It seemed like a good idea at the time.

With Sue on the back, my sister too this picture the day after the police chase.

Funeral leads to arrests

ANAHEIM, Calif. (Reuter) — An uneasy peace reigned between motorcycle gangs in this city 20 miles southeast of Los Angeles Sunday after a spectacular biker funeral Saturday led to 34 arrests.

The gang war has pitted the Hangmen and their allies, the Hessians, D e v i l 's Disciples and Nuggets, against a beach-side gang called the Seekers.

More than 200 members of the Hangmen and their girl-friends turned up at a funeral ceremony for murdered Terry Chuck Powell, 24, and more than 100 cyclists dressed in gaudy club outfits roared in a c o r t e g e behind Powell's hearse.

Powell was killed two weeks ago when unidentified motor-cyclists shot him on an Ana-heim street corner, also injur-ing one of Powell's friends and a 13-year-old boy.

The incident touched off an apparent r e v e n g e shooting Friday when 19 bullets were fired into a wooden house, se-riously w o u n d i n g Dennis Decker, 25, a one-time Hells Angel and Hessian who re-cently affiliated with the Seek-ers.

The Phoenix Star, March 6, 1972. As usual, they didn't get it right about the shooting.

Chapter 28

The Ambush

After the funeral fracas, most of the brothers who had gone to jail were back out in just a day or two. Most charges were minor, like failure to yield to emergency vehicles, running red lights, or speeding. They were diffi-cult to prove in a situation in which fifty or more bikes were riding in a mob.

A couple of people got nailed for small amounts of drugs or concealed weapons, mainly folding Buck knives. These were completely legal, but that never stopped them from booking us for 'possession of a switchblade.' Those usually got dismissed too.

During this whole mess, one of our brothers, Mark, my old high school buddy, had been serving time in jail for a traffic warrant. He was due to get out just as things were heating up. We had intel that the Seekers knew he was getting out of jail on the proposed date and that there would be an ambush, so we decided to plan a surprise of our own.

It was an elaborate plan. We reconned a location in a quiet orange grove a couple of miles east of Angel Stadium in east Anaheim, or it might have been in the City of Orange or Santa Ana.

That location is now all residential neighborhoods full of houses, busi-nesses, and fast-food drive-throughs, but then it was relatively remote and nothing but orange trees. That's why it is called Orange County.

I volunteered to drive the car to pick up Mark at the appointed time at the Orange County Jail at 550 North Flower Street in Santa Ana. He walked out at noon, right on time, and we pulled away from the jail.

I handed Mark a fifteen-shot Browning High Power nine-millimeter pistol. He checked the chamber, making sure it was ready for action, and I filled him in on the plan. Under a jacket on the seat next to me was a Smith & Wesson .357 magnum revolver, loaded with hollow points.

Driving a pre-planned route, we made our way to the remote orange grove. Our senses were on maximum alert and the tension and adrenaline built as we watched for anything suspicious, knowing the shit was about to hit the fan.

We turned onto the quiet lane lined with tall eucalyptus trees along one side. On both sides were nothing but orange trees packed densely as far as you could see, which wasn't very far. It was a beautiful, quiet, and peaceful spot.

Suddenly, a car came out of nowhere, pulled abruptly into our path, and lurched to a stop in the middle of the narrow two-lane road. I grabbed my revolver with my right hand while I slammed on the brakes and skid-ded to a halt by shoving the parking brake all the way down.

Before we came to a complete stop, Mark and I bailed out of the car and ran for our lives into the orange grove, ducking under the branches of the trees as we went. Hot on our heels was the driver of the car that had pulled out in front of us.

Just two rows of trees into the orange grove, we met our brothers, who were waiting in the kneeling position, two with AR-15s and one with a twelve-gauge pump shotgun shouldered and ready to fire, aiming into the kill zone.

When Curt, the driver of the car that had pulled out in front of us, and Mark and I were safely behind the ambush shooters, we knelt and waited for the pursuers to arrive in our trap.

We didn't have long to wait before a car appeared in our field of fire.

Being ready to rock and roll, we all held our breaths while waiting for the fireworks to start.

The vehicle pulled slowly into the ambush zone and stopped. Fingers came off the triggers, and everyone in the orange grove finally took a big breath and let it out. It was the "blocking car," driven by two more heavily armed Hangmen.

Their job was to keep the Seekers from getting away. They would trap them while the others in the grove opened fire, Bonnie and Clyde/ Frank Hamer-style. But nobody showed up. We didn't know whether to be disappointed or relieved. We just 'knew' that they would plan to follow Mark when he got out, and we were anxious for revenge for Terry. We had convinced ourselves that this was going to happen.

After a minute, we started to laugh, letting out the tension and realizing that all the drama had been in our heads. Oh well, at least we were prepared and weren't going to get caught unaware again.

Now we just had to get the cars out of the road and get the hell out of there before someone came along and started asking questions.

The drive-by.

One of the things you see in situations like this is that both the police and the news media try to have all the answers, even when they don't, which is most of the time. But they both want everyone to think they do.

It was amazing to read in the papers what we were doing when we weren't doing it. Well, not all of it anyway.

All of the newspapers were talking about the "Cycle Gang War."

There were stories about a guy in Santa Ana who had been shot in the head while sleeping in his front bedroom.

Somebody pulled up and pumped a bunch of rounds through the bedroom wall, missing his wife, but hitting him in the head.

One day, they reported that he was a Hells Angel; the next, he was a Hessian, neither of whom we were at war with. The next day, he was said to be a Seeker. He probably wasn't any of the three. We didn't know who the hell he was, but we did know that we didn't shoot him.

Pooch opening up at the gas station doesn't count. We did not do drive-bys on houses. Never! Ever! It had nothing to do with our disagreement with the Seekers, but the media didn't care. It was one more victim they could add to the list of casualties to sell papers.

Death on the porch.

Just a night or two after that, at a rented house in Anaheim, at about midnight, a couple of Hangmen were hanging out, staying on the alert while peacefully watching Ozzie and Harriet reruns on the TV.

Or maybe they were busy with the naked drugged-up girl in the bedroom when someone started pounding on the front door.

Dan'l was tough enough without the twelve-gauge shotgun he had loaded with slugs. He brought it along when he answered the door, figuring it wouldn't hurt to be ready. But, hey, it may have been Seekers.

It turned out to be a doper named Robert Clair, according to the newspapers. He was pounding on the door, demanding drugs. He was not a Seeker; he wasn't even a biker.

Holding the inner door open with his left hand, the shotgun in his right, Dan'l told him, "Get the fuck out of here."

Instead of realizing that this could be a life-changing event, ol' Robert, thinking that whatever drugs he wanted were more important than his life, decided to insist.

He flung the screen door open. Light flashed off the knife blade in his other hand as he started to walk through the door.

Big mistake. Dan'l was one of those hard asses, and so was Lurch standing behind him. Knife or no knife, I am sure Dan'l could have easily knocked that guy completely off the porch with one punch. It was kind of a hobby of his.

But tonight, he must have been bored and wanted to do something different, and he did. He lifted that shotgun and blasted that guy square in the chest. It displaced him backward about eight feet onto the lawn. He was deader than last Sunday's church sermon.

When their ears stopped ringing, Dan'l and Lurch decided that it wouldn't be a good idea to leave their new lawn ornament lying around, so they decided to load him into the panel truck he arrived in.

Dan'l was holding him under the arms while Lurch had his legs when suddenly police cars were all around them. Talk about awkward!

"Hi, officers. What, oh, this? I can explain... Uh, we just found him lying on the lawn and thought we'd drive him home."

It should have been a pretty clear-cut case of self-defense. Still, when you're a Hangman, and there's a gang war going on, and you're standing there holding a dead body, trying to load him up like a piece of old carpet, the easy answer is that the police are probably not going to believe you.

The naked, unconscious, and drugged young lady they found in the bedroom probably didn't help either. So, of course, the newspapers kept saying this guy was a Seeker too, and they were all over the part about the naked girl. Along with that drive-by in Santa Ana, the rapidly growing 'Cycle Gang War' body count increased by one more.

The police rounded up several other brothers who lived nearby, and all were charged with first-degree murder. Eventually, charges were dropped for everyone except Dan'l.

He stayed locked up as they held him over for trial. During that trial, he was able to prove that it was self-defense and was later released.

In the meantime, it was kind of nice to have Dan'l locked up for a while. It gave us a respite from having him kill people. He could be so difficult sometimes.

An invitation to a meeting.

One of the most essential things in any war is intelligence. I don't mean intelligence as in smarts, which certainly helps, but is sometimes lacking. I'm talking about intel as in knowing where the enemy is and what he is doing. We needed to know where more of the Seekers were. The ones whom we knew about didn't seem to be home anymore.

There were a pair of brothers, as in real brothers, loners, whom we knew hung around those guys, so we put out the word that we would like to Frankie and his brother, whose name I don't recall.

It wasn't long before we got a phone call that they had shown up at the house of someone who was a friend of the club. Two Hangmen were immediately dispatched with a panel truck to collect them.

They burst through the front door with guns tucked obviously in their waistbands. The guy whose house this was and who had given us the tip was treated as if he didn't know what was going on. He was told to not move, keep his hands in sight, and keep his mouth shut.

The Hangmen said that the brothers' motorcycles had been recognized in the driveway. The two brothers were invited to accompany the intruders out to the panel truck, where they were hogtied and blindfolded.

After a ride across town, during which they were not told where they were going or why, they were finally unloaded at our new secret headquarters and sat in chairs in the middle of a dimly lit room full of Hangmen. There, they were questioned for hours. When the desired information was obtained, the return trip across town was much the same: They were retied and could not see where they were going.

The vehicle stopped in an alley a block from where they had been picked up. They were let out, untied, and told to stand still as the truck pulled away. Their orders were to not take the blindfolds off until they were alone. They complied.

A pickup truck backfires.

A few days later, the newspapers had a front-page headline about a man who had gone out to start his pickup before work, and there was a massive explosion.

They found the hood of the truck on the street the next block over. What was left of him was taken to the hospital. Surprisingly, he survived, but he would probably never be the same.

Newspapers and television reports said that he was a member of the Seekers, their president, newly elected since their last one was still in the hospital with bullet wounds.

Maybe the truck had something wrong with it. Or perhaps he had built up that motor too much to have it do that. Within a few days, we started hearing from other clubs, other bikers, and even cops or detectives who would frequently sit outside our houses, engaging in conversation.

They told us that the Seekers had disappeared – left town or gone into hiding.

We were seeing the same thing, as all our surveillance was turning up zero. We wanted to track down every one of them and make them pay for Terry, but we just couldn't find them.

Eventually, the tension and stress began to subside like a bad hangover. We never heard anything about them again.

Outnumbered Seekers Go Into Hiding in Cycle Gang Feud

BY BILL HAZLETT
Times Staff Writer

The Seekers have gone underground.

Fearing reprisals, the smallest of at least two motorcycle packs involved in a gang feud has parked its choppers and abandoned its turf.

"They've gone so deep you could be standing right next to one and never know he was a Seeker," said Det. Sgt. Phil Mason of the Garden Grove Police Department.

"Most of them have shaved their beards, gotten haircuts and traded their motorcycles for Volkswagens to avoid recognition.

"And I don't blame them," he added.

The Seekers, a newcomer among California motorcycle clubs, is en-gaged in a bitter rivalry with the Hangmen.

Violence flared into the open Feb. 20, in Anaheim, when a burst of gunfire wounded three persons, including the president of the Seekers and a 15-year-old bystander, and damaged two automobiles.

The first outbreak was followed a week later by the shotgun slaying of a 24-year-old member of the Hangmen, blasted off his motorcycle as he left the Garden Grove Freeway at Fairview Ave.

A 25-year-old Santa Ana man, identified by police as a Hangmen member and former rider with Hells Angels, was critically wounded March 3 when his house became a target for 19 bullets.

The next day the feuding motorcycle gangs called a brief truce to bury their dead.

Two days later—last Monday—the body of a 27-year-old Anaheim man was found sprawled in the back of his panel truck. He had been shot once in the chest with a shotgun.

PART II INDEX

Police have been unable to establish a concrete link between the second slaying and the continuing gang warfare, although two members of the Hangmen have been arrested as suspects.

"The feud, which has resulted in more than 40 arrests—most on traffic and disturbance charges, following the funeral for the slain Hangmen—has spurred demands for an investigation at the local, county and state level.

Although the reasons behind the rivalry are not clear, both the Seekers and the Hangmen, along with several other motorcycle groups in Orange County, are under scrutiny from the Organized Crime and Criminal Intelligence Section of the Attorney General's office, investi-

gators from Dist. Atty. Cecil Hicks' staff, and detectives from Garden Grove, Anaheim, Santa Ana, and Costa Mesa.

"The Hangmen have been around Southern California for a long time, so we're familiar with them," said an intelligence officer from Sacramento.

"But the Seekers are new to this area. Their 'mother' club is in Altoona, Pa., so they've apparently moved into Orange County to recruit for a new chapter.

"The Seekers' invasion, he added, possibly sparked the feud by forcing the larger Hangmen club to stage a power play to demonstrate local dominance.

Please Turn to Page 8, Col. 3

Back to Modesto.

War over or not, I had a court date in Modesto. I was supposed to go on trial for the attempted murder charge, so I saddled up with Sue on the back, and we were ready to hit the road.

Gentleman Jim was still in So.Cal. for the festivities. Knowing that it would be a cold ride, he insisted that I wear his handmade leather pants to help keep me warm.

Even with another pair of jeans under them, they were a little loose on me, but I tightened up the belt, knowing that they would provide plenty of wind-breaking protection when it got cold.

Pointing my chopper north onto Interstate 5, I traveled through Los Angeles, then Hollywood, the San Fernando Valley, Saugus, and up the Grapevine. We stopped at the Gorman Pass to get gas.

I noticed that the bucket holding the squeegees had a layer of ice on it. I'd seen that before, and I knew it would warm up when we got down the hill on the north side to lower elevations.

As we cruised quickly through the curves down the north side of the Grapevine, it did warm up some. At Bakersfield, I-5 turned into Highway 99. The interstate was still under construction, and unless you were over on Highway 1 or 101 on the coast, Highway 99 was the only northbound route.

The San Joaquin Valley was mostly farmland and ranch land and still is today. Dotted with small towns between the larger ones like Fresno, it was prone to fog. That was what we encountered that night.

I thought that I could make Modesto by midnight, so I kept pressing on. The comfort of my shivering date on the back of my bike was not as important as my court date the next day. It would not look good to miss it.

The fog was not that bad. I could see about a quarter of a mile, and we were keeping up a good speed. It was too dark for my sunglasses, and I didn't have clear goggles, so I just kept squinting, blinking, and wiping my eyes with my gloved hands as the moisture built up on my eyelashes.

Two and a half hours later, Sue started complaining that she was cold. Wearing Jim's leather pants, I was the one in front taking most of the wind and fog. I just told her to hang in there.

As DeVinch used to say, "It's mind over matter. If you don't mind, it don't matter."

Cold or not, I needed gas. The 3.1-gallon Sportster tank I was running at the time would go only so far, so I took the off-ramp at Clovis. Pulling into a Shell station, I coasted up to the pumps and shut 'er down. When I climbed off the bike, I heard a crackling sound. Looking down, I saw thin sheets of ice at my feet.

When I turned to look at Sue, she was still shivering, but she started laughing and pointing at my face. Not used to people laughing at my face, I looked into the mirror of my bike to see what was so funny. I found that a thin film of ice had covered my mustache, my eyebrows, and the hair on the front of my head.

I had no beard at this time because being semi-clean-cut could be helpful during the covert operations that we had just been doing.

Stepping back to look at the bike, I saw that the whole front end, except the tire and the headlight, was covered in a sheet of ice. Well, maybe Sue was right. It WAS fucking cold!

This phenomenon was called structural icing. It was very common in aviation, but at that time it was entirely new to me. Water droplets in the air cling to a surface. On airplanes, it is on the wings and propellers. In the accelerated cold air called wind chill, it freezes, causing clear ice to form.

In extreme situations, due to excess weight and a deteriorated aerodynamic surface, it can cause the airplane to crash. Fortunately, I don't think it can cause a motorcycle to crash unless the rider freezes solid.

Through the fog, I saw a neon sign across the street, glowing in the misty night. It said MOTEL. The building was a small, old motel so typical along America's older highways, probably built in the '40s.

Another sign said "Vacancy." Seeing where I was looking, Sue nodded hopefully, so I decided that we had come far enough that night.

When I quickly did the math, which was not my strong suit, it seemed we were only about two and a half hours from Modesto, and my court appointment wasn't until early afternoon.

After getting gas, we rode over to the motel and stopped in front of the small office. I parked the bike, walked in, and enquired about a room. It cost the exorbitant sum of eight dollars. I didn't have much on me, but I had enough for that and for gas to Modesto, so I got the room.

Wanting to get my money's worth, I also wanted indoor parking, so I just rode the bike inside the room and locked the door.

Still fighting off the chill, Sue and I wasted no time in stripping down and sharing a very hot shower. It felt like heaven. The rest of the night did too.

Day in court.

Back on the road at dawn, neither one of us had the money for breakfast. We were again charging up Highway 99, with the sun peeking over the horizon. It was a little warmer and now there was no fog. Arriving at Manteca, we stopped by Sue's parents' house, where she lived.

Promising to see her someday, I dropped her off, then headed north for another twenty minutes to get to Jim's place. I parked my bike in the garage, ran inside, took off my riding gear, and peeled Jim's leather pants off, leaving my relatively clean Levi's underneath.

I tried to brush the knots out of my long hair. Then I waited for one of the local hang-arounds to come by and drive me to the Stanislaus County Courthouse.

I got there with time to spare, about twenty minutes before my trial was supposed to begin. I found my public defender waiting in the hallway outside the courtroom. He had a big smile on his face as he told me that the district attorney wanted to make a deal.

I listened with a mixture of anticipation and concern. Instead of the felony charge of attempted murder, the DA would drop all of the lightweight charges like burglary and receiving stolen property if I pled guilty to "misdemeanor assault with a deadly weapon."

The DA's office would recommend 'time served,' which was the two months that I had already been a guest of the county, and then I would be free to go that day! It sounded too good to be true.

If I didn't take the deal, they would proceed with the trial on the felony charge of attempted murder. If convicted, I could get locked up for years. PRISON! The Big House, Leavenworth, Sing Sing. Well, okay, that's Kansas and New York.

It seemed like a good deal, and any chance of getting away from a felony seemed like a great deal. I didn't ask why there was a change of heart from the DA's office. Maybe I should have. I just said, "I'll take it."

A short time later, I found myself standing in front of the judge. He asked, "How do you plead to the charge of misdemeanor assault with a deadly weapon?"

"Guilty, Your Honor."

"I now sentence you to five months in the county jail," he said.

Eyebrows raised like a suspension bridge, I turned to look at my public defender. He returned my stupefied stare with a smile and shrugged.

"Judge's discretion" was all he said.

Chapter 29
Summer Vacation, 1972

I was immediately taken back into custody and returned to my alma mater, the Stanislaus County lockup, AKA, the Modesto city jail. Still in kind of a daze, I thought this would be a very long five months.

However, within hours, I found that I was to be awarded those two months in the county jail as time served. That meant I was looking at only another three months. Then came the excellent news: I was not going to be staying there.

I was going to be shipped off to the Stanislaus County Road Camp, a minimum-security work camp in the countryside west of town.

It was more like a summer camp, just one that you could not leave. You were fed and housed, and you had to work, but not very hard. It was pretty easy.

You did some job to keep the camp operating, like cooking, cleaning, doing laundry, or mowing lawns, or you would be cleaning up parks and roadsides. For the county, it was free labor.

For us, it sure beat the hell out of sitting in a cell all day every day talking shit with losers who didn't know how long they would be there. I know, I had just been one of them.

It was pretty nice. Being as this was county time, it was only for misdemeanor offenses, meaning doing time of less than a year. Any felony carried at least a year. Those offenders were usually in places like San Quentin, Folsom, Vacaville, or many others around the state.

This place was lightweight. There was a chain-link fence, but no guard towers. It wouldn't be hard to escape, and some did, but anybody who would want to leave this was out of their minds, as they would be charged with a felony and then have to do real-time prison.

Most of the other occupants were in for minor stuff: drug possession, traffic warrants, non-support, drunk driving, etc. The accommodations were large barracks with metal bunk beds. It wasn't even that crowded. Most people got a bottom bunk. I did right off the bat.

When we weren't working at whatever our jobs were, the guards left us alone to hang out in groups or read books. There were even televisions in the barracks. Three times a day, we would wander down to the big cafeteria for breakfast, lunch, and dinner.

On my first day at work, after breakfast, we gathered in the parking lot and loaded into the back of a large truck, an old Army 'Deuce and a Half' from World War II.

I was put on a crew hoeing weeds along a highway near the camp. At about ten o'clock, we'd been there about two hours. Looking at his wristwatch, the guard hollered to us, "Okay, load up."

Climbing into the back of the truck, I asked the guy next to me, "Where are we going?"

He said, "Coffee break."

I laughed and said, "Yeah right,"

Imagine my surprise when we pulled up next to the cafeteria and walked inside to see that all of the cooks and their helpers, who were other inmates, had pots of coffee and cups lined up on the tables along with containers of cream (cans of Carnation Condensed Milk) and sugar.

I couldn't believe it!

Of course, we disliked the guards. It was kind of required, but they were pretty good guys. Still, we liked to complain about them and make fun of them. After all, we were the cool guys and they were the worthless losers. Funny how perspectives change over time – or maybe I should say, with a little maturity.

My job opportunities advanced quickly. I started with a shovel and a rake, but I did that for only about a week. One day, I was whacking weeds in the hot sun along the side of a country road out in the farmlands when the guard shouted out the question, "Who can drive a tractor?"

Four or five hands went up. Mine was not one of them. The guard just said, "Okay," and walked off. About twenty minutes later, he walked up to me and quietly asked, "Can you drive a tractor,"

I said, "Yes."

He replied, "Good, the job is yours."

I have no idea why he picked me, but I was happy to be relieved of a shovel. It was the second time I had been promoted to a tractor. I must have had a tractor driver look about me.

Driving the tractor was fun. It had a big, wide mower on the back that mowed about an eight-foot path wherever you went. I got assigned to mow parks, baseball fields, along the side of highways, and even the lawns in the road camp compound.

It was a big tractor too. I don't remember the make or model, and I don't know much about them, so I can't give any details about it. But it was a lot bigger than the one I had driven in the apple orchards in Prosser, Washington. There seemed to be a real status to getting to be the operator. A lot of guys were envious. I didn't see it that way. I just thought it was fun.

When I was off motoring around on that big machine, it felt like I was on my own. It didn't seem like I was locked up. It was more like a regular job.

The laundry.

After about a month of being on the tractor, for some reason, I got offered the job of running the laundry. Not working in it – RUNNING it.

I would have people to work the machines for me. I thought, 'Why would I want to do that? I am out here in the sunshine, operating a big machine. I'm happy here, three meals a day plus coffee breaks.'

But my new friends said, "You've got to take it. The laundry is a great deal. One of the most prestigious jobs in the road camp."

I thought that was weird. I said, "Doing laundry is prestigious? You gotta be kidding me."

But they insisted, and I listened to their advice. When you are in the laundry, people need favors from you – proper-fitting clothes, etc. I still thought that was kind of dumb, but they kept saying, "If you do favors for people, you get favors back." That is the way it works when you're locked up, just like in the real world.

So, I accepted the job. As promised, my assigned crew did all the work, loading sheets, pillowcases, towels, and clothes into the giant washers, and then into the dryers. When the laundry was done, the crew folded it. I just made sure they did the job right.

I had a desk, a radio, and a large swamp cooler that blew straight on me when the summertime temperatures in the San Joaquin Valley hit one hundred and ten degrees Fahrenheit. I was surprised when I found out that I didn't need to eat in the cafeteria with everybody else. The cooks brought my food to me in my office in the laundry.

It turned out the cooks were very picky about their clothes. I don't know why; it wasn't as if we were all going out to the bars to pick up chicks in our jail wear. But whatever they asked for, I gave them. No skin off my nose.

I soon found out that their appreciation involved my being given all the best food from the kitchen, all brought to my 'office.' The best meats, freshly baked bread with butter, whole pies, cherry or apple, and always a fresh pot of coffee. Best of all was something they secretly made in the kitchen. They called it potato wine.

I think it would qualify more as vodka.

Once again, I found myself happy in my new existence. I was enjoying the unexpected perks. Time went fast while I was there.

When I wasn't sitting in my laundry office, drinking coffee and eating pie, I was hanging out on the mowed lawns, talking with people in my clique, who were mostly either bikers or druggies who thought the bikers were cool.

Sometimes we would get into fake slapping fights, just playing around. When the guards came running, thinking they had some real shit going down, we would wait until they got to us and then turn and laugh at them.

They seemed relieved that they didn't have to break up a real fight. After telling us to "Knock that shit off" and threatening us with some kind of punishment, they would walk away.

I happened to find out something interesting about my case.

Talking with a new arrival who asked what I was in for, I gave him the rundown of the charges and the plea deal.

When he found out I was a Hangman, he said, "Oh, so you're the guy from the pizza parlor thing."

I said, "What do you mean by that?"

Somehow, he knew the whole story of the fight at the Outer Limits on Oakdale Road. He said, "You're going to be mad when I tell you this."

I said, "Tell me what?"

"The witnesses they had against you, the guy you stabbed, his buddy, and the two 'witness' girlfriends, had all left town. The prosecution could not find any of them. They had no witnesses to testify against you. If you had gone to trial, they would have had to dismiss the case."

I asked how he knew this. He declined to give any details, but he seemed to have all the facts down.

I just shook my head and laughed, saying, "My public defender was probably in on the deal. I wouldn't be surprised if he's buddies with the district attorney."

It was like a poker game. They bluffed and I folded. The high stakes were all on my side.

But it was only a misdemeanor, and a couple of months out of my life in summer camp. I didn't get upset. It could have been way worse. That guillotine of a felony hanging over my head was gone, and besides, I had never gotten to go to summer camp when I was a kid. This was the closest I ever got.

Work furlough.

At some point, just as I was enjoying the cushy job in the laundry, one of the guards walked into my 'office' and said, "You've qualified for work furlough."

I said, "What's that?"

He explained, "If you used to have a job, or if you can get a job, you can leave here five days a week and go work in town instead of here."

I said, "I don't have a job in town."

He said, "There are some guys here who work in town. You might be able to get a job with one of them."

I asked, "Who and where?"

It turned out that there was a guy who worked at the Ralston Purina plant, where they processed turkeys. Being a local guy, he was there for 'non-support,' meaning he had not paid his child support payments. He had a car and drove to work every day.

I said, "Sounds good. Count me in!"

They arranged for me to ride to work with him, and the plant hired me on the spot. I even got a paycheck. Wow, like an honest job!

I got to learn how turkeys were killed, gutted, de-feathered, and frozen to prepare for millions of thanksgiving dinners.

There were some funny stories about working in a place like this, but I won't go into detail. Mostly, I kept thinking that it was better than sitting in a cell in the Stanislaus County lockup.

The guy I rode in with was a real nerd, and I don't remember his name. He was a nice enough guy but a total citizen. I think he was afraid of me and had probably heard stories about me in the camp. Most of them probably were not true... Probably.

Some days, I coerced him to drive fast on the way into town, to visit a girl I knew. He would wait outside in the car while I went in the house, which was unlocked, stripped out of my clothes, got into bed, and woke her up to give her a little morning sunshine.

All the while, he was freaking out that we were going to be late, and the factory would report us to the road camp. Talk about a quicky! All too soon, he was pounding on the door. Then I would pull my pants on, run out to the car barefoot, hop in, and get my boots back on as we raced to work. I got him to do this several times, but for some reason, he never seemed to get used to it.

After work, we had a finite time to get back to the camp. We got off work at 4:30, and the guards expected us to arrive at camp at 5:03. Fortunately, he liked to drink beer. I didn't have to talk him into that.

With my companion driving as fast as he could, the first stop after leaving the plant was a liquor store to buy three sixteen-ounce cans of malt liquor. As the designated driver, he sipped his one can on the way back to the road camp; I would slug down my first one as fast as I could, then toss it out in the farmlands outside of town. I would savor the next can until we were almost 'home.'

Driving along with the windows down on a hot summer day, the cold beer tasted great. It was a rare interlude from being incarcerated. For a short time, it made us feel almost free.

Before getting to the gate, I would drain what was left of my second can and throw both of them out the window.

When we got back into the compound, my chauffeur seemed to be fine with one beer, but I was pretty drunk. I must have covered it well because I never got in trouble for it.

If they had discovered that I was drunk, I would have been taken off work furlough and would probably have been back on a rake and shovel along the side of the highways – or maybe, worst-case scenario, back to the city lockup. For some reason, I just couldn't help but take chances.

One funny incident happened when I was back from a day of working in town and enjoying the effects of the beer while playing with a needle and thread.

I'd learned that if you pull up the skin on your forearm and push the needle through it, it doesn't hurt much. There are so few nerves in that area, or maybe it was just the alcohol.

I started sewing stitches on the top of my forearm. Yeah, I know, but you can do some stupid shit when you're bored and/or drunk. Besides, when you are locked up, it doesn't hurt to have a reputation for being a little crazy.

I was walking around, showing the other inmates my handiwork, getting lots of oohs and aahs and a few "holy shits!" Eventually, the commotion attracted Officer Trout, one of the guards we all knew and loved... to make fun of.

He was actually a nice guy. Very strait-laced and quite lame, trying to do a good job, I'm sure, but that just made it more fun to pick on him.

When he came over to inquire what was going on, I proudly showed him the stitches I had put in my arm, with the needle still protruding from the skin. He looked shocked and said, "Oh my God," as he stared at my arm. Seeing this, I decided to push the issue.

I told him, "It doesn't hurt, really." He just shook his head and backed up, so I said, "Here, I'll show you." With my right hand, I jerked the needle out of my arm, breaking the thread. With my left hand, I grabbed his right arm.

That was all it took. He pulled away and yelled, "NO, NO," then turned and ran away, down the sidewalk, all the way to the office at the front of the camp. He never slowed down until he was in the safety of the front office.

The people around me laughed and laughed. I was surprised. I had not intended to scare him like that. I was just having fun and wanted to show him that a little needle through your skin in the right place was not a big deal. He must have been one of those people who could not handle needles. I felt kind of bad for scaring him.

Twenty-first birthday in jail.

June 1972. Earlier, I'd spent Christmas and brought in the New Year in jail. Somewhere during this little summer adventure, my birthday came along. I turned twenty-one while at the Stanislaus County Road Camp.

Usually, it might have been a big deal. What might one do? Go out to a bar legally for the first time? I had been going to bars for the last four years. Get drunk? I was doing that every day, coming back from the work furlough.

No, when you are a guest of the county, your twenty-first birthday just kind of comes and goes like any other day.

There was a guy I knew in the work camp with the nickname of Dog. He looked like a biker, but was more like one of the local doper class. Some of the inmates had gotten a hold of some belladonna root, or maybe it was locoweed because it will make cattle crazy.

I'm not sure what it was, and they probably didn't know either. It appeared that they took this root, boiled it into a mixture and drank it. I guess Dog got most of it, and the results were not good.

The next day, he was gone. The story going around was that he was found about four o'clock in the morning, behind the barracks, out in a field in the compound, under his mattress, trying to dig a hole in the ground to get away from whatever was after him.

It sounded like a bad trip. He ended up being loaded into an ambulance in the middle of the night and was never heard from again, at least not by any of us in the road camp.

Sunday was visitor day. Many times, brothers would come out from town, sometimes bringing one of my girlfriends with them (preferably not more than one at the same time). That was how the morning visits on the way to the packing plant were arranged.

These visits, of course, boosted not only my morale, but also my status in the camp, as the other inmates were always impressed at Hangmen showing up on motorcycles.

Time flew by. Before I knew it, my three months were up, and they were letting me go. I almost wanted to tell them, "Wait a minute, can I stay a little longer? I am having such a good time here."

Unfortunately, real prison is a fact of life for too many in the biker world. I don't mean to make light of it, and I consider myself very fortunate to have avoided that part of the lifestyle.

Visitor's day at the road camp. Only this time I am visiting Pugh.

Chapter 30
Free Again, Grand Canyon, 1972

Just like that, life changes. I was free again! And, in time for the 1972 National Run, once again at the Grand Canyon. I suddenly went from being locked up to blasting down the wide-open highways in a pack, with my brothers, on my Harley. It's hard to explain how good it felt, like from dream to reality.

Or, maybe I should say, it was like going to sleep, away from reality, and getting back to the dream. Either way, it was hard to keep the smile from my face as I rode with the Modesto crew.

We left early one morning for an all-day ride to get to the big party. Riding, drinking, and camping with our brothers. What could be better? This was what we lived for.

The memory of having been locked up was fading fast.

The trip to the Canyon was kind of a blur, and I enjoyed every minute of it. We were riding hard and fast, back down Highway 99 to Bakersfield, where we turned east on Highway 58 to Barstow.

It was summertime, and it got hotter as we rode into the Mojave Desert, but we didn't care. Our minds were on the destination and having a good time. We kept moving; none of the bikes broke down.

At Barstow, we picked up Interstate 40 and Route 66, riding through the middle of the towns along the way, like Needles, on the eastern border of California, into Arizona at Kingman, and through the smaller towns of Seligman and Ash Fork.

There was no time to stop and sit in a cafe or diner. Lunch was a quick cheeseburger and fries at a small malt shop after gassing the bikes up. Rumbling through the town of Williams, Arizona, we turned north again on that crappy road with all of the seams in it, Highway 64.

As the sun was going down, we rolled into the Grand Canyon, or at least, the pre-arranged location to meet the rest of the chapters, So.Cal. and OKLA. We were dirty, tired, and sunburned, but everyone had smiles on their faces as we greeted each other again.

Having heard that we were coming for the second year in a row, the National Park Service was ready and waiting. They still weren't going to let us in the park except for two bikes at a time.

Once again, they directed us to a place to camp outside the park. It wasn't the same spot, but it was close, so we proceeded to set up camp. Back then, that meant parking the bikes, building a firepit, and maybe picking a spot to throw your sleeping bag. Nobody brought tents. The party started immediately.

Somebody had bought a bunch of chicken parts in the town of Tusayan just down the road. We had drumsticks, thighs, and breasts. Trying to cook it in the dark was a nightmare. Maybe it was the drugs that were going around, but it seemed to take forever, holding it over the fire on a stick.

No matter how long you waited and cooked, when you took a bite of it, it was still raw on the inside. At some point, you just gave up and ate it anyway. Afterward, I think we made a new bylaw that said only steak and hot dogs on runs. No damn chicken!

Late one night, with the bright starlit sky overhead, we sat around the fire, with its light reflecting off the chrome of the motorcycles and the tall pine trees surrounding the camp. We were tired and mellowed out, no doubt drunk and stoned. Gremlin said something that Mike from OKLA either didn't like or simply misunderstood.

Gremlin was sitting on the ground in front of the firepit with his back to a fallen log, and Mike was standing near the fire. I wasn't paying attention to what was said and was surprised when, suddenly, Mike turned and kicked Gremlin in the face, catching him in the jaw and knocking him out cold.

From the way Gremlin went limp, we weren't sure if he was unconscious or dead. Suddenly, the camp erupted into pushing and shoving, with the So.Cal. guys going after Mike and the Oklahoma guys trying to keep us from killing him. We started surging back and forth like waves on the beach, seemingly with just as much power – lots of shouting and cursing and squaring off.

Knives flicked open and guns were being cocked here and there in the darkness. Gremlin was still not moving. I remember having my knife out and open, wanting very much to plant it into Mike, hoping to cut 'deep, wide, and continuously,' as Gentleman Jim liked to say.

This eerie scene took place by the flickering light of a campfire with dust rising into the air from scuffling feet and shadows reflecting in the remote dark woods of Northern Arizona.

The cops couldn't care less about what we did to each other. We were on our own, but of course, we were comfortable there. We sure as hell didn't need anybody's help. Well... Maybe an ambulance when it was over.

Just when the confrontation seemed to be getting completely out of control, Gremlin came to and said, "Hey, what the fuck is going on? Where's my drink?"

Realizing that he was still alive did a lot to calm down the So.Cal. and No.Cal. sides.

Suddenly, cooler heads prevailed, and tensions relaxed. We started putting the knives and guns away. Before long, we were pounding each other on the backs and opening more beers and whiskey. Pretty soon, all was back to normal. Fortunately, no ambulance was needed.

When it was over, I asked Gremlin what he had said, but he didn't know. He didn't remember a thing about what happened. I think Mike was part Indian, from Oklahoma; Cherokee, perhaps? It doesn't matter. He was one of these guys who didn't hold their alcohol well. Not long after that, Mike was gone from the club.

Suddenly, it was Friday morning, and already the second National Run was over. After hugs and goodbyes, we all headed our separate ways. Gremlin talked me into riding with him back to his home in Phoenix for a visit. Being as I had no plans or no place to be, I was happy to go with him and relax at his place for a while.

Back to Modesto with Jim and Major.

After a few quiet days in Phoenix with Gremlin, I was taking it easy over the weekend. Life was good. The run was over. It was nice not having that whole 'attempted murder' thing over my head and we didn't seem to be at war with any clubs.

But I needed to head west again. I dropped by So.Cal. and hung out for a few days, but at some point, I decided to go back to Modesto. There were always exciting times in Motown, or maybe it was the girls I knew there.

Even though I was part of the So.Cal. Chapter, I had no place to live there, and I knew that I was welcome at Jim's house. It was always fun hanging out with the crew and getting into trouble, as long as you didn't go to jail... Again.

There were many times back then when the only thing in my life seemed to be riding down the highway. I often felt that it was the only thing I was good for.

A strange thought, I know, but when you spent day after day riding and riding, and at the end of the day you looked for a place to sleep and, if you were lucky, something to eat, it just seemed that way at times.

When I arrived back in Modesto, Jim and Major had rented a three-bedroom house; they gave me one of the bedrooms. Wow, life was good again. I got back into the routine of riding and partying, and there were always girls.

One night, Jim and I had left a bar in downtown Modesto, drunk, of course. We went right through downtown, racing from one light to the next as the red lights seemed to catch us every time, so it was one one-block drag race after another.

Being as it was about two o'clock in the morning, with the thundering noise from our exhaust pipes echoing off the buildings, of course we attracted the attention of our buddies, the local police.

One car with two cops pulled us over. The cops got out and called us both by our first names before they asked for driver's licenses and registration. That was not unusual. It wasn't that big a town, and we had a lot of contact with them. They all knew who we were.

But they didn't write us up and they didn't ask us if we'd been drinking, which was kind of obvious at that time of night. We chatted back and forth for a while, and then they let us go on our way, telling us to slow down a little.

That happened a lot. We were part of their world, and they were part of ours. I also think that, like everybody else, they had a lot of respect for Jim.

There was a lovely young girl I met when she showed up with another girl at the rented house. Her nickname was Mouse.

She was probably eighteen years old (I hope), and she was small and thin, with the cutest pointed nose, pouty lips, and the reddest hair and whitest skin. She used to come over to Jim's house to see me and spend the night, sometimes dropped off by her mother. I thought that was a little odd, but was not about to complain. That was Modesto for you.

In the meantime, another girl was living at Jim's house. Her name was Sue, but she was not the same one I had taken on the wild police chase at Terry's funeral. This Sue was from Oklahoma and had just been to the 1972 run with the OKLA guys.

She had somehow ended up with the No.Cal. guys. Being as I had come back to Modesto via Arizona, I was not involved in how she got there, but she was now living at Jim's house.

I didn't have anything to do with her because I was involved with Mouse at the time. Unfortunately, things like money and valuables of any kind started disappearing.

I had been back in Modesto about two weeks when Curt and Hipster showed up. They had driven up in Curt's panel truck, the one with the Corvette engine. With them was a cute blonde-haired young lady, also from Oklahoma, named Jan.

The So.Cal. chapter had sent them to bring me back home, saying that it had 'been decided' at the last meeting that I belonged down there.

After they presented their case, my response was that I had nowhere to live down there. Poking his thumb in Jan's direction, Curt said, "You can live with her. She has an apartment, a car, and a job."

Taken aback, I looked at Jan. She smiled and said, "Yeah, that will be fine."

Not knowing what else to say, I just mumbled, "Why not."

I think it was a setup.

The next day, the three of them loaded up into Curt's panel truck while I packed my sleeping bag onto my bike, a little sad that I probably wouldn't see Mouse again.

I gave her a call. Her mother answered and said she wasn't home, so I asked her to tell Mouse that I was leaving town and didn't know when I would be back. Such was the temporary nature of life back then.

After saying goodbyes to Jim and Major, we headed southbound. The weather was perfect. The trip back down Highway 99 and Interstate 5 went quickly and smoothly as I followed them back to Anaheim.

When I moved in with Jan, I found that her place was a small, modern, and comfy one-bedroom apartment. It was a semi-permanent place to stay, almost like a home. Although I didn't consider it my home, still, it was something I had not experienced for a while.

For the last four years, the most time I had spent in one place was when I was locked up.

Settling down was not something I had in mind. I would see how long this relationship lasted.

A couple of days later, I got a call from Modesto, telling me that the night I left, Jim and Major had confronted Sue about the thefts that had been going on in the house. They had applied a little physical discipline to try to persuade her not to do it anymore.

It wasn't malicious. They were just trying to get her attention, like a parent spanking a child. Unfortunately, it didn't have the desired effect. She climbed out a bedroom window and went to a neighbor's house, where she told them she needed help. They called the police.

Jim and Major were arrested on several charges including kidnapping. Eventually, they were both convicted of felony assault and battery. They ended up doing several years over the whole thing.

It was sad and ironic, after all the men they had both beaten to a pulp, for them to go to prison for slapping a girl.

I've always wondered what would have happened if I had stayed one more night, if Hipster and Curt and Jan had not come and pulled me out of there, taking me back to So.Cal. Would I have also been charged? Prison for me too?

Or might I have been a voice of reason and stopped what happened? There is no way to know.

Chapter 31
Partying, Too Much of a Good Thing

The author at Randsburg Ghost Town, 1972.

I awoke lying on my back with the morning sun just starting to peek over a distant desert mountain range. I squinted through painful eyelids to see that it was getting light.

My head was pounding, probably from dehydration and maybe a lack of food, but certainly whatever I had been drinking the night before was a significant contributor.

My neck hurt from the uncomfortable position of my head on the rolled-up leather jacket that I used for a pillow, and my back hurt from lying on the hard sand. I was lucky to have pulled the sleeping bag off my bike and thrown it on the ground.

Though I hadn't gotten in the bag and still had my boots on, at least I wasn't lying in the dirt, which was a common practice back then. I had a little dignity, ya know.

I was in the Mojave Desert just outside the ghost town of Randsburg. There were some abandoned buildings that we used to camp out in and around. A dozen of us had ridden out the day before so we could shoot guns, have fun, party, drink, and take whatever recreational medications we might have brought with us.

As I sat up on my sleeping bag, I had to figure out where I was. Nothing looked familiar as I scanned in all directions. I never crashed around the campsite; I always wandered off into the darkness to be alone and feel secure, even if I wasn't.

I quickly rolled up the sleeping bag. Just as I was about to set off in the wrong direction, somebody fired up a motorcycle back off to the east, so I just had to follow the sound back to the camp.

Others were climbing out of their sleeping bags, swearing at whoever had made them drink so much, while the die-hards who had never given in all night were still standing around the dwindling campfire. Walt, a new patch holder, was one of them, along with Mark and Earl.

Somebody said, "Let's go find some coffee and breakfast." Although I preferred to sit around and hold my head for a while, coffee and food did sound pretty good.

The guys who were still unconscious, uh, I mean asleep, were roused and told to "saddle up." They grumbled and moaned, claiming it was too early. "Who's idea was this anyway?"

It wasn't long before the dozen of us were lined up and making our way single file down the dusty sand of the dirt road, wrestling long front ends with skinny front tires and, for most of us, suicide clutches until we hit the pavement and then formed up two abreast and headed down California Highway 395.

Pulling into a gas station at Kramer Junction, then known as Four Corners, we found that the little diner was closed. After gassing up, we decided to head south down Highway 395 in search of a place to eat.

Uncle Tom was leading, and I was riding right front beside him. About twenty minutes out of Four Corners, we noticed, in our rear-view mirrors, that the pack was pulling over and stopping; someone must have broken down. We also braked hard and hung a U-turn in the middle of the highway, then hauled ass back to see what had happened.

It was worse than we thought. We found a line of bikes parked on the shoulder of the road. Off in the soft desert sand was Walt and his bike, lying in a mess.

Mark was leaning over him, talking to him, reassuring him, begging him, and even threatening, "You better not die on me! Don't you fucking die on me. If you die, I will kill you."

Walt's body seemed intact, with no apparent broken limbs and no blood. His breathing was shallow, and his pulse was weak. His eyes were closed and he was not conscious as his brothers huddled around him and Mark.

Curt was already riding balls out back to Four Corners to find the nearest phone and get an ambulance on the way. The rest of us were helpless to do anything except stand around, hanging our heads and kicking the sand with the toes of our boots.

Everyone was feeling guilty. Could we have done something to prevent it? If only...

Walt must have fallen asleep, or you might say passed out, after the long night of partying. Or maybe he just wasn't paying attention for a second. That's all it takes.

His bike had drifted right, and as bad luck would have it, he center-punched a paddle marker, one of those little upright reflectors along the shoulder that mark the edge of the road at night.

It seemed a perfect storm of bad luck. That paddle marker had snapped off the lower aluminum legs just above the axle. With the front wheel gone, the bottom of the forks dug into the soft sand along the side of the road, and the bike flipped, cartwheeling both of them into the desert.

No amount of talking, begging, or threatening would awaken Walt. Of course, he wasn't wearing a helmet. He was brain-dead. We didn't know it yet, but found out after a couple of days in a hospital.

He was in ICU, and they kept him breathing on a ventilator. Even though we would talk to him, he just wasn't there, and the doctors said he was never going to be.

We got to go in and talk to him one last time to say goodbye. After a week, his family decided to terminate life support, and he was gone.

Hangmen Walt.

Another funeral.

1972 was not a very good year. After the Seeker war earlier in the year, we found ourselves planning a second funeral. In previous years, we had never held funerals for our members. We had only attended the funerals of other clubs. Terry and Walt were the first Hangmen to die in the line of duty, so to speak.

At a church in the city of Orange, the turnout was huge. Hangmen from So.Cal., No.Cal., and OKLA, Berdoo Hells Angels, Hessians, So. Cal. Outlaws, Iron Horsemen, a new club called the Vagos, and many hang-arounds and loners produced a pack of about two hundred bikes lining the road outside the church where the service was taking place.

Not wanting to listen to a eulogy by some preacher who didn't even know Walt, some of us stood outside the chapel and passed a bottle of whiskey around. Unfortunately, I took several hard pulls off that bottle.

When it came time to saddle up and head for the cemetery, I was feeling pretty good while sitting backed into the curb in a long line of bikes on both sides of the street. Hangman Art was on the back because his bike was down at the moment.

Most of us had our engines running and were waiting impatiently for the procession to get going. Right across the street from me, parked smack dab in front of the church, was a police car with a cop sitting in it.

I don't know what I was thinking, other than perhaps that doing a wheelie in front of all of those bikes would look cool. Damn that whiskey! Without saying anything to Art, I put my foot on the clutch and whacked the jockey shifter into first gear with my left hand, then revved the motor and popped the clutch.

The extra weight of Art on the back made the bike go straight up as it left the curb. I didn't have to worry about sticking to the plan because I didn't have one. I headed across the street toward the police car.

The cop inside was looking at me with his eyes getting bigger and bigger. I couldn't see where I was going with the bike pointing straight up. The expression on the cop's face was described to me later by people who had seen it.

With the front wheel about seven feet in the air, I had no control, only enough energy to keep moving forward, balancing precariously like a redwood that had already been cut and was just waiting to fall.

Realizing that hitting a police car would cause problems, I reluctantly closed the throttle and reached up with my right foot to hit the rear brake, hoping that there was enough forward motion to bring the front wheel down so I could steer away from the police car. There wasn't.

Before anyone could yell, "Timber," the bike fell to the right like that fallen redwood and landed on my lower leg with a crash. Seeing what was about to happen, Art put his foot down, and stepped off, and stood aside before the bike hit the ground. He wasn't hurt at all. However, my right leg was pinned underneath the bike as I lay there, thoroughly embarrassed.

The whole street erupted with cheers, applause, and raucous laughter from the hundreds of other bikers. They seemed to think my little stunt was the most entertaining and funniest thing they had seen all day. The cop never got out of his car; I glanced up at him as I was lying in the street and saw that he had a smirk on his face.

A couple of brothers ran up and helped Art pick the bike up and off me. Other than a few scratches, it was not damaged. I staggered to my feet, hopping on my left leg. They asked if I wanted someone else to ride it for me, but I said, "No, just get it started, and I'll ride it."

Surprisingly, Art got back on with me. We rode with several hundred bikes and a police escort in the long, slow funeral procession to the Holy Sepulcher Cemetery overlooking Irvine Lake on Santiago Canyon Road in the eastern foothills of Orange County. I was able to limp to the ceremony at the gravesite.

As usual, the newspapers were there to record the event. Afterward, as we headed with a group of Hessians to a memorial party in Riverside, we rode in an orderly pack, mostly obeying speed limits and stopping for red lights. Nobody wanted a repeat of the melee after Terry's funeral, when so many went to jail.

Using my rear brake was torture, but I was still able to ride. Walking hurt like hell, and I was limping badly, but I was pretty sure I had not broken my leg. I didn't take my boot off, as I knew that if I did, I would never get it back on. Finally, at about one o'clock in the morning, I rode to Jan's apartment, where I was now staying. She was shocked when I came limping in and fell onto the bed.

The next morning, I could not put the foot down. When I tried, the blood rushed into it, and the pain was unbelievable. The only way I could get around was to hop on my left foot while holding my right foot up behind me. It still hurt, but to put it down was unbearable.

With my leg swelled up twice its normal size and having turned vibrant hues of purple and a rather sickly yellow, Jan dragged me to the Orange County Municipal Hospital, the same one where I had been dropped off after my motorcycle accident three years before.

After viewing the X-rays, the doctor came in and said, "You didn't break the bone, but it would have been better if you had. It would have healed quicker than the bone bruise that you have."

"What should I do?" I asked.

He said, "There's no reason to put on a cast. Just stay off it as long as you can."

I was up and around in about three weeks. I shouldn't have been, but I was. The two puncture marks made by the footpeg healed quickly, but the large bone in the lower leg, the tibia, was soft to the touch for over a year. You could press on it with your finger, and it would leave an indention that would stay for an hour or more. Jan, my new roommate, nursed me back to health. I think she was wondering what she had gotten herself into.

Walt had been such a good addition to the club. A big, strong guy at six-foot-three, and a Vietnam veteran, tough and fun to be around, he loved the brotherhood, and we loved him. His loss left a big hole in his family, the chapter, the club, and our hearts.

L to R, Charlie, Mark, Clark, Zero, Curt, the author, Billy and Gremlin.

Chapter 32
Daisy Mae's

One thing that kind of grated on our nerves was fake bikers or side-walk bikers, as we called them. These guys dressed like bikers and hung out in bars, but didn't own a bike. They were pretenders. I don't know why it pissed us off so much, but it did. As if we needed a reason.

Some of us spent a lot of time at a bar called Daisy Mae's. It was a big place with lots of pool tables, frequently with live bands, located on Knott Avenue, named after Knott's Berry Farm a few miles away.

The bar was right next to the '22' Garden Grove Freeway. It was al-ways nice to have a bar alongside a freeway with convenient escape routes. In addition to the bouncers who worked there, a group of black belt in-structors from one of Ed Parker's karate schools frequented the place.

These guys were badasses and loved to get into fights just to practice their skills. I got to know them well and trained with them for about six months.

Whenever there was trouble in the bar, any Hangmen and these black belts would assist the bouncers, so it was all free 'no harm, no foul' fight-ing. As long as you didn't get carried away, you probably wouldn't get arrested if you were assisting the establishment.

As we got to know these guys, it was only natural to join in when the action started, which seemed to be every night.

We had some great brawls, even though there were usually only five or six of us, bouncers, black belts, and a Hangman or two. More than once, a group of drunks outnumbered us, but we always won, and nobody ever got in trouble for it.

It was a rowdy bar, and the management was happy for the help. The movie Roadhouse with Patrick Swayze reminded me of Daisy Mae's.

One night I was there with one other brother, named Zeke, a tall, lean Navy veteran. We were just hanging out, drinking beer, when one of the bouncers came over and told us that they were having a problem with some guy.

He was being pushy with other customers and giving the waitresses shit. I asked the bouncer to point him out. It turned out that it was this fake biker whom I had already spotted walking around.

He was wearing a Levi's cut (but with no patches), a wallet on a chain, motorcycle boots, no beard, and a sleeveless T-shirt displaying an impressive set of biceps.

He was strutting around, playing the tough guy. I think the bouncers, who were no lightweights, were a little worried about him. After discussing the situation, they said they would like him gone. I said I would see what we could do.

I found out his name was Bo. Soon, he walked out the front door and into the parking lot. Zeke and I followed him out. We cornered him and told him that the bar wasn't happy with the way he was treating the girls. They wanted him to leave. His response was a simple "Fuck you!"

It was considered a bad idea to say that to a Hangman, so I hit him as hard as I could, which didn't seem to faze him. The fight was now on, and fortunately, I had help.

Zeke was a six-foot-three Navy veteran and a good man to have at your side.

I was glad to have the help because this guy, Bo, was good. He knew what he was doing. Looking back, I'm not proud of the two-on-one thing, but it's just the way things are with brothers, especially back then.

If a brother needs money, you help him out. If a brother needs to work on his bike, you help him out. If a brother is in a fight, you help him out. In most clubs, it is required that you join in.

We had one only rule: "We win, you lose."

This two-on-one brawl went from one end of the parking lot to the other, bouncing off cars and fences and trees. It was like

Obi-Wan and Qui-Gon Jinn against Darth Maul. The guy was solid as a rock.

Between the two of us, I can't say we kicked his ass. He got in a lot of licks himself, but we put some hurt on him and wore his ass out until he finally gave up and cried uncle.

We also took his Levi's cut simply because we didn't like sidewalk bikers and told him not to come back to that bar.

As the word got around about the fight, I started getting some feedback from people who knew him. It turned out this guy Bo was a former Golden Gloves boxer! Shit! No wonder he knew what he was doing. I was lucky I had some help.

Fast forward about six weeks. Out on my bike one afternoon, I got arrested for a traffic warrant for a ticket that I had forgotten. Crap. I thought I had tossed that I.D., but no, I was still using it, and off to jail I went.

After I was booked at the Anaheim city jail, they drove me to the giant Orange County facility. I was processed and they put me into the usual large O.C. jail facility with smaller cells holding six people. They also had 'day rooms' with televisions and metal tables and chairs fastened to the concrete floor, like what you might find in a fast-food restaurant.

They locked the cells at night, but usually, during the day, they were all open for the inmates to mingle in the day room or each other's cells.

I found the room with my bunk and met my new cellmates, shaking hands all around. One of them decided to be the welcoming committee and started asking all of the usual questions,

"What are you in for? How long? Where do you live?" etc. He then took me around to some of the other open cells to introduce me to the inhabitants of this part of the jail. In one of them, he introduced me to a guy whom I recognized

This guy looked at me with a smile and a puzzled expression, saying, "Where do I know you from?"

I said, "Hello, Bo. Remember Daisy Mae's?"

The realization came into his face as his whole demeanor went from friendly to "I'm gonna get you."

Which just happened to be exactly what he said.

I said, "Okay, whatever."

About an hour later, I was sitting in the day room, watching television with my back to the open cell door, which was not very smart, when I heard the footsteps of someone racing into the room. Before I could turn to look, I got socked in the back of the head.

Fortunately, as I have related previously, I seem to have a pretty thick skull. Instead of knocking me out, it just propelled me onto my feet. I turned to meet him and the fight was on, with the whole jail yelling and cheering... for him.

Nobody knew who I was, but he had been there for about a month, and everyone knew him. He seemed to have a lot of friends.

I fought a lot back then. Like riding motorcycles, it was our sport. Plus, I had trained for about six months with those black belts who hung out at Daisy Mae's. It was a good thing too, because, like I found out in our first encounter, this guy could fight! I was definitely out of my league. The last time it was two against one, but now I was on my own.

You know how fights are; things happen so fast that it is hard to re-member just what all went down. I do remember that I would hit him once, then I would get punched three or four times.

And that does not include the ones I was able to block or duck. At one point, he got a hold of me and pulled my county-issue sweatshirt over my head.

Knowing that he would try to blind me and use my head for a speed bag, I instantly jumped back, getting out of the sweatshirt, and we went back at it again.

After what seemed like an hour, which means probably about five minutes, I was exhausted and needed a solution. I wasn't going to outbox this guy. Sidestepping a right hook, I caught his arm and swung around behind him, then got his other arm and put him in a full nelson with my hands clasped behind his head.

It was a move that he was not used to in boxing. I had him now; there was nothing he could do. The crowd, his crowd, began yelling at me to "Let him go, let him go," as they started closing in on us. I whispered in his ear, "Are we done?"

He said, "Yes."

So, I released my headlock on him. He stepped forward, turned to face me, smiled, and punched me again right in the face.

We started all over again, brawling around the day room with his fan club cheering him on. As we got near a corner of the cell with bars on two sides and those steel tables and stools, getting desperate, once again, I was able to sidestep a punch and do the same trick a second time.

I trapped his arm and jumped behind him for another full nelson headlock. This time, I put one foot against a metal table and locked the other foot into the cell bars. Wedging myself into the corner so that no one could get behind me, this time I whispered in his ear, "We can call this quits right now, or I can break your fucking neck. Take your pick."

His buddies started closing in again, telling me to let him go or else. What they didn't know was that I was totally bluffing. I was already holding him as tight as I could. He was so strong, I couldn't have broken that thick neck of his if my life depended on it. And for a while there, it seemed like it did. Maybe he believed me, or possibly he was just as tired as I was.

Finally, he said, "Okay."

I said, "Really? Cuz I can just kill you right now. What's it gonna be?"

He said, "Yeah, okay, we're done."

So, taking another chance before his fan club closed in, I let him go.

This time, he didn't turn back. He just walked away, with most of his crowd following him out of the day room. A couple of guys who were not part of the fan club came up to me, saying things like, "Holy shit! What a fight! That was awesome!"

Between gulps for air, I said, "That fucking sucked."

It suddenly got quiet, and the thought occurred to me: 'Where are the guards?' They had never shown up with all that noise. Perhaps they were watching television in a soundproof room. Or maybe they just didn't care; I had seen that before in jail.

I didn't care that much either. I didn't want their help. I didn't win the fight, but I didn't lose either, so I was satisfied. I went back to my assigned cell and climbed into my bunk. Only then did the aches and pains from all of the punches set in.

Lying still on the steel bunk with the thin mattress, I reminded myself about what DeVinch always said about mind over matter: "If you don't mind, it don't matter."

I had nothing more to do with Bo after that. I only saw him from a distance. In the chow hall or across the day room, we didn't speak and succeeded in ignoring each other. I guess he felt he had gotten his revenge.

Or at least as much as he was going to get. I was there for only three days before I went to court and the judge gave me the three days "time served" for the traffic warrant. I got released back out into the world. Bo was serving a sentence and got to stay as a guest of the county for a while longer.

That might have been the end of the story, but there is a twist. About three months after the battle of the day room, I was in a bar one night in Santa Ana with some of the boys, having a few beers.

Whom should I run into? My old buddy Bo. But this time, the dynamics were quite different. When we met in the bar, I thought the fight would be back on all over again.

He had proven that he was very tough and not afraid of anyone. But when he saw me, we recognized each other. He walked up, put out his hand, and smiled.

This was probably a trap, but I thought, 'Hell, I'm game,' so I took his hand and shook it, expecting him to hit me with the other. Cautiously, I said, "How have you been?"

He said, "Good, and you?"

I said, "I've been okay."

He said, "It's good to see you again."

At first, I was floored. 'He's just going to forget all of that,' I thought to myself. But I realized, for trained fighters, when you fight for sport, in his case, boxing, it is not personal.

They can beat the hell out of each other to try to win a match and be friends afterward. It was a concept I had never learned and was not used to.

Just about that time, some of my brothers appeared and recognized Bo. They knew he was the guy from Daisy Mae's and they had heard about the fight at the jail.

Three of them grabbed him and said they were going to take him out to the parking lot. But after what had just transpired, I told them, "No! Wait, he and I are good. There's no problem. We're friends."

Surprised and disappointed, they looked at me sideways with raised eyebrows. "Friends?" Deprived of some fun, they reluctantly let him go and walked off.

Bo said, "Thanks for that."

I said, "No problem, but you might want to take off before they change their minds."

He said, "Yeah, I was just leaving anyway, but I saw you, and I wanted to say hi."

I told him, "I'm glad you did. you take care of yourself. I'll see ya around."

He said, "You too."

We shook hands again, and he left.

I guess he had decided that he respected me, and I certainly had learned to respect him and his ability to fight.

Contrary to first impressions, he seemed to be a stand-up guy.

I never saw him again.

Chapter 33
National Run, 1973, and a New Bike

In 1973 I sold the 'Panelhead' that I had been riding for five years and built a whole new bike using a 1957 'Straight Leg' frame, which was rare because it was the last rigid frame from Harley before they came out with the Duo Glide in 1958. The frames now had shock absorbers. None of us wanted any part of rear suspension. It didn't look cool.

Using the money from the bike I sold, I bought a brand-new 1973 Shovelhead motor, which arrived in a wooden crate at the Fullerton Harley dealership.

I built the new bike on the coffee table in the apartment I shared with Jan in what we called the Ghetto, a group of apartments on the corner of Vermont and Dakota in Anaheim.

Having already collected other parts, like a transmission, gas tank, rear fender, and new seat, I kept the long fifteen over wide glide of my old bike, replacing it with a shorter one before selling it.

I had been saving a rare set of rake-able sidecar triple trees, which allowed you a three-quarter-inch rake without cutting that rare frame. Ten-inch dog-bone handlebar risers held a set of eight bend pullback handlebars.

DeVinch, with his welding skills, helped me fashion a new sissy bar out of flat steel. It was very strong and had two legs for mounting to the rear frame. It was already in the chrome shop. Rather than run the old tin primary cover or, like many were going to, an open primary, I opted for the bulky, unsightly stock aluminum cover because the primary chain ran in a quart of oil and was kept lubricated and adjusted across a Teflon pad.

It was the same system that Harley uses today. It didn't look as slick, but it was great for dependability, and it didn't leak oil.

When the frame, gas tank, and rear fender were ready, I took them to my painter, a paramedic named Tim, and told him that I wanted the red to be as close to the color of blood as he could get. Mixing paint until he got it right, he did great and like any good paint job, it had a lot of depth.

That became the red bike that I rode for years; Tim had painted Yosemite Sam on the gas tank, only he was holding a pistol in one hand and a noose in the other. It was ready to go for the big summer run.

The newly finished Yosemite Sam bike.

We loved to ride our bikes, the farther the better. We'd blast along on our choppers, usually in a tight formation with any number over one, but sometimes in a disorganized mob if we were drunk, or maybe running from the police.

We'd ignore the speed limit, feel the wind on our faces, and hear the roaring sound from the wind and our loud exhaust pipes.

Sometimes it was out into the high desert or the mountains around Idyllwild, or maybe up to Modesto. But the long run for the year was now the National Run with all chapters. This year, in June, it was going to be in Taos, New Mexico.

The So.Cal. president leading the pack was now Uncle Tom. We'd been riding all day, from early that morning, through the desert heat. I've talked about that heat before and it is always the same. You just endure it to get to the other side, where you know, eventually, it will cool off. In the meantime, you do what you gotta do, stay alert, and keep riding.

Late in the day, we were eastbound on I-40 in New Mexico when, just east of Gallup, the sky started to darken with storm clouds. Our moods darkened accordingly. The rain was only light at first, but soon it got heavier. Sometimes, if you keep riding, you can get through it until it quits, and you will dry out. Sometimes it doesn't quit.

It wasn't our habit to pull over and hide from rain. We would just plow right on through. But there seemed to be no back side to this storm and before long before we were soaked.

Most guys didn't run front fenders, so your sunglasses or goggles, if you planned ahead, would quickly get obscured with dirty water and road grit from your front wheel.

We developed a riding style: You would hold your head to the side, and with your left hand up in front of you, try to ward off the spray from the front wheel to see where you were going.

Our idea of rain gear was a leather jacket. We kept riding and riding, and it got cold. When you are soaking wet, it doesn't have to be very cold to be 'really fucking cold!' The accelerated air creates 'wind chill.'

Without rain gear, it doesn't take long for the water to soak in, even through leather.

It is bad enough to have the water soak through to your torso, but the worst part is when it finally soaks down into your crotch, normally the warmest part of your body. That's when you really start to feel miserable, but frequently there is nothing you can do except keep going.

Anyone who has ridden a motorcycle for any length of time has probably experienced this unpleasant sensation.

Since eight o'clock in the morning from Anaheim, we'd been riding, some of the guys packing Ol Ladies. By seven in the evening, the rain had finally stopped, but we were still wet.

It was getting dark and we were approaching the western edge of Albuquerque. A gas stop was in order. We had several priorities on our minds: First, gas the bikes and try to dry out, and second, find a place to spend the night that would be out of the rain if it started again.

Of course, getting some food, the usual canned Dinty Moore Beef Stew or Campbell's Pork and Beans, as well as hot dogs and buns, was always good, but it was difficult to pack the buns without squishing them flat.

Plenty of beer was also high on the list, but most of all, we wanted to dry out! Staying in motels never seemed to be an option.

Uninvited guests.

Our plan was to find a place to camp, but first we needed to find a laundromat where we could throw our clothes in the dryers so that we wouldn't have to sleep wet that night.

Pulling into a gas station that had a convenience store, we filled up the bikes, then went inside for supplies. We asked the cashier about possible places to camp and if he knew of a laundromat nearby.

From the looks of us, he seemed surprised that we wanted to wash our clothes. We explained that we just needed the dryers.

Fortunately for us, not necessarily for him, another customer in line, also holding a case of beer, blurted out, "Well, I have a dryer at my house, but…"

He realized his mistake, but it was too late. Barry threw his arm around the guy's neck, gave him that Barry grin, which was more scary than friendly, and said, "Take us there." It wasn't a request!

None of his excuses would change our minds. This guy was given no choice as he drove ahead with a pack of soaking-wet bikers rumbling ominously behind.

He pulled into his neighborhood, then into his driveway. We lined up our bikes in the street in front of his house and went inside with our new hostage, I mean, friend.

He pointed out the dryer, probably hoping that we would dry our clothes and leave. We proceeded to get out of our wet clothes as we broke out the beer and the party was on. It was nice to use his stove and micro-wave, instead of a campfire, to heat our food. He had not invited us to stay the night, but it quickly became apparent that we weren't leaving.

Our 'host' was basically freaking out about having twenty hardcore bikers plus the girls camping out in his living room, on the floors, and in the garage, stripping down and gulping down cans of beer.

He seemed like he was trying to decide whether he should call the police or just get it over with and commit suicide. But then some of our women started stripping down and dancing to the music, showing more and more. Some of them were strippers anyway and they weren't shy.

As he had his share of beer, soon his attitude changed. He happily stared at the girls wearing little or nothing while running around his house drinking beer and having fun. Pretty soon, he was getting into the whole idea and having a good time. He was no longer a hostage. They call it Stockholm syndrome.

We took turns with his dryer; we had so many wet clothes. We prob-ably increased his electric bill for the month by at least one hundred percent. We couldn't put our leathers in the dryer, so the next morning, our jackets and boots were still damp, but they would soon dry out in the seventy-five-mile-an-hour air and the sunshine.

The party lasted late into the night. When we ran out of beer, our host broke out a large bottle of Jack Daniels whiskey. He got at least as drunk as the rest of us. Maybe more.

The next morning, as we were saddling up in front of his house, his neighbors came out of their homes, staring and pointing at the spectacle of shiny motorcycles and dirty bikers that had turned their quiet neighborhood into a bike rally.

We were busy getting our bikes packed up, but we noticed that our host had his chest puffed up and was strutting up and down the line of bikes like the cock of the walk. He seemed happy, so we asked him what was up. He said he'd had some issues with the neighbors in the past and they had not gotten along, but now, because of his new friends, they would have more respect for him.

We laughed and wished him well. He stood waving as we roared off. We were now dry and rested, maybe a little hungover, but once again on our way to the run, on the road again, the wind in our hair and our ears along with the roar of Harley engine exhaust.

It felt great as we pointed our long front forks eastward on Interstate 40, into the morning sun, not getting rained on. Life was good.

Taos.

The author's motorcycle in front of the Taos Pueblo.

Arriving in Taos, we quickly met up with the Oklahoma boys, led by Muther, who was still OKLA president, and the No.Cal. crew led by Gentleman Jim. After greeting each other in a large vacant lot and sending prospects for cases of beer, we lined up into one big pack about fifty-strong and headed to a campground that had been scouted for us outside of town.

Keeping it reasonably slow, from Highway 68 where we had come into town, we turned on the Paseo Del Canon, heading east until it dead-ended on Highway 64. Taking a right, the pack rumbled along slowly as we wound up into the hills alongside the Fernando de Taos River. Before long, we found the campgrounds and turned off onto the dirt road, then dispersed from the formation as we parked our bikes under big cottonwood trees on the banks of the fast-flowing river. The few campers who were there started packing up as soon as we pulled in.

Because no one ever brought tents, there was no setup to do, and the party started immediately.

We didn't wait for the beer to show up. Bottles of whiskey from No. Cal., mezcal tequila from So.Cal., plus moonshine and Everclear from Oklahoma started getting passed around, not to mention a joint or two.

We were happy to see each other again. It had been months for some or even last year for others.

The prospects started a campfire. It was now early evening. One was lucky if he remembered to open a can of stew or cook hot dogs over the fire before getting too drunk or stoned and completely forgetting to have some dinner. Lodging was your sleeping bag if you were conscious enough to take it off your bike and get in it.

Hanging out together, getting drunk, and having fun. Those were the planned activities for the next four days. We kept the prospects busy fetching firewood and tending the fire when they weren't running errands into town for supplies or helping someone work on their motorcycle. Some of us found time to ride into town to sit and drink in a bar, meet some of the locals, or visit the small park to see Kit Carson's grave.

Others rode out the north end of town on the highway to the town of Taos to visit the historic Taos Pueblo, continuously inhabited for over one thousand years. A few of us spent some time in the old downtown Taos Plaza with its shops, farmer's market, and restaurants.

It was a good run, with no fights among us or in town with the locals. They weren't the fighting type anyway: mostly artists, merchants, and hippies, gentle people. It was a nice place to relax. Surprisingly, unlike the Grand Canyon, the local police and state troopers didn't seem concerned with our presence. They left us alone most of the time, only stopping a few guys for speeding and just telling them to slow down.

In town one afternoon, we met some friendly local Native Americans in their late teens and early twenties. They were probably from the Puebloan tribe, which has its own language.

They were excited to meet real California bikers and treated us like celebrities.

They pronounced Earl's name as 'Arrow,' which became his nickname for a while. Following us around the downtown plaza as we hung out, they were fun people, laughing and happy. We said adios to them when we went back to our campground that evening.

Finally, it was time to head out. For some, that meant going home, heading east and west. But a small group of us was not yet ready to call it quits, as we were having too much fun. It was time to hit the road, and we didn't care where.

A small pack of nine bikes rode east on Highway 64, winding through the mountains alongside the river, through Eagles Nest and Cimarron and then Raton, New Mexico, before heading north into Colorado.

We took Interstate 25 north to Walensburg before turning northwest on Highway 69. We drove along two-lane roads through some of the most beautiful mountains in America, just riding to ride. At Texas Creek, we finally turned back west on Hwy 50 toward Monarch Pass. Our carbureted bikes were running rich at that high altitude, but they still pulled strong in the thin air.

Uncle Tom was leading, along with Big Greg, who looked like Bob Seger, with hair down to his waist, only much more muscular. He could bench press four hundred pounds, and at that time, was OKLA sergeant of arms. Also from Oklahoma was Papa Joe. The rest were from So.Cal.: Curt, Sportster Jack, Joe, Earl, Pugh, and me.

We'd had to kidnap Sportster Jack. He said he only had money to get home, so we jumped him and took his wallet so he couldn't leave. He was now along for the ride, whether he liked it or not. He had a great time and kept thanking us for the kidnapping.

We camped wherever we could find at the end of the day, remembering at the last gas stop to get provisions, either canned goods or maybe hot dogs and buns, or even a steak.

Sometimes it would be a campground beside the narrow mountain road and alongside a river. Other times, it was an abandoned house in a ghost town, or just a vacant barn alongside the road.

We were there for the ride and the brotherhood, always enjoying each other's company, laughing, joking, telling stories, and, when we settled down for the night, partying.

I lost track of the days and the names of most of the towns. I remember only the fine riding on great roads through the incredible country of mountains, rivers, and forests.

We'd go single file on the tight, twisty roads, downshifting, leaning hard right or hard left, accelerating, braking, repeat. It was great fun, but don't try to do any sightseeing in that beautiful countryside until you stop. Everybody in the pack depends on you to do your part. Everyone being expert riders, we had no issues.

We were spending all day, every day riding our bikes with our brothers. It was perfect. Finally, turning south at Montrose, we took Highway 550 south through more beautiful country, including Ouray and Silverton.

We stopped in the old mining towns, getting lunch and a few beers in one-hundred-year-old saloons. We were tourists like most of the folks in town. We just looked a little different. When we hit Durango, we turned west on Highway 160. Finally, when we headed out through the Navajo Nation, it turned hot.

Ten days after leaving the campground at Taos, in Southwest Colorado, just before Four Corners, we turned off of 160 and took a right on Highway 41 toward Blanding, Utah. We made frequent gas stops because of our small tanks, usually three gallons. We didn't always know how far the next gas station would be.

Highway 41 merged into 162 at the tiny community of Aneth, where we filled up. As we rode back into the hot desert, Highway 162 paralleled the San Juan River. It was late afternoon when we stopped in the little town of Bluff, Utah, not only to gas up but also to buy some provisions for spending the night. Where? We did not yet know.

Highway 162 turned into 163. We still rode southwest, mostly long straightaways with a few sharp curves. The bikes were running great, and the sun was low in the western sky. Off to our right, it was casting long shadows from the sandstone buttes, mesas, and pinnacles at the Valley of the Gods National Monument.

It was barren of trees, but with its scenic desolation, it was great country to ride through just the same.

Finally, Highway 163 turned south again. Off to our left, we saw an unusual sight, so we slowed and pulled into a dirt lot on the left side of the road. Putting down our kickstands, we climbed off and started taking pictures.

Mexican Hat Rock loomed large even though it was half a mile away. It is named that because it looks exactly like a huge Mexican sombrero placed upside down, balanced on top of a small mountain next to the San Juan River.

We noticed a dirt road running off to the left that went down to the river below the hat. It was getting late, so we decided that this would be it for the night.

Single file, bouncing down that dirt road on our bikes, among the five-foot-high grass right next to the river, we found a clearing just big enough for us. It even had a fire pit, a perfect camping spot. It always amazed me how we found these places.

We got organized for the night, collecting driftwood and building a fire pit with stones before throwing down sleeping bags and popping open cans of beer.

We weren't there long when five local Indians showed up in a pickup truck. Almost certainly, they were Navajo: two girls and three guys. They were excited to find us there. Like most of the Indians we had met, they were friendly and seemed to like us.

They were sneaking off from their parents and tribal elders to party for the night and take peyote. They asked if we would like some peyote. I think everyone except me said yes.

I had other plans.

As the other guys got acquainted with the local teenagers, I felt that there was still enough daylight to climb up to Mexican Hat Rock, so off I went. With the sun dropping below the horizon, the temperature cooled slightly.

The journey wasn't bad, mostly just walking up steep slopes with only a little climbing straight up, hand over hand on solid rock. It wasn't that high, maybe seven hundred feet above the river where we had camped. The climb took about an hour.

When I got to the base of the rock, the view was incredible in all directions. I pulled out my cheap Kodak 110 pocket camera and took several scenic shots, including looking down on the river where the boys were partying with their new friends.

I pulled my knife from its sheath, snapped it open, and in the slanting evening light proceeded to carve my name into the soft sandstone rock at the bottom of the 'Hat,' along with all the other graffiti that was there.

It was dark when I got back down to the riverside campground. A campfire illuminated the surrounding tall grass and reflected off the waves in the fast-flowing San Juan River.

The party didn't need a soundtrack because the river's constant flow and the wind whistling through the tall grass created all the music we needed. Somebody handed me a cold beer.

Some of our guys were lusting over the young, pretty Navajo girls, who were flirting back, smiling, laughing, and sometimes touching, but the young men – or maybe I should say braves or warriors – who were with them were not going to let anything happen. It was all good-natured, and there was no friction.

Finally, at about midnight, the local kids piled into their pickup truck and waved goodbye as they left in a cloud of dust.

At the end of another long day of riding, not to mention mountain climbing, I was done in. I took my well-used sleeping bag from my sissy bar and slinked off to find a quiet place to sleep.

The psychedelic party continued with the rest of the boys well into the night.

The party on the San Juan River under Mexican Hat Rock.

On to Phoenix.

I woke with the sun in my eyes. Already, I was hot and sweating in my sleeping bag. Thinking I may be holding up the rest of the guys, I quickly got up, pulled on my boots, and rolled up my sleeping bag.

Finding my way out of the clearing in the long grass, I walked down to the river and followed it until I got back to the camp. I was partly disappointed to find that everyone else was still asleep, either in their bags or just lying in the dirt next to the now cold, burned-out fire.

I sat down next to the campfire and waited. It wasn't long before the rest of the guys started to come alive, if you could call it that. Joe was first to stir. He rolled over and squinted with one eye in my direction.

Seeing me sitting there, he said in a raspy voice, "Where am I?"

I said, "I think we're in Utah."

"How did we get here?"

"We rode. Don't you remember?"

"The last thing I remember is being on some other planet."

"Which one?"

"Damned if I know. All I remember is that it was very dark and had a lot of tall grass."

One at a time, others were slowly coming back to life. We had no coffee, no breakfast, and no reason to hang around this place anymore.

As we packed up our bikes, they entertained me with stories of the wild night, at least in their minds. How some had gotten lost in the dark and the long grass.

During the night, Sportster Jack had somehow fallen into the river and was almost swept away in the fast current. Fortunately, Earl heard the splash and ran downstream, jumping in to pull him out.

Getting ready to go, both were still wearing wet clothes. They would dry out quickly in the desert air.

The psychedelic fantasy and Twilight Zone images from the previous night were hilarious – the confusion, the imagination, the fun, the fears. I guess it had been quite a night and we were lucky to still be in one piece.

But just like a dream that is gone thirty seconds after you wake up, none of that mattered anymore. Our priority was to be on the road again. Second was to find coffee and a place to eat.

Two miles down the road, we pulled into the Hat Rock Cafe. After more than two weeks on the road and sleeping on the ground, we looked dirty and weather-worn. Ignoring the staring tourists, we found a big table and got comfortable.

After many nights of sitting on the ground, a rock, or a wooden log, it felt nice to sit on padded chairs. We scarfed down eggs, bacon, pancakes, hash-browned potatoes, and, of course, as much hot coffee as we could drink.

Fed and rested, we pulled out of the dirt parking lot, got into formation on the highway, and headed south once again. Nine o'clock in the morning and it was already hot.

Just after the wide spot in the road called Oljato, which was not even a town, just an elementary school and a high school, US 163 turns a slight right and then proceeds straight as an arrow for thirty miles as you head into Monument Valley.

The giant rock formations loom larger as you get closer. Even if you've never been there before, the scenery is familiar. Hollywood filmed so many Western movies there. It was one of those deja vu moments, all over again.

Here we were, outlaws riding our steel horses into a Western movie set. At least we didn't have to worry about fighting Indians. They had all been friendly.

US 163 dead-ended in the town of Kayenta, now in Arizona, still part of the vast Navajo Reservation. After a quick gas stop, we headed westbound on Highway 160 through the Painted Desert until Tuba City, where we gassed up again before turning southbound on US 89 toward Flagstaff.

Our destination was Gremlin's house in Phoenix, where we could visit, sleep indoors in air conditioning, and hang out with him for a couple of days. He had not been able to make the run to Taos, so people wanted to see him.

It was a long day of riding, three hundred and fifty miles, over six hours, most of it in the heat of over one hundred degrees.

Once we were in the city of Phoenix, stopping at red lights and sitting over that big, hot engine was almost more than we So.Cal. boys could stand. We felt like shrimp that had just been thrown on the barbie.

After two nights at Gremlin's, we hit the road early, wanting to beat the heat. However, that was impossible because we had to ride through the middle of the Mojave Desert most of the way back.

We stopped several times during the day to take advantage of air conditioning whenever possible. We stopped at several diners for lunch or just to sit and drink cold water or sodas.

It was another hot six-hour day through Blythe on the California border, over the mountains at Desert Center, Indio, and then Palm Springs. Finally, we reached Banning Pass, where the temperatures started cooling off.

Not wanting to give in yet, Greg and Papa Joe from Oklahoma were still with us as we pulled into Anaheim. A high overcast was blocking most of the sun, and the mid-afternoon temperatures from the cooling ocean breeze were only seventy-five degrees. No wonder we lived here!

We were all tanned and dirty, with greasy hair and beards. It had been three weeks since we had left, and we'd been on the road almost every day. We felt hard as nails, creatures of the highway.

It was nice to be back. Some of us started splitting off as we rode into town, heading home to our Ol Ladies and some rest.

Greg and Papa Joe would be staying with Uncle Tom.

It had been a great run, with a lot of great riding, no arrests, and no accidents, and the bikes had held together.

For us, the small pack just getting home. It had been a typical summer ride.

In Phoenix, the author, Earl, Papa Joe, Pugh, Gremlin, Greg & Uncle Tom.

Chapter 34
Packing a Pistol in All the Wrong Places

It was time for me to get back to business as usual, which meant trying to figure out how to get into trouble again.

Back in So.Cal., in 1974, I had a pullover leather jacket with zippers down the sides. Sometimes I would carry a small .22 caliber snub-nosed revolver that would fit into the top front pocket of that jacket. The gun belonged to Jan, my current girlfriend. I still have that jacket.

One evening, I was invited to a party in the city of Orange, and I decided to take that gun along. In California back then, just like now, it's frowned upon by the police.

Stopping my bike in front of a dozen other bikes at the front of the house, I shut it down and backed into a space at the curb, then threw out the kickstand, pulled out the key, and strolled into the house.

Once I was inside, someone showed me a bedroom where I could throw my jacket on a bed and wear just my cut. Other jackets were there too. It must have been a good party, as I don't remember much about it. I stayed so late, it was getting light when I finally decided to head out.

Picking up my jacket off the bed, I checked that the pistol was still in the pocket. When I walked out to the curb, I jumped on the kick-starter, whacked the transmission into gear, and roared off down the street.

It was about six AM, and I was almost out of the Orange city limits when red lights lit up behind me in the early morning sky. Oops, the local PoPo. It was not unusual to get stopped for no reason back then.

Most of the time they wanted to know who you were and would do what they called a Field Interrogation card on you, known as an F.I. It also gave them a chance to run a warrant check on you, which this cop was happy to do. Damned if one didn't come up for a ticket for expired registration.

I had gotten the registration taken care of, but had forgotten to take care of the ticket. At times I had used so many fake I.D.s that I lost track of some of them. A hazard of multiple personalities. I really needed to start paying more attention to that kind of thing. But fixed registration or not, a warrant is a warrant.

"Up against the car, you know the position." Happy to have scored on his watch, he said, "You're under arrest."

As he gave me a quick pat down. I was sure he would find the pistol in the front pocket of my jacket. He had already taken my knife, and now I knew that I would be facing another concealed weapon charge for the gun.

Imagine my surprise when he slapped the cuffs on me. He had completely missed the gun. I waited in the back of the car while he called for a tow truck to pick up my bike. Fortunately, the tow truck driver knew how to handle motorcycles and was careful with it.

Sitting there, I pondered what the hell I was going to do with the gun. I considered getting my hands under my feet. Then, with them in front of me, I could get to my handcuff key and take the cuffs off. But the windows were up, so I couldn't throw it out.

Nor could I just leave it in the back seat because they always search it after taking you out to see if you dumped anything.

Usually it was drugs, but it could be weapons, too – anything the arrestee does not want to get caught with.

The cop drove me to the city police station on Batavia Street. Today it's a large facility, but back then, it was relatively small and informal in comparison.

He took me into the office. This early in the morning, no one else was there as he started typing to process the arrest report.

With just the two of us in the room, he took the handcuffs off for the fingerprinting, then left them off as he had me sit in a chair next to his desk. He asked me questions for the report form.

He was an okay guy, and we talked amiably. I was usually respectful and friendly to cops, for two reasons. One, though this isn't always the case, usually you get back what you give, and it just makes life easier.

Two, it was a good way to keep from getting shot.

I was still wearing my cut over my leather jacket with that damn gun still in the pocket. My mind was going a million miles per hour, trying to figure out what to do with it. I hoped that he would leave me alone for a moment so I could ditch it into a trash can or slide it under the desk, anywhere out of sight.

But soon other cops arrived at the small office for the new shift and I never got the opportunity to make my move. I knew if I tried the old 'using the bathroom' trick, he would either watch me or search it afterward.

No way was even a small pistol going to get flushed down a toilet, and a urinal was definitely out of the question.

With the paperwork done, my first host was going off duty. He put a guy on the morning shift in charge of delivering me to the county lockup.

I was cuffed again and given another quick pat-down. I thought, 'Here it comes,' and couldn't believe it when he missed it too. He put me into the back seat of another patrol car and we were off to my home away from home, the Orange County Jail.

It was only a fifteen-minute ride and, of course, I had no opportunity to get rid of the gun. Pulling up to the guard shack, my chauffeur handed over the paperwork.

The guard lifted the barricade and we drove into the vast, very secure facility. I was thinking that no matter how this played out, it was going to get interesting.

My driver backed into the receiving location like he had done it a hundred times. A sergeant came out and greeted the cop. When he opened the back door, I slid out with my hands behind my back. They led me through the double doors to a small room, where the Orange City cop stowed his gun in a little locker and put the key in his pocket.

Arriving in a large room at the prisoner induction station, I was amused knowing that the only one who had a gun in there was me.

However, I was not amused by the charges I knew were sure to come. After signing a clipboard and handing me off, the Orange City cop removed his handcuffs and left.

The county deputy gave me another cursory search and I was amazed again. He missed it too. Still wearing my leather jacket and cut, I was led to a large room with bare concrete walls and floors along with about twenty-five other new arrivals: the night's catch from various cities in the county.

Also present were eight guards who started shouting orders to start stripping down and putting our clothes in separate piles in the middle of the room. Everything!

My mind was reeling. There was no longer any solution. All I could do was keep hoping these guards would miss the gun as the Orange City cops had. I kicked off my boots and started peeling off my cut, jacket, pants, and shirt (no underwear).

Naked, I lined up with my back against the wall along with the rest of the other equally bare new arrivals. I stood there with my arms folded and watched as the guards started going through our clothing, probably looking mainly for drugs.

My focus on the search heightened when they got to my pile of clothes.

The guard went through all my stuff, pocket by pocket. He was very thorough. Patting down my jacket, he felt the lump in the front pocket. Opening the zipper, he reached in and pulled out my little pistol.

"GUN!" The deputies' screams echoed off the bare walls of the large room. The guards must have practiced for this because, as one, they all bolted for the locked door in a mini stampede.

A deputy on the other side of the glass hit a switch that unlocked it, and they ran out of the room.

The new arrivals had a good laugh at them, but I was more interested than the rest, knowing what was going to happen next.

There was a big glass window where we could see into the outer room. We new arrivals stood around talking for the next ten or fifteen minutes while the guards had a pow-wow.

Finally, a lieutenant came into the room. He was followed by the other guards. The lieutenant asked where the pistol had been found. Walking past the piles of clothes, the guard pointed to mine.

The lieutenant demanded to know whose clothing this was. Knowing it was inevitable, I put up my hand.

Ordered forward, I padded across the cold concrete on bare feet to the center of the line of guards. Mr. Lieutenant demanded to know why and how I had gotten a loaded gun into a secure facility.

I said, "What gun?"

"This is your jacket?"

"Yes."

"Then that was your gun!"

"No."

"What the fuck do you mean it's not yours?"

"I've never seen it before."

I explained that I had been at a party all night, where I had laid my jacket on a bed. Putting it on before I left, I didn't check it.

"Someone 'obviously' thought it was their jacket and put the pistol in there by mistake. It was so small, I didn't know it was there. Which was evident by the Orange City cops and your deputy not finding it."

"I don't believe you," he said.

"I don't blame you. I probably wouldn't believe me either, but how was I supposed to know it was there? I've been searched three times, and they didn't find it. Besides, if I had known it was there, I obviously would have said something."

They couldn't prove the gun was mine, as there was no sales record.

Also, I don't doubt that they thought if I had known that I had a loaded gun with me, this dangerous Hangman biker surely would have used it to escape and maybe kill a cop or two in the process. It was an embarrassing situation for them.

I lounged in the county lockup for a few days, reading, watching television, and enjoying three meals a day of what I thought was pretty good food. There were no fights this time.

Monday morning, they took me to court for an arraignment hearing. I was expecting a multitude of charges ranging from carrying a concealed weapon to possibly attempted murder of police officers. After the usual preliminaries, the prosecutor read the charges.

"Failure to appear in court for the traffic citation of expired registration."

The judge said, "How do you plead?"

Thinking this was only the beginning, and being well-versed in these situations, I said, "Guilty, Your Honor."

The judge said, "I sentence you to three days in the county jail. Time served, you're free to go."

I stood there with my mouth open until the bailiff pulled me away and led me out of the courtroom as the judge slammed his gavel down and said, "Next case."

A huge weight had been lifted from my shoulders as the realization crept in. Once again, I had dodged a bullet.

I had expected to get locked up for a while, possibly for some kind of felony.

I guess the jail guards and the Orange City Police Department were embarrassed by what had happened. They wanted to sweep it under the rug and forget about it.

I didn't ask for the pistol back.

City of Orange P.D. Different cop, different day.

Chapter 35
Red Dog

Oklahoma City, July 1973. Most of So.Cal. and a few No.Cal. had ridden for days when we got to Oklahoma in the heat and humidity of July. Just like with the run to Blyth, California in 1969, we started wondering, "Whose fucking idea was this?"

But we had a good time with the OKLA boys, as usual, whether it was hanging out at their current and temporary "clubhouse," which was a rented farmhouse in the country on the city's outskirts, or at some of the bars they frequented in town.

We preferred the bars because, unlike the farmhouse-clubhouse, they were air-conditioned. Anything to get out of the heat.

One of those bars was the famous Red Dog Saloon, a large strip joint on 10th Avenue in Oklahoma City that is still there to this day. We had been there several times during the week, but one day was a little more memorable than the others.

It was mid-afternoon and I was hanging out near the front door when one of the patrons stomped past me, heading outside.

Following right behind him were Joe and Earl, both So.Cal. brothers. Earl stopped long enough to say to me, "C'mon, this guy says he's going to get a gun. We need to get it away from him."

I found out later that this dude had a lot to drink and was talking shit, saying he "wasn't afraid of us fucking bikers because he had a gun."

Joe said, "Really? Let's see it."

As he pulled up his shirt to reveal a revolver, Joe grabbed his arms while Earl snatched the pistol out from his waistband. It wasn't very smart to make threats and then tip your hand. They let him go, telling him to get the fuck out of the bar.

His answer was, "There's more where that came from. I'll be back," as he stalked away.

After giving me the heads-up, Joe and Earl followed him into the bright sunshine and blazing heat of the parking lot. I went straight to my bike and reached down into the sleeping bag, pulling out a 1911 Colt .45 semi-automatic pistol that I had brought from California in case of emergencies.

The guy had gone straight to his Volkswagen van, climbed into the passenger seat, and grabbed another pistol. Turning to his right to exit the vehicle, he was surprised to find Joe and Earl in front of him.

They grabbed him again and reached for the gun, trying to pry it out of his hands. However, this time he had a vise-like grip on it. In the small space of the van's doorway, the three of them began struggling over the loaded gun.

By the time I retrieved my pistol and got over to the VW van, the struggle was going on at the right side. I knew he had not seen me, so I snuck up the left side to the driver's door and pulled on the handle to open it. It was locked.

The wrestling match on the other side of the van continued. My plan (yes, I had one for once) was to get the drop on him from behind, forcing him to let go of the gun. However, that was foiled due to the locked door.

Then I spied the open wind wing. Remember those? I thought I could reach through it and unlock the door.

So, I found myself pointing my .45 at the guy through the glass of the window while reaching in through the wind wing, up to my armpit, searching by feel to unlock the door.

That was exactly how I was standing when the parking lot suddenly filled with police cars from every direction. No sirens; it was a complete surprise.

The other three continued to grapple for the gun. Upon the arrival of the police cars, our opponent turned and saw me behind him with a gun pointed at his head.

His eyes got wide and he started firing rounds straight up through the roof. I suppose he was afraid that if Joe and Earl got the gun away from him, they would shoot him with it, and he wanted to leave them an unloaded gun.

Or maybe he was signaling the police for help. I don't know which it was.

The cops swarmed out of their cars like a hive of killer bees.

Given that they had been greeted by gunfire, and that they didn't know the situation as they charged toward us, I'm still amazed they did not pull their guns and start shooting.

Cops on the passenger side did draw down on the other three guys, forcing them to put their hands up. Van Guy had already emptied his six-shot revolver and it was now unloaded.

For all the black and white cars that filled the parking lot, you would have thought the Red Dog had announced free donuts.

When the guy started popping caps, I quickly withdrew my arm, put my .45 inside my cut under my left armpit, squeezing it against my body with both hands empty and at my sides.

I casually started to walk away, trying to look innocent, like I was just passing by. That didn't work.

The nearest cop grabbed me from behind and pushed me up against a nearby parked car's fender. At the same time, I tried to keep the gun anchored under my arm so I wouldn't drop it.

I was leaning down on the fender, but as the cop kicked out my feet and forced me to straighten my arms, the .45 clattered to the ground at my feet.

It was cocked, but not locked, and the safety was off. The cop did a little dance of surprise and made a funny little noise. I guess I couldn't blame him. That was all he needed to pull my arms behind my back and slap the cuffs on.

This was a Wednesday afternoon, so Joe, Earl, and I got put in a four-man cell that would be our home for a while.

We were charged with assault, armed robbery, and carrying concealed weapons, not only for the numerous guns, but also for our folding knives.

After getting booked, we were each interviewed by the local police. I got an additional visit from an FBI agent. My .45 had come up stolen and from out of state. I guess the fifty bucks I paid for it was not such a good deal after all.

Van Guy had told them that we had stolen a pistol from him inside the bar, hence the robbery charges. Of course, he conveniently forgot to mention that he was threatening to shoot bikers. He told the police he was innocently leaving when we followed him out to his van.

The police had taken three guns from all of us. Nothing was registered and none of them had a paper trail of having been sold to any of us. When the FBI agent asked me where I had gotten the .45, I said I had taken it from the guy in the van.

This happened to jive with what the cops knew or thought they knew so far.

Fortunately, a brother had gotten on my bike and taken it to the clubhouse, so the police didn't get to search it and find the two loaded .45 caliber magazines rolled up in my sleeping bag.

The three of us spent the next few days lounging in the four-man cell, playing cards and enjoying the free food. The bologna and cheese sandwiches were awesome.

None of us wanted to have to pay bail yet. Earl used his phone call to get a hold of the boys at the clubhouse and tell them not to do anything until we saw what happened when we were arraigned in court. They had to arraign us within seventy-two hours.

Friday morning, an officer came just before lunch, unlocked the cell, and told all three of us, "Let's go."

We asked, "Time for court?"

"No, the charges are being dropped, and you're being fined twenty-five dollars each for carrying concealed weapons."

Surprised, we looked at each other, "Okay! That's fine with us." Within twenty minutes, we had been processed, our fines were paid, and we were out the door.

They even gave us our knives back, the ones we had just been fined for carrying. I thought it best not to ask for the gun.

We asked about Van Guy and were told he had warrants. They were going to be keeping him for a while. Maybe they believed us when we told them that he was the instigator of the whole thing.

Soon, we were back partying it up with the rest of the brothers as if nothing had happened.

Motorcycle Gang Members Arrested

Police consficated six weapons and arrested three members of a California motorcycle gang Wednesday night after a disturbance at a westside Oklahoma City tavern.

Several shots were fired during the incident, officers said, but there were no injuries.

Officers said they seized three guns, a switchblade and two daggers when they responded to an early evening call at the Red Dog Saloon, 6417 NW 10.

Arrested on suspicion of armed robbery were, Joseph A. Steele, 26, James E. Earls, 27, and Tommy Dale Wilson, 25, all of Anaheim, Calif., and all members of the Hangmen Motorcycle Club, which has an Oklahoma City chapter.

Police said Stephen C. Ludner, 19, and Donald Bradley, 22, told them they were in the bar discussing a pistol they had purchased Wednesday morning when the three Hangmen and several other motorcycle riders confronted them with a demand that they give them the gun.

The dispute moved to the parking lot, where Bradley fired several shots into the air in an effort to frighten the Hangmen. One of them reportedly produced a knife and attempted to seize the pistol.

Police arrived moments later and halted further violence. They said the two victims expressed a desire to prosecute the suspects, and charges were pending late Wednesday night.

Joseph Steele is actually Joe Heller. And of course, Tommy Dale Wilson is me.

Chapter 36
More Bar Fights

We would frequent certain bars for a while, places like Daisy Mae's and the Crystal Pistol. Invariably, we would get into fights and tear the place up.

Maybe not after the first fight, but after it happened repeatedly, we would not be welcomed back. There were exceptions, of course, when we were friends of the bar and would help with "security" by assisting the bouncers whenever there was trouble.

People who go to bars normally consider it 'their bar' and resent a bunch of outsiders coming in and acting like they own the place. And we always owned the place.

Getting into fights in bars was so common that, besides riding motorcycles, it was our official sport. Not that we went looking for trouble. Well, at least not most of us.

We did have a couple of hot-headed troublemakers who frequently started shit, but we also knew that if the police got involved, the bikers always got the blame whether we started it or not. We didn't have anything to prove, and for the most part, the fights came to us.

On our side, there was always that drunk brother who was looking to have some fun. On the other side, drunks, who for some reason, we always seemed to find in bars, were often willing to volunteer.

To us, they were known as a "dial-a-victim."

Then there were always the karate experts, former football players, or high school wrestlers, claiming, "You bikers aren't so tough. I ain't afraid of you. I'll take you all on!"

Sometimes, we would just laugh it off, but that didn't always work. It could embolden the tough guy, making him think we were afraid of him and not up to the task. That was always a mistake.

Most of the time, if they had friends in the bar, they would join in. Unless it was a quick knockout or beatdown, it was rarely one-on-one.

What would start that way could quickly turn into a melee with not just fists flying, but also beer bottles, cue balls, chairs, you name it. Often, it looked like the saloon fights depicted in Western movies.

As long as nobody got too serious and pulled a knife, or worse, a gun, it was usually fun. We never lost a fight, even if it was just two Hangmen against a bar full of people.

It could get touch and go at times, but we would do anything to win, or at the very least, walk out on our own two feet. That also meant racing away on our bikes as police sirens wailed.

Naturally, as I've said, we always got the blame, partly because we tried not to be there when the cops showed up, so they got only one side of the story. Most of the time, we didn't care what story they got as long as none of us were arrested.

Some of the Oklahoma Hangmen have a great story about a guy in Colorado who started shooting up a bar. Eventually, they got the gun away from him while he was reloading and almost beat him to death with it.

The police arrived before they could escape, but they arrested him instead of the Hangmen. After sending the shooter to the hospital, the police made the club leave town.

La Grange, California.

Alongside the Tuolumne River, thirty miles east of Modesto, is the historic little town of La Grange, which is French for "The Farm." With rolling hills with parched yellow grasslands in the summer, rich with oak and cottonwood trees alongside the river as well as in the old town, this was California's gold country.

I was with the Motown crew. There were six others besides me, and none of them were patch holders yet. We were looking to get out of town for a leisurely motorcycle ride.

Due to a lot of heat from the police at the time, we were trying to lay low. I hated to ride without my patch, so I was wearing a thigh-length overcoat with my cut underneath.

We wanted to enjoy the ride, not spend half the day alongside the road, getting checked for warrants. Gentleman Jim had business elsewhere and couldn't make it that day.

Motoring north out of town on McHenry Avenue, which turned into Highway 108, we followed it as it turned eastbound through Riverbank and then Oakdale, merging with Highway 120. With Chuck leading front left because he knew where we were going, I rode right front. We blasted along in a tight pack. Nobody ran speedometers, but we tried to stay near the speed limit. After years of riding, we were good at getting close.

About thirty miles out of Modesto, we hooked a right onto La Grange Road, a two-lane ribbon of easy curves that lasted for fifteen miles.

Flying in formation, we were a group of great-looking bikes, spotless, with flashy paint jobs and flashing chrome, blasting that Harley thunder. By contrast, the bikes were ridden by a bunch of ragged, dirty, long-haired, bearded misfits.

We rode together as one. Finally, we hit the intersection of Highway 132 and made a left turn. In a quarter of a mile, the pack rumbled into the small town.

We moved into single file, lined up, swung out into the road, and backed up to the curb. We parked in front of the La Grange Saloon and Grill, a two-story stone building built in the late 1890s.

Sitting in the old bar, we relaxed from our short ride and enjoyed some beers. Some of the guys ordered hamburgers while others played pool on the two tables toward the back of the room.

Bullshitting and laughing, we were having a good time. After about twenty minutes, we heard the roar of more motorcycles coming into town. They parked in front of the bar alongside ours.

Nine guys walked in. Mostly, they ignored us, so we paid them no mind. None were wearing patches and I saw no need to let them see mine.

We avoided each other in the small bar, but it wasn't long before an altercation started. It was something simple, like their guy bumping into one of our guys. No apology, angry stares, a shove, a punch, and the fight was on.

There were the familiar sounds of glass breaking and furniture hitting the floor, the bartender yelling for calm as everyone on both sides converged. Soon, as often happens, it was all of us against all of them, like one of those cowboy movie saloon brawls minus the exciting music.

At one point, I was duking it out with a guy next to one of the pool tables. I got in a lucky shot and knocked him down. One of his buddies across the table didn't seem to like that. He started picking up pool balls from the table and heaving them at me as hard as he could from about four feet away.

I used my arms to deflect them and was successful at keeping from being hit in the face or head. Chuck Chapman was behind him. Having just floored his opponent, he had some free time, so he laid into the guy and took him off my hands.

One of our guys, named Dave, the guy who drove the truck during the getaway from the pizza parlor, was being outmatched near the middle of the room by a big guy who had him pinned against the bar while repeatedly punching him.

I raced over to them and grabbed the guy from behind, pinning his arms and pulling him away.

While I had a hold of him, another one of the opposing team grabbed a beer glass, broke it against the bar, and jabbed it into my side as hard as he could while twisting it.

When I was a kid, fighting my older brothers or the Mexicans in the neighborhoods where we lived, I learned that getting mad during a fight was unproductive. Being a redhead, I had a ferocious temper, which I thought I had learned to control... Most of the time.

But like the fight in the pizza parlor parking lot, once I felt that someone was trying to kill me, the game changed, and so did my attitude.

Fortunately, the heavy coat I was wearing, and my leather cut underneath, prevented the broken glass from hurting me. However, now I was angry. Turning into him, I shoved the guy I was holding into Guy Number Two, which knocked him away from me.

As he and I faced each other, he dropped the broken glass, reached to his belt, and pulled out a knife. Stepping back, I flung off the long coat I was wearing and pulled my knife from its scabbard. With a flick of the wrist, it snapped it open. This was about to get serious.

As he and I started advancing toward each other, I heard shouting around the bar, but paid no attention. That whole adrenaline thing, you know. Just as we were about to engage, I was grabbed from behind and pulled backward.

Two guys from the other side took hold of my opponent and started dragging him toward the front door. It was a bit bewildering, but I saw that the fighting had stopped, and the bar was quiet.

I finally realized it was Chuck who had a hold of me and pulled me across the bar. He let me go, and I turned on him, madder than a Democrat at a Republican convention.

"Why the fuck did you do that?" I demanded.

"Because I knew you were going to try to kill him," he replied.

"And what's wrong with that?"

"First of all, there are too many witnesses. Second, these guys are with Tasty, who is a Gypsy Joker. He's not here, but they shut it down when they saw your patch. Tasty and Gentleman Jim are friends. Nobody knew who the fuck we were until you took off the coat."

There were some apologies from both sides.

"Sorry about that, if we had known who you were..."

We respected the Gypsy Jokers and were formally friends. No wonder these guys were so tough and fought well.

It was all just a mistake, which luckily was corrected before things got out of hand and someone got badly hurt.

The guy whom I had faced off with was taken outside and never came back in. I guess he didn't want to be friends.

After some discussions, it was something like, "Tell Gentleman Jim it was a mistake."

"Yeah, no problem, same here, tell Tasty that as well."

"No hard feelings?"

"None at all. What's little fisticuffs among friends?" The tension was broken and everyone laughed.

Rounding up their people, they went outside and started kicking over their bikes. As the noise of their motorcycles faded into the distance, we started picking up chairs and tables and ordered more beer, but the bartender shook his head.

"No, you guys need to leave too. The cops are on the way."

Shit! We'd rather not stick around for that conversation. Only then did I notice that I had big lumps on my forearms from blocking those pool balls. It was like I had chicken eggs under the skin on my forearms just above my wrists.

We went out and put on our gear, meaning sunglasses and gloves. I put my patch on over my coat this time.

Lesson learned, police or not: Sometimes people need to know who you are. We could have avoided the whole thing if we had started a conversation with them.

When we fired up our bikes, the noise built to that satisfying Harley rumble and we pulled away from the curb, then got into formation and headed west on Highway 132. I was a little lightheaded, from either the fight or the beer. Maybe both.

I tried to ignore the pain from the bumps and bruises, and I noticed my jaw was sore. I didn't remember getting hit in the face.

We followed 132 alongside the Tuolumne River, eventually through the town of Waterford, and finally back to Modesto.

What was supposed to be a nice, pleasant getaway had turned out to be a rather long day with many wounds to nurse. But it could have been much worse. Another day in the life.

The beer pitcher.

One night, at a bar on Western Avenue in west Anaheim, six of us got into a brawl with a whole bar of locals. I don't remember the name of the bar or why the fight started. We were outnumbered, which was often the case.

Near the front of the bar, I was mixing it up with a couple of guys from the opposing team when, somehow, we tumbled out through the front door and onto the sidewalk in front of the bar.

Once outside, as we squared off, one of these guys grabbed me from behind and pinned my arms to my sides while the other guy was about to swing at me. I was able to plant a good hard front kick to the middle of his chest, knocking him down.

Spinning to my right, I broke the other guy's hold. With his arms around me, he had been bending forward, exposing his back to me.

Jerking my arms free, I let my legs fall out from under me as I dropped and planted an elbow between his shoulder blades.

That put him down to his knees, so I grabbed his jacket and assisted him with a little forward momentum. I slammed his head into the stucco wall, which made a large hole the same size as his head.

Absentmindedly, I noticed the chicken wire inside the stucco lining of the hole in the wall. He started to crawl away, and I let him go. That left me with only one guy to deal with. Suddenly, life was easy.

But I guess, after getting up, he'd had enough. Putting up both hands as kind of a surrender, he turned and walked away.

Flinging open the door to charge back inside, I was almost knocked down by my brothers, who were charging out and saying to me, "We gotta go, now!" No one followed them. We headed for the bikes.

One of the brothers inside the bar found himself surrounded. Punching and kicking against three guys at once, he was outnumbered with his back to the bar.

Out of the corner of his eye, he noticed an almost full pitcher of beer. Grabbing it by the handle, he brought it down over the head of the guy on his right. It shattered with the handle still in his hand. The jagged pieces that were left continued down the side of the guy's head and sliced his left ear clean off. Oops!

That ugly scene with copious amounts of blood kind of took the wind out of our opponents' sails. That was our cue to get the hell out of there, and they seemed happy to let us go.

Oddly enough, this incident was never mentioned in the newspapers. Today it would probably make the local news, and cell phone and surveillance camera videos would be called evidence. I hope that guy took his ear to a hospital and got it sewn back on.

Collecting scalps... almost.

I saw a meme once that said, "I don't like to make plans for the day because then the word premeditated starts getting thrown around the courtroom."

At a bar in Livingston, California, I was hanging out with Gentleman Jim on one of my days off when I worked up in Sonora.

We started drinking at his house before going to the bar. It was now late evening. Just a week before, after leaving a bar, Jim's buddy, SS, who was not a Hangmen, had crashed right beside him and been killed.

So, Jim was still in kind of a bad mood.

But he was trying to have a good time and forget about it. By now, he was getting rather drunk.

He always handled it well and was able to function, even riding his motorcycle. He never crashed because of too much alcohol.

He could always fight in that condition too, maybe even better, because he was fighting by instinct instead of thinking about it

I had to drive back to Sonora that night, so I was taking it easy on the beer.

At this bar, there was a volunteer dial-a-victim: a big guy about Jim's size with longish hair and a beard.

He seemed to be showing off for his friends and trying to act tough. He wasn't afraid of no stinking bikers!

Apparently, he was drunk and didn't have enough sense to stay away from us. He was with a group of friends, all probably regulars there. There were about ten of them and only two of us.

They stood in a cluster across the bar, some leaning on the far wall, staring us down. After strutting around the bar looking our way, Mister D. A. Victim would go over and tell them something. Then they would all look at us and laugh.

We had no idea what they were saying, and they had no idea what kind of fire they were playing with.

A couple more times, Mr. Victim walked across the bar and cruised by Jim and me, eyeballing us like he was daring us to do something about it. Perhaps he was gaining courage because we hadn't done anything since he and his friends had us outnumbered.

He would then repeat the little game of talking shit to his buddies and they would laugh.

Finally, on his third pass around the bar, he was still glaring at us, obviously looking for trouble. Jim was more than happy to give it to him.

Sliding off his barstool, Jim stepped directly into his path. A little surprised, the guy stopped and put his beer down on a table next to him.

Jim reached down with his left hand, grabbed his own crotch, and said, "Here, I've got something for you." The guy looked down and never saw it coming.

In the blink of an eye, Jim's right fist flashed out with perfect accuracy, an uppercut to the side of the jaw. As so often happened from one of his punches, the guy was knocked off his feet, horizontal in the air, before he landed on his back with a loud thud. He was out cold.

The only sound in the bar was the jukebox.

I jumped from my barstool, expecting the guy's buddies to be all over us, but they just stood and stared, not moving.

Normally, Jimmy would have been satisfied with his handiwork, but not this time. This guy must have really made him angry.

There were about twenty people in the bar, including Mr. Victim's crowd.

As everyone watched, Jim stepped across the unconscious form and pulled his razor-sharp Puma folding knife from its custom leather scabbard. With a flick of his wrist, it opened with a loud click.

Going down to one knee, he grabbed a head full of hair. Lifting the guy's head, he put the blade to his forehead.

An audible gasp went through the bar, but still nobody moved. A chill went through me when I realized that Jim wasn't just showing off. He intended to scalp this guy.

Stepping close to him, I leaned down and grabbed his arm, trying to pull him away, but he had a firm hold on the trophy he intended to claim. It looked like he was trying to decide the right angle for the best cut to get the most hair.

Leaning closer to his face, I whispered loudly, "Jim, don't do it!"

He turned his head to look up at me, squinting with an expression that seemed to say, "Why not?"

Answering the look on his face, I said, "There are too many witnesses!" He stared at me for a couple of seconds. Finally, that seemed to make sense to him.

He gave me a little nod and released the still-unconscious guy's hair. His head fell back to the floor with another loud, hollow thunk. Still, no one in the bar moved.

As Jim stood and turned back to his barstool, I quickly strode over to Mr. Victim's friends and told them, "Get your buddy up and get him out of here, right now!"

They seemed only too happy to do it. He started coming to as they gathered him up and escorted him out to the parking lot with a guy on each side.

I watched through the open door as they piled him into a white Ford van and drove it away. The rest of them got into pickup trucks and followed.

Jimmy was in no mood to call it quits for the night. He was just starting to have fun. We continued drinking as the rest of the bar got back to normal. For him, it was tequila collins, with just beer for me. I was keeping it on the light side for my drive.

It's not unusual for someone who just got their ass kicked to come back to a bar looking for revenge. It had happened to us before, sometimes with a crowd of support, or with a gun.

For that reason, I made frequent walks over to the door to check out the parking lot. I was not surprised when that white van came pulling back into the lot, parking in the same space it had been in before.

I thought it was just one of his friends, but when the driver stepped out, it was none other than Mr. D. A. Victim himself.

Since he did not bring an army with him, I was sure he had brought a gun and was looking for payback.

I didn't tell Jim what was happening because I was unsure of what he would do this time. This could get ugly. Instead of his scalp, Jim might just take his whole head.

I let the bar door close and stood in the relative darkness next to it. Thirty seconds later, when the door swung open, the guy stepped through it. I grabbed him by his right arm, using his forward momentum to pull him into the bar in an arch, then swung him one hundred and eighty degrees until I slammed him against the wall face first.

Stepping behind him, I said, "Don't move." As I held him pressed against the wall with one hand, I patted him down with the other, looking for weapons.

Still quite drunk, he didn't resist. Not finding a gun or even a knife, I turned him around, continuing to hold him against the wall. As quietly as possible, I said, "What the fuck are you doing back here?"

He slurred, "I want to have another beer."

I wondered if he even remembered what had happened to him. He didn't seem to, and I realized he probably had a concussion.

I couldn't trust whatever he might have planned, if anything, but I was more worried about what Jim would do if he saw that the guy was back.

I told him, "Not here. Go somewhere else to have a beer, and don't come back here tonight."

Looking at me with that glazed-eyed, far-away look, a look I had seen more than once that night, he nodded as if he understood.

I let him go and he turned and walked back out the door. I watched him wobble out to his van and climb into the driver's seat. He backed out and slowly drove away.

The other people in the bar had been giving Jim and me a wide berth. They didn't even want to look at us, but nobody had called the police either.

About a half-hour after Mr. Dial-A-Victim left, the barmaid was shouting, "Last call."

We slugged down our drinks and people filtered out into the parking lot. Jim and I weaved our way out as well. We never saw our buddy or his friends again.

Gentleman Jim.

Chapter 37
RICO

One evening, early in 1974, I was standing outside the Crystal Pistol bar in Anaheim. I noticed an unmarked police car sitting in the parking lot with two men in it, staking out the bar, so I strolled over and said hello.

The detectives immediately hopped out of the car and said hello back, calling me by my first name.

Taken aback a little, I said, "Oh, you know who I am?"

Smiling, they said, "Of course, we know who all of you are."

To prove their point, they pulled out a large photo album, laid it on the hood of their car, and opened it. The pages were full of surveillance photos of most of the Hangmen, plus mug shots, criminal charges, newspaper articles, arrest records, and suspected crimes that they had no proof of yet.

One surveillance photo of me was pretty good. I said, "Can I get a copy of that?"

Laughing, they said, "No."

There was even my blood brother Neil. I said, "He's not a member of the club, what's he doing in there?"

"He's a known associate. That's good enough."

They described crimes, real or imagined, that we had done and told me how they would take us down and send us all to prison.

They were cocky and full of themselves. Posturing like this from the police was very common, but it was also evident that these guys were serious.

Today you might call them the Gang Task Force. Either way, these detectives were assigned to us, and their goal was to destroy the club.

They were oddly friendly while at the same time telling me they were going to send me to prison. They enjoyed their job, even telling me about a rape case they were investigating that I was supposedly involved in.

I had certainly never raped anyone. Nor had I heard about this alleged incident. And I was not the only one in So.Cal. with red hair, so I had a suspicion about whom they were talking about.

Sometimes, as I have said, what they don't know, they make up. Like the newspapers or TV news.

Law enforcement was feeling their oats using federal laws designed for organized crime, the mob.

Now the feds had decided RICO – the Racketeer Influenced and Corrupt Organizations Act – was the way to go after motorcycle clubs.

In the early '70s, the FBI had rounded up Sonny Barger and about one hundred Hells Angels in the state of California alone and had charged them with every crime they could think of.

They thought they had a solution to use against bikers to destroy us. The police and the feds started using RICO against bikers as their new weapon.

After a long, expensive trial, they did not get a single conviction of any Hells Angels on RICO charges. But even if they don't get any convictions, the district attorneys and feds are happy to bankrupt someone by having them pay bail and legal fees.

They have unlimited funds, and they feel that they win either way.

RICO charges have been filed against not only the mob, which included the Gambino family, the Lucchese family, and the Bonanno family, but also the Key West Police Department, the LAPD, and Major League Baseball.

I could also recommend some politicians in Washington.

These detectives told me they were going to use RICO against us. They were just waiting for the right crime at the right time.

The coon hunters.

Up in the hills just west of Elsinore was an old, abandoned house made of stone. It was very remote, and the only access was a dead-end dirt road.

It was surrounded by golden California grass and huge oak trees. We used to go there to get away and party by ourselves. We would drink, take whatever drugs were on the menu, shoot guns, and target practice.

We had gone there several times and it was a fun getaway, being closer and cooler than the high desert of Randsburg. Some of us would ride our bikes, bouncing up a steep dirt road with our long front ends and suicide clutches, up the escarpment west of Lake Elsinore.

Some drove pickup trucks and vans with supplies, beer, food, and guns. We'd bring sleeping bags to camp out, as there was not much left of the house except for the stone walls and the dilapidated roof. However, it was a nice campsite.

We would always have a big bonfire of dried oak firewood in front of the old house.

One evening, after copious amounts of shooting during the day, we were relaxed and mellowed out well after dark. Stoned at the stone house, as it were. As we stood around the fire, drinking and smoking, we saw headlights in the dark coming our way.

The location was kind of isolated, so we were curious as to what was going on.

The lights came to a halt about one hundred yards away and sat shining in the dark, but not pointed at us.

Mark volunteered to go check it out. Off he went, trotting down the dirt road toward the lights.

It wasn't long before we heard loud, excited barking from what sounded like large dogs coming down the road. And then, pop, pop, pop – gunshots! The rest of us scrambled in the dark to find our weapons and get ready... for what? We didn't know.

While preparing to mount an armed charge down the road to find Mark, we were relieved when he came flying back down the road.

In the dim light, we could see a little cloud of dust trailing from his feet like the Road Runner cartoon character.

We grabbed him and tried to check for bullet holes, but he waved us off. Breathlessly, he gave us a quick briefing.

He had approached the headlights of two vehicles and entered a patch of scrub oak for concealment to watch and listen. Then, suddenly, almost invisible in the darkness, two large black coon dogs appeared right in front of him, growling and barking.

I guess they couldn't tell that he wasn't a raccoon, and now, they didn't seem prepared to debate the matter.

He was confronted in the dark at very close range with glowing eyes and flashing white teeth that emitted fierce growls and loud barks. He said that he could smell their hot breath.

Mark drew his pistol and fired three shots into the ground between him and the dogs, who had the common sense to retreat. Mission accomplished. However, the coon hunters to whom the dogs belonged didn't seem to have as much sense.

Yelling and swearing furiously, they called their dogs back as Mark, hearing weapons being loaded and cocked, departed back to our camp as fast as he could go. No sooner had he completed his briefing than the lights again caught our attention.

Down the dirt road came two Jeeps barreling upon us with headlights on high beam. Roof-mounted off-road lights illuminated our campsite as if the sun had come up.

Nineteen Hangmen stood in line abreast behind the fire, all armed with pistols, rifles, and shotguns as the Jeeps came to a sliding stop in a cloud of dust.

Six men piled out with guns. We could see only pistols. You didn't need much gun for a treed raccoon. It was an eerie scene as dust hung in the air.

They walked into the light in front of their vehicles and stood silhouetted like gunfighters, side by side on the other side of the fire.

I faded back off to the side of our line toward a large oak tree, brought up my AR-15, and flicked off the safety. Bracing it across a branch for a steady rest, I put the front post of my open sights on the guy in the middle, who started doing the talking.

I don't know what they expected to find, but I suspect that running into a bunch of hairy, heavily armed bikers in the dark in the middle of nowhere didn't exactly make their day. But they stood their ground, as did we.

With a Southern twang, he loudly stated, "What the hell do y'all thank you're doin', tryin' to kill our dawgs?"

I wondered, 'What are these rednecks doing in Southern California?'

Charlie, who was So.Cal. president at the time, spoke from the middle of our defensive line, calmly telling him, "Nobody tried to kill your dogs. Our guy just fired into the ground to scare them off. If he wanted to kill 'em, they'd be dead."

The lead coon hunter said, "I know you might kill us, but we ain't gonna let no one kill our dawgs."

I guess he wasn't listening.

Charlie said, "Nobody killed your dogs, but you're right, if you don't turn around and leave, we will kill you, and then we'll kill your dogs too."

If they didn't value their own lives, maybe they valued the dogs.

Mr. Lead Coon Hunter stood in the middle of the six guys. All of their weapons were held pointing at the ground. From my position in relative darkness about thirty feet away and off to the side, I had a clear field of fire on all six of them.

I held my front sight on their leader's chest, with my finger on the trigger. If he had raised that large, long-barreled revolver, I would have instantly fired, as would have everyone there.

It would have been a blood bath, worse than the O.K. Corral. They might have killed some of us too, but there was no doubt that the coon hunters would have lost, and we would have been left with quite a mess to clean up.

They had probably been drinking, as had we.

As if to try to help us understand his position, their leader said, "We ain't afraid of you."

Charlie said, "In a little bit, it's not going to matter one way or the other."

Silence.

After that exchange, the standoff continued. The seconds ticked by very slowly as we stared each other down across the fire. I had pulled the slack out of the two-stage AR trigger. It would not take much to fire that first round.

At that range, the front post of my sight seemed huge on the middle of his chest. I was mostly holding my breath, not only to keep a steady aim, but also because it seemed like time was standing still.

Charlie broke the silence by asking, "What the fuck are you doing out here anyway?"

Their spokesman announced, as if it should have been obvious, "Huntin' coons. What else?"

More silence. The ball was in their court.

Finally, I guess they decided that they had made their point, or maybe they figured out that it wasn't worth getting killed because someone had shot at their dogs.

The lead guy quietly said something to his buddies. Then, keeping their guns pointed down, they turned their backs, walked to their Jeeps, and climbed in.

Spinning their wheels while backing up and turning, they threw more dust and gravel into the firelight. We kept our guns on them, fingers on the triggers as they blasted off down the dirt road in the direction from which they had come.

Watching their taillights fade away through the dust and into the darkness, we took deep breaths and clicked the safeties back on our weapons. Somebody remarked, "I'm sure glad they left. We didn't bring any shovels."

Chapter 38
Another Hostage Situation

In the late '60s, a new club started up in Southern California. It is still active today and has grown quite large. In 1974, they were not nation-wide yet. The So.Cal. Hangmen had been invited to their bar/clubhouse in Norwalk, L.A. County, and about ten of us rode there to party with them.

By the time we got there, the bar was packed with about fifty of them. All was going well for a while. Uncle Tom was our So.Cal. president and was sitting with their president at a table in the middle of the room.

The rest of us ordered beers and got acquainted with some of the members. Many of them seemed like they were new to the biker scene and inexperienced.

Feeling their oats and their superior numbers, the more these guys drank, the more belligerent they got. Having Joe with us didn't help. He got belligerent back real fast.

Pretty soon, the two clubs were growling at each other near the back of the room. Tom, sitting with the other president, was trying to keep things light-hearted, laughing and joking.

It seemed to be working for a while, but there was some friction going on in the back of the bar. Finally, Joe socked one of their guys.

Instead of fighting back, the guy backed off as both sides rushed in and squared off. However, no one threw any more punches. There was a lot of tension and yelling, but no more fighting... yet.

Right after Joe hit the guy, Mark spotted a dude sneak out the back door of the bar. Though the room was about to explode, Mark had the tactical awareness to keep an eye on that back door. Sure enough, it wasn't long before the same guy came back in carrying a briefcase.

Being pretty sure he had a gun in there, Mark walked close to the guy as he put the case on a table and prepared to open it.

Slamming his hand on the lid, Mark pulled his snub-nosed .38 and told him, "You're not opening that."

The guy stared back at Mark, but didn't try to open the case. Letting go of it, he stepped back with his hands out and open.

Members of the other club, seeing the gun, got a little bit quieter, but the confrontation showed no signs of abating as they started pulling knives and chain belts.

We stood our ground with our backs against the wall. There was a lot of shoving and jostling among them.

As usual, Joe was happy to make things worse when he walked over to Mark and said, "Give me that. I'm gonna shoot this fucker." He was referring to the guy he had hit.

Knowing he would do it, Mark said, "No."

Joe said, "Yes," and grabbed for Mark's gun, but Mark hung onto it.

In the middle of this standoff, Mark and Joe had a ridiculous back-and-forth tug of war.

"Gimme it!"

"No!"

"Gimme it!"

"No!"

After about four tugs, pow, it went off. The bar got very quiet, but even tenser. Or maybe it was just the ringing in my ears.

Swearing loudly, Joe looked down, seeing a hole in his boot. Blood started to leak out onto the dirty linoleum floor. He said, "Fuck, you shot me!"

Suddenly, the place erupted with more yelling, which became even louder than before as the crowd started closing in.

Still sitting next to their president, Uncle Tom, hearing that someone had shot one of his guys, and knowing we were outnumbered five to one, decided to act.

In one smooth move, he jumped out of his chair, pulled his Buck knife, and snapped it open with one hand. He stepped behind their president, grabbed him by the collar, and pulled his chair back on two legs, getting him completely off balance.

Putting the razor-sharp knife to his throat, Tom yelled, "Nobody move or I'll kill him."

Their pres held his arms up, palms out, signaling for calm.

Once again, the bar quieted down. Tom leaned over and spoke into the president's ear. "One of my guys is hurt. We're walking out of here, and you're coming with me."

Always thinking outside the box, Tom decided to use brains instead of brawn. Maybe it would have been more hardcore to just fight it out with them, but with those odds, it would have gotten very messy, for them and for us.

Blood pounded in my ears and I could feel adrenaline flooding my body as the rest of us circled the wagons around Joe and Mark, staring back into angry faces that looked like junkyard dogs straining at their chains.

Tom yelled at us, "We're leaving, NOW!"

Not wanting their prey to escape, the other bikers erupted again. They were outraged and probably feeling helpless about the new hostage situation. Yelling and swearing, they made a lot of noise, but nobody seemed to want to make the first move.

Mark pointed his pistol at the guy with the briefcase and said, "I'm taking this. I'll leave it outside." The guy nodded once.

In single file, the Hangmen started through the bar toward the front door. The crowd parted and let us through. Joe was limping and leaving a trail of blood.

Uncle Tom let the president stand up and the two of them followed us out.

The other club was still making a lot of noise, screaming at us and brandishing knives and other weapons, but they didn't try to stop us. Reaching the door, we filed out into the parking lot.

Once we were outside, the whole bar spilled out behind, then spread out around us, waiting for their chance to make a move.

Jumping on our kick-starters, we got our bikes running. Tom's bike was right next to mine, so I started it for him since his hands were full.

We weren't sure how this would go once he had to let go of their president. Putting him on the back of Tom's bike just wouldn't work.

Sitting there with our motors running, anxious to get the hell out of there, Tom announced, "Shit! I left my leather jacket in there."

Thinking, 'That settles it, we're not going to get out of here,' I put my kickstand down, pulled my Buck knife out, and opened it. I got ready to fight.

Instead of sending someone to get it, Tom marched his hostage back into the bar, then had the guy pick up his jacket from the back of his chair and carry it out to the bikes.

With the angry crowd all around us, we fully expected that we would get jumped as soon as Tom let go.

But suddenly police cars, a whole bunch of them, came flooding into the parking lot. They were Los Angeles County sheriffs.

The cavalry had arrived, just in time.

The bartender must have called them.

I folded my Buck and put it in its scabbard.

Joe said he was able to ride, even with a bullet hole in his foot.

Putting his pistol inside his jacket, Mark tossed the briefcase into a planter.

The other club stood by helplessly as Tom let go of their president, said, "See ya around," and holstered his knife.

Throwing his jacket onto his seat and sitting on it, he whacked the shift lever into first gear and led the way single file as we wove through the arriving cavalry.

Police cars were slamming on the brakes and cops started piling out.

I almost hit one of them, but fortunately, he jumped out of the way.

We roared off. None of the cops tried to stop us or follow us.

We haven't had very good relations with that club since then.

Sometimes you wonder how many more sunrises you will see.

Chapter 39
National Run 1974

The national runs were always in the summer around Independence Day, July 4. You could ride north or south from Los Angeles or Orange County, and while it may have gotten hot in Bakersfield and the San Joaquin Valley, it was still nothing like the desert.

Being on the West Coast, you can't head east without crossing that damned Mojave Desert. It was 1974 and we were about to ride to the national run, this time in Rock Springs, Wyoming.

We decided to get smart and start the first leg of the trip at night when the temperatures would be only about ninety-five degrees, with no brutal sun beating down on us.

Leaving at eight o'clock at night, we pulled out from Uncle Tom's house with a pack of twenty bikes. As president, he was leading. Our VP couldn't make the run, so as an officer, So.Cal. treasurer, I rode right front.

Traffic was light and it got lighter as we thundered through San Bernardino and climbed up the Cajon Pass on Interstate 15.

After an hour, we stopped for gas in Victorville. There, we made some adjustments, checking that our packs and sleeping bags were still holding tight and that nothing was falling off.

Leather jackets were rolled up and strapped to sissy bars or handlebars. Nobody needed them, even at night that time of year.

Ninety-five miles later, we pulled into Baker, California for another gas stop. Baker is home to the world's largest thermometer: one hundred and thirty-four feet high.

They picked that number because it was the highest temperature ever recorded on earth, not in Baker, but in nearby Death Valley in 1913.

When you're riding with any big pack and stop for gas, it can be like herding cats. The bigger the group, the more delays you have. People pull out smokes, wander off, buy food if the station has a store, and distribute cans of beer from six-packs.

It was nice to break up the monotony of the ride. However, Tom and I tried to keep things moving and soon we were back on I-15 heading northeast.

It was about midnight. After passing Halloran Springs, we climbed up into the hills toward a mountain pass. We were making good time. There was a high overcast, the moon was not up yet, and we had no light from the stars.

With only our headlights for illumination, it was quite dark in that lonely desert. Cresting the mountain pass, we motored down the other side in the right lane, feeling the bikes coasting fast and easy downhill.

Running at about eighty miles per hour, I saw in front of us a car with no taillights, just barely silhouetted in front of its dim headlights. It was no more than a quarter of a mile ahead.

I looked over at Tom to see if he was moving over, but he had not yet seen the car. We were gaining on him fast and the car was going much slower than we were, maybe forty-five or fifty.

With eighteen Harleys close behind me, slamming on the brakes was not an option. I swerved to my left, coming so close to Tom's bike that I put my left hand on his arm and started yelling at the top of my lungs, "NO TAILLIGHTS, MOVE OVER!"

He looked over at me like I'd had too much beer at the last gas stop. I pointed ahead and hollered even louder. He got the message and swerved hard into the left lane, with me right next to him.

The rest of the pack followed us, and we ended up missing that idiot's car by no more than a few feet as we roared past him. It was a very close call, but everybody in the pack did what they were supposed to.

It was nice having a bunch of expert riders in the club. It could have been quite a mess.

An hour later, we were riding up Las Vegas Boulevard. Even at that time of night, it was busy.

The interstate did not bypass the strip back then, so we had to go from light to light through the middle of town with our long front ends, suicide clutches, and jockey shifters. Not a big deal; we did it all the time.

The casinos advertised entertainers like Frank Sinatra, Dean Martin, Andy Williams, and Elvis.

Some of the guys yelled, "Let's stop and do some gambling," or "Hey, let's pick up some hookers," but Tom was having none of that. He kept us moving.

The hookers were a joke anyway. None of us could afford that. But then, if they had seen Curt's blue eyes, they might have come along for free.

Finally, on the north side of town, we picked up the highway and accelerated. It was good to be moving fast again.

Away from the distractions of Sin City, Tom chose a truck stop for gas. Of course, there were more delays in trying to get us moving again. Still hot in the middle of the night, we blasted through Mesquite, Nevada without stopping. Briefly, we cut the corner of Arizona and then entered Utah at St. George and another gas stop.

When we pulled into Cedar City, it was getting light. Because we were getting away from the desert, the temperature started to drop off a bit.

Not cool, just not quite as hot.

Going through the middle of town, we spotted a city park. Tom led the pack down a side street. Almost as one, we lined up and backed into the curb, threw out our kickstands, and shut down.

Everyone was tired from riding all night with that hot desert wind in our eyes. It was time to get some rest. Some took sleeping bags off bikes. Others sat with their backs against a tree or just laid on the grass or a picnic table and went to sleep.

It was good to get some shut-eye, but after a couple of hours, two local police cars showed up. The cops told us we couldn't sleep there and we couldn't stay.

As we packed up to leave, Gremlin, riding up from Phoenix, came cruising through town, saw the bikes, and pulled in. He had been riding throughout the night to avoid the heat as well. Soon we were all heading north again.

North of Beaver, Utah, we'd had enough of interstate highways and turned east into the mountains on what is now Interstate 70. Back then, it was mostly two-lane roads.

The riding was a lot nicer and the gas stops were easier in the small towns. Plus, places to eat, diners, cafes, and local saloons were easier to come by.

Ice cream break.

Whether it was blasting down the interstate or off in the countryside on smaller roads, we just did our thing. Speed limits were not the most important thing to us, but the local cops thought they were.

Most cops didn't know how to pull over a pack. They would come up behind us with their red lights on and maybe hit their siren so that one or two bikes in the back would pull over. The rest of us would just keep going.

The cop had a choice of writing tickets for those who stopped or chasing the ones who didn't. If he continued to chase the pack, again, the back two bikes would stop and then the other guys who had previously stopped would go flying by.

It got to be a game, at least to us. Just doing the math, one vehicle trying to pull over one or two dozen motorcycles just doesn't work – most of the time.

On this day, just south of Richfield, Utah, heading northbound, we were happily cruising along. I don't know how fast, probably speeding.

We were surprised to see a police car passing the pack in the left lane. Then he pulled in front of us and turned on his red lights. Through the back window, we could see him point to the right side of the road as he started slowing down. It took us by surprise because no cop had ever done that before.

This guy seemed to know what he was doing! So, we just pulled over and stopped. Oddly, he did not write us tickets, but explained that we were all charged with speeding.

Because we were from out of state, he said we had to follow him to the nearest county magistrate, where we would pay the fine. If we didn't pay up, he would put us in jail. Of course, it was a small municipality, and they just wanted our money.

We weren't sure how he planned to enforce that, but rather than jump him on the side of the road, we took the easy way out. Pulling in behind him, we rode along after his police car as he led us into town.

When we got to the town square, riding up Main Street, I could see the courthouse up ahead. Because I could not afford to pay a speeding ticket, I hooked a right, thinking the rest of the pack would follow me. They didn't.

After a short block, I turned left, went two blocks, turned left again, went two more blocks, then made another left turn. I came to a Tasty Freeze across the street from the local park.

I swung my bike behind the ice cream parlor and parked close behind it. Taking off my patch, I pulled my hair back into a ponytail, walked around front to the window, and ordered an ice cream cone.

Without the patch, I looked like just another hippy, from a distance at least. That probably would not have passed a closer inspection.

There were some picnic tables out front, so I sat down at one. While eating my ice cream, I could see the front of the courthouse building just down the street. I watched the rest of the guys go into the courthouse and pay their fines.

Obviously, the cop had not seen me leave the pack, and he must not have taken a headcount before we left the side of the highway.

When they all finished paying their fines, they rode off. Trying to ride out of that small town as quietly as possible, I slipped away from the ice cream place to catch up with them.

As I passed the pack to get to my place at the front, they all saluted me with middle fingers.

I took a lot of shit from the guys because they had to pay fines and I didn't. But it was all good-natured and was well worth it.

I enjoyed the ice cream cone.

Highway 89 petered out from the nice mountain riding and descended into the city at Spanish Fork, putting us back into the traffic on Interstate 15.

But we didn't stay in it for long. Breaking off again on Highway 189, we headed northeast through Heber City and finally Park City.

It was late afternoon and people stopped and stared as we rumbled into the old mining town, which is now a ski resort. After lining up against the curb in front of the hundred-plus-year-old buildings, we found a bar where we could get some food and beer.

We had been riding for a long time with little sleep and we were exhausted.

As we relaxed and chatted with the locals, drinking beer in ice-cold mugs, we asked where we could spend the night. They told us there was an old, abandoned ski resort nearby in the mountains, and they were sure we could stay there with no problem.

After getting written directions, we sent a prospect to a store for more beer for the night, then set off before it got dark so that we would be sure to find the place.

Once we left the pavement getting up to the ski lodge, it turned into a dirt road and then a hill climb that most Harley riders today wouldn't even try, but it didn't slow us down.

We stopped at the bottom, and our guys took off one at a time to get to the top. Certainly it was not as steep as a real hill climb, but it was a challenge to try it with our choppers and suicide clutches.

Everybody made it and no one fell. I was once again impressed with the quality of the riders in our club.

The townsfolk were right; it was an abandoned ski resort, an ancient building, with no door. The windows were broken out and nobody was around.

After we made a campfire in a pit near the bikes, some of us stood around it, drinking cans of beer and enjoying the cooler weather in the Wasatch National Forest's high country.

We were able to sleep inside the old building. There was not much of a party that night, as everyone was anxious to get some sleep.

Barney crossing the finish line at the Park City Hill Climb.
Joe Heller waving the checkered flag.

Rock Springs.

The next day was a piece of cake. After breakfast in town, we wound our way north, found 189, and followed it until we hit Interstate 80, which turned north, then northeast, then east. It was beautiful country.

After living in the cities of Southern California, many of us talked about how nice it might be to live there.

When we left Park City, the countryside dried out, turning into treeless rolling hills. After riding for an hour, we crossed into Wyoming. It got drier still, but it was nothing like the deserts we had ridden through the first day.

After a short three-hour ride, we pulled into the town of Rock Springs. Finding a bar on the main highway, we pulled in and parked the bikes out front. OKLA was due to show up at any minute, so that would make it easy for them to find us.

We were surprised to find that this small town was booming, like an old mining town. The bars were busy in the middle of the day. There were people from all over the country and across the globe.

Like any boomtown, there were hookers in the saloons, as well as gamblers, con artists, and tough miners. There were also rumors of a very corrupt police department.

Before getting into town, we had passed a large, obviously abandoned building on the right side of the road. While we ordered beer and hamburgers and waited for the rest of the brothers to show up, we sent a prospect to check out the building, to see if the roads to it were accessible and if it would be a suitable place for us to stay.

He was not gone long when the Oklahoma boys showed up, roughly doubling our numbers. Hearing the bikes pulling in with Muther and Greg in the lead, we spilled out of the bar to greet them and immediately started swapping stories about how the ride had gone from both directions.

An hour later, after more beers, the Modesto crew showed up with ten bikes, and the rendezvous was complete. There was a little friction with some of the locals about us coming in and 'taking over their bar,' but nothing came of it.

Nobody wanted to take on all of us, but then it was early in the day. Maybe they weren't drunk enough yet.

Soon, the prospect was back with his report on the abandoned building. It turned out that it was the old train depot. The roads going to it were reasonably smooth dirt roads and it was empty. We decided that would be our location for the rest of the run if nobody threw us out.

By this time, it was late afternoon, and we made the usual preparations: cans of food for some, hot dogs and buns, and cases of beer. Anybody wanting wine or whiskey would bring their own.

We lined up in a big pack with Uncle Tom and Muther leading and roared out of town to our new home for the next few days.

The old train depot was all by itself about two miles west of town. With no parking lot or other buildings, it was surrounded by dirt, sagebrush, and tumbleweeds. Huge and mostly gutted inside, it had three large rooms.

We unloaded our bikes, brought our gear inside, and threw everything on the floor, then chose our spots along the outside walls. There was a fire pit in the middle of the main room.

We weren't the first ones to use it for temporary lodging.

The old train depot in Rock Springs, Wyoming.

We started a fire in the pit and handed out cans of beer. Some guys broke out cans of food for dinner. I had a better idea. I wanted fresh meat, so I went out to my bike and got my Armalite AR-7, chambered in .22 long rifle.

It's a small survival rifle that comes apart and fits into the stock. In the movie From Russia with Love, James Bond uses one to shoot down a helicopter.

Actually, he shoots a guy in the helicopter, causing him to drop a hand grenade, and then it blows up.

After pulling the rifle out of the leather scabbard I'd made, which matched my heavy leather saddlebags, I assembled it, inserted a loaded magazine, and went off in search of dinner. In this part of the country, that probably meant sage grouse or rabbits.

Outside of a close-range headshot, this caliber was too small for deer, although that would have provided our whole camp with plenty of fresh meat for several days.

California law enforcement was paranoid about anybody having guns, especially 'criminal' bikers like us. Frequently, when I got stopped by the police, whether for something else or because they saw the rifle scabbard, they would think they had me for carrying an illegal gun on my bike.

But I kept the sales receipt in my wallet to prove I had purchased it legally. It was unloaded, disassembled, and in plain sight.

No matter how hard they tried to find something, there was nothing they could do. It was fun to carry it on the bike for that reason alone – as long as I didn't have warrants for something else, of course.

It was sunset as I strolled through the sagebrush about one hundred yards from camp. Soon I spotted a cottontail rabbit about fifty yards away. After a brief stalk and a headshot at ten yards, I showed up back at the depot camp with my kill.

Quickly cleaning the carcass and washing it with water from my G.I. canteen, I placed it on a stick and started cooking it over the open fire.

Other mouths were watering as they cooked hot dogs or pork and beans from a can. It wasn't a very big rabbit, and I ate it all, washing it down with cold beer. It was great.

Over the four days, we frequently went into town and hung out in the air-conditioned bars during the days and evenings. We got into a few small scuffles with the locals at the bars in town, though nothing major or anything to write home about.

Nobody on either side got badly hurt. The local police did not seem concerned. It happened a lot in that town.

The temperatures were moderate the whole time we were there, averaging eighty degrees, with only the occasional rainstorm. Evenings and nights were pleasant, about fifty-five to sixty degrees, frequently with lightning shows in the distance. It was a good location even without shade trees or a river nearby.

One night a car came charging up the road toward the depot. We watched the headlights bouncing in the dark and heard the motor racing. Was it some of the local tough guys who didn't like us?

We didn't know. Not wanting to take any chances, I ran to my bike, pulled my rifle out of its scabbard, and assembled it in record time.

Snapping in a loaded magazine, I chambered a round and knelt behind my motorcycle, resting the AR-7 over the seat. A couple of the guys who had pistols pulled them out and got ready as well.

I watched through the sights as the car got fifty yards from the building and the bikes. Then it suddenly slammed on the brakes and sat still a moment. It backed up, did a three-point turn, and headed back toward town.

False alarm, maybe teenagers looking for a place to party. But it gave us a little excitement for the night.

On the third day, while a few of us were outside with the bikes, we noticed movement on the hill off to the west. Coming down a powerline trail was a man on horseback, leading another horse.

Well, this was Wyoming, so we weren't too surprised. We watched the lone horseman as he got closer. We expected him to pass us by, but he rode right up to where we stood.

He was a grizzled old man, riding a grey horse and leading another grey as his packhorse.

"Howdy," he said. "Where are you boys from?"

"California for some, Oklahoma for some. How about you?"

"Yuma, Arizona."

Curt said, "Holy shit! That's a long way on a horse. Where are you going?"

"On my way to Washington State."

We were impressed. The guy looked to us like he was eighty years old.

"What'er y'all doin' here?"

"Just camping for a few days, hangin' out, partying."

"Mind if I join you?"

"Hell no, happy to have you."

"Thanks. I'm about done in for the day anyway." Stepping down from the saddle, he stuck out his hand and said, "Name's Bob, Bob Seney."

We shook hands all around, introducing ourselves.

Someone asked, "Are you a cowboy?"

Bob said, "No, son, I don't own any cows. I'm an old cavalryman. Used to be in the Army when they still had horses back in the thirties."

It was mid-afternoon. He hobbled his horses, loosened the cinches, took the bedroll and boxes off the packhorse, and laid them on the ground. He worked easily, as if he had done it a thousand times before.

Intrigued by this stranger we continued to ask him questions.

"Why are you riding to Washington?"

"My daughter lives in Port Angeles. It's too hot in Yuma for my horses, so I'm going to live up there with her for a while."

Rock Springs, Wyoming is not exactly on a straight line from Yuma to Port Angeles, so it was apparent that he was not in a hurry. He was making the most out of this trip – kind of like being on a motorcycle, just riding to ride, enjoying the journey.

After taking care of his horses, Bob asked, "You got any whiskey?"

That we did. Bob liked whiskey. After a couple of long pulls on the bottle, he looked up at Oklahoma Greg, who was the biggest one of us, and said with a sly smile, "I'd sure like to fight you."

Bob was about five-foot-six with his cowboy hat and boots on, while Greg was six-foot-three and buff. He could bench press four hundred pounds. But the way Bob said it, we could tell he just wanted to have some fun. Greg took it that way too. The rest of us just laughed. We liked his spunky attitude.

Some of the guys were heading into town, firing up their bikes. Bob asked if he could go along. Somebody said, "Sure, get on the back." Bob climbed on and off they went. Talk about being ready to live life in the moment. That was Bob.

After they left, a thunderstorm swooped in and it started to rain hard. Before the downpour, Pugh had decided to go into town also.

Not about to let a little rain stop him, he tried to ride out the dirt road, which quickly turned into a mess of slippery mud. Seeing that he was having problems, I put on my G.I.-issue rain poncho, undid the hobbles on Bob's saddle horse, threw them across the pommel, tightened the cinch, and swung up into the saddle.

Using just the lead rope on his halter for reins I galloped out to where Pugh and his bike were on their side in the mud.

Of course, I didn't go to help him. I just took pictures to record his misery as he swore at his motorcycle, at the muddy road, and at me. Even in the downpour, it was all worth it.

Eventually, Pugh got his bike up and pointed in the right direction. Although he kept slipping and sliding, this time it stayed upright as he headed off toward town.

I trotted Bob's horse back to the depot. It was still raining hard, so I rode him through the front door into the building.

Stepping off, I tied him up to an exposed stud in the wall inside the big room where most of us were staying, then went out and got the pack-horse, brought him in, and unsaddled them both.

I placed the saddles against the wall, far enough away so the horses wouldn't step on them. It seemed to be a pretty good bet that they would be spending the night. I also brought Bob's pack boxes and bedroll inside.

An hour later, the bikes came roaring back from town. Once the rain had stopped, the road quickly dried out. It was still wet, but not the slimy mess that Pugh had decided to take on.

Big paper grocery bags were bungee-corded onto the sissy bars of most of the bikes. They had gone to the market and Bob had bought steaks, potatoes, and ears of corn for everyone. They'd also bought more beer and whiskey.

Bob walked up to me and said, "You're the one who brought my horses inside?"

I said, "Yeah, I didn't want your gear to get wet. We've all been there and done that. It's not fun."

Bob said, "Well, you're a good man. I sure thank you for that."

I said, "Happy to help. I love horses too."

Later that night, some of the boys were outside with the motorcycles. They had another campfire whose flames reflected off chrome and shiny paint jobs.

Some of us sat around the fire in the middle of the big room in the depot, wishing the smoke would draft better.

Contented horses stood tied against the wall, eating grain out of feed bags that Bob had pulled out of his pack. We cooked steaks on a stick and put potatoes into the fire along with ears of corn still in the husks.

There was butter for the potatoes and corn. It was one of the best meals I'd ever had.

Between pulls on the whiskey bottle as it was passed around, Uncle Tom asked Bob, "Did you fight in the war?"

Bob proudly said, "Yup, I was in the infantry in Europe, General Patton's Third Army."

"Did you see any combat?"

"Every day it seemed like." The smile left his face.

Someone asked, "Were you on horses?"

Bob's mood changed again, and he laughed, "Oh no, son, the Army had gotten rid of the horses back in the thirties." He lived up to my expectations when he again looked at Greg with that sly smile and said, "I'd still like to fight you."

Then we all laughed. I thought, 'What an amazing person.'

Greg laughed it off too, and that fight never happened. Bob was just looking for some fun, and Greg knew it. I think he took it as a compliment.

Joe asked Bob, "Have you ever done this before? Taking a long trip with your horses?"

Bob chuckled again and said, "This is my fourth trip on horseback. I've ridden through seventeen Western states, about ten thousand miles in the last five years."

I was amazed and asked, "Are you going to retire when you get to Washington?"

Bob's eyes narrowed and he focused past me as he seemed to contemplate his future. "Maybe. Ya know, I hadn't thought about it."

I had to wonder, if I were lucky enough to make it to his age, would I have his adventurous spirit, independence, stamina, and vitality?

When Bob had enough whiskey, he bid us goodnight and rolled out his bedroll right between his horses. I worried about him getting stepped on during the night, but that didn't happen.

He probably slept that way all the time.

The next morning, he made a pot of cowboy coffee on the fire and shared it with us. It was the best coffee I'd ever had.

After getting his horses saddled and the packhorse loaded, we took some pictures together.

Before mounting up, Bob pulled out a newspaper article about him that a reporter had forwarded to him on his trip.

He handed it to me and said, "Thank you for taking care of my horses and putting them inside during the storm. I want you to have this."

I was humbled and thanked him. I accepted the clipping and put it in my album when I got home. It is still there.

We watched him ride off to the east and disappear into the distance among the sagebrush. We were happy that we had gotten to meet such a man and such a character.

Meeting memorable people. That's what happens when you travel around the country on a motorcycle. Or a horse.

I wouldn't have been surprised if Bob got bored after getting to Port Angeles and decided to climb Mount Everest.

The author with Bob Seney and Curt.

Chapter 40
Out on the Road Again

A s the run wound down, people started heading home. Most of Okla-homa headed east on Interstate 80. So.Cal. and Modesto headed west.

At noon seven of us went north. We'd heard there was a World's Fair in Spokane. Once again, it was Uncle Tom, Curt, Earl, Joe, Barney, Pugh, and me – just So.Cal. guys this time.

We rode north out of town on US 191. The temperatures cooled a bit, and an hour out of town we had the Wind River Range on our right. The country got prettier and more forested.

After a short gas stop in Pinedale, we pressed on. Late in the after-noon, we pulled into downtown Jackson Hole and parked our bikes in front of the Million Dollar Cowboy Bar.

It was across from a park that had arches made from thousands of elk antlers shed every winter and collected from a refuge near town. The thorny-looking arches were on all four corners of the park.

The Million Dollar Cowboy Bar was a historic location. It had rich lacquered wood everywhere, shiny with a deep luster. Columns of trees supported the roof, with burl wood protruding from them. The bar had saddles for stools.

Hundreds, if not thousands, of silver dollars were embedded in resin on the bar.

The friendly inhabitants were locals and some tourists. Asking around, we soon found a location where we could stay for the night – a free campground just outside of town. In the meantime, we ordered beer and food in the bar, which soon filled up. It was Friday night.

I got into a conversation with a guy who was from out of town, but was working locally. The conversation turned to hunting and guns. Having a lot in common, we got along great.

He had a Smith & Wesson .44 Magnum, and I did too. He had a .300 Weatherby Magnum rifle and I wanted one.

Later in the evening, when we'd had enough beer, he said he had to leave so that he could get up for work in the morning. Telling me his .44 was in his truck, he said to listen for a parting salute.

Standing on the porch of the saloon, I watched him reach into his pickup, pull out his .44, and fire four shots into the air. It was loud, like thunder in that small quiet town as it echoed off the buildings' flat walls.

Firing a gun in the air is never a good idea in a populated area. He jumped into his pickup and hauled ass out of town.

It was not long before the local police showed up. They walked into the bar, came straight up to us, and wanted to know who was shooting off a gun in town. We told them we had no idea. They said, "We know it was you and you need to leave town. Now!"

We'd had enough to drink, and it was getting late. Rather than argue, Tom said, "We were just leaving anyway." We got on our bikes, fired them up, and headed out into the night, following the written directions to the campground.

The cops followed us to make sure we didn't get lost or stop at another bar. Surprisingly, we rode so well, even after many beers, that no DUIs were issued.

In the small park beside the highway, we threw our sleeping bags on the ground. The cops left, and we called it a night.

The next morning, lying in our sleeping bags, our puffy eyes tried to ignore the fact that the sun had come up. It, too, seemed to want us to leave town.

As the temperature increased, we started sweating, so we painfully crawled out of our bags and started packing up the bikes, grumbling and cursing the person who made us drink so much.

Then we rode back into town to get breakfast and our fill of much-needed coffee.

Before leaving, we walked across the street to the park in the middle of town with the elk antler arches. Each of us pulled one out for a souvenir. We strapped them across the front of our bikes.

Nobody said a word or tried to stop us. Mounted in front of the handlebars, they looked kind of like a set of bull horns, only with a lot more points. We rode with that garish display of horns on our bikes for the next two weeks all the way back to California.

Pointing north from Jackson Hole, we got back on 191 and enjoyed the beautiful country, riding next to Jackson Lake with the Grand Tetons reflected in the water.

We wondered why we didn't live there, but logic reminded us that there was such a thing as winter. We weren't familiar with it because we were from Southern California, whose winters were nothing like Wyoming or Montana winters.

If you wanted to ride a motorcycle year-round like we were used to, this was not the place.

An hour later, we were riding through Yellowstone National Park. It was beautiful, with mountains, trees, and geysers. Elk, deer, and bears all wandered around in the open in broad daylight.

Dodging buffalo and tourists, we stopped for a couple of photo ops, but otherwise kept on moving.

It was a wonderful country to ride through. Following US 191 past Old Faithful, we continued north, eventually leaving the park, crossing into Montana, and riding the rest of the day in more beautiful countryside.

Grey ribbons of asphalt were lined by pine trees. We rode in valleys and alongside fast-flowing rivers on two-lane roads, far from the interstate.

The western sky was turning to gold as we were still in the mountains just south of Bozeman and the sun was setting. We found a campground alongside the highway.

Having bought provisions at the last gas stop, we made camp, then drank beer or whiskey and cooked food around the fire as its light reflected off the pine trees and our motorcycles.

We talked about the day's ride and what we had seen in Yellowstone.

I didn't go hunting. I was afraid that even the rabbits in that part of the country might be too big for my .22 rifle.

Up early the next morning, we packed up and headed north again toward Interstate 90 at Bozeman, not stopping for breakfast. It was a decision that almost got us all killed, timing-wise.

We picked up I-90 and turned west again. We had been riding for half an hour and the sun was still low at our backs. At an area called Three Forks, several bridges crossed the Jefferson and Madison Rivers.

Entering the narrow two-lane bridge, we saw a semi-tractor-trailer rig coming in the opposite direction. At first, no problem, except that suddenly, from behind the semi, appeared a white pick-up truck wanting to pass.

No doubt blinded by the low sun in his eyes, he probably didn't see us. We were rolling at about sixty-five, and he was going even faster, trying to pass. It was only a few hundred yards that disappeared quickly as he came at us in our lane.

Riding two abreast, our pack became chaotic. We backed off the throttles, but didn't hit the brakes, as that could cause a pileup.

We crowded toward the steel framework on the side of the bridge. We were bumping into each other while trying to maintain control of our bikes. Seeing what was happening, the semi-truck driver laid on his horn, trying to warn the idiot in the pickup to back off. However, instead of slowing down, he just floored it, determined to pass.

There was absolutely no room for seven motorcycles and one pickup truck in that lane. We had nowhere to go.

All at once, it got very noisy with the rumble of our bikes, the engines, the whining tires, the blasting horn of the semi, and the screaming engine of the pickup truck in passing gear. All of us, at the top of our lungs, screamed curses and threats at the stupid driver. We figured if we were going to die, we would at least give him a piece of our minds first.

Then my world turned to slow motion. Suddenly, I felt calm, and the noise became distant and muffled. I thought, 'This must be what it is like at the moment of death,' which I believed was imminent.

I could see the deep red paint job of my gas tank, the radiant blue water of the river below, the emerald-green forest in the distance, and the expansive, endless blue sky above, streaked with white cirrus clouds.

I also noticed the bright, slanting rays of morning sunlight from behind us, shining on the walls of buildings across the river.

I seemed to see all those things at the same time without focusing on any of them.

I think I even saw our pack of bikes on the bridge from above, looking down. Or maybe that was just my imagination.

As luck would have it, I think the semi-driver slowed down to let him in. Just before impact with our motorcycles, the pickup was barely past the front of the semi when he dove back into his lane.

We felt the blast of air as he passed within a foot of our pack, crowded against the railing. Just as suddenly, he was gone. The singing tires and the blasting air horn faded behind us. We were surprised to find ourselves still alive.

At some point, we realized that we might as well get back into our normal formation. We had bunched up so tightly to the right side of the lane that it was a miracle we didn't get tangled up and crash on our own. It took me a while to pull out of that odd trance. Everything was back to normal, but I didn't feel normal.

On the other side of the bridge, we pulled off the highway into the small town of Three Forks, where we found a coffee shop to get breakfast. By this time, my weird out-of-body experience was gone.

We were quiet and subdued, knowing what a close call it had been. Nobody really wanted to talk about it. I don't think anyone wanted to admit how scared they had been. I know I didn't.

After breakfast, we continued our westbound journey, each of us lost in our thoughts, trying to get back to business as usual, rolling down the road together as we loved to do and enjoying the break from not having someone try to kill us.

Somewhere in Idaho.

Eight hours and four hundred miles later, after riding in still more wonderful country, only faster this time, since we were back on the interstate, we found a campsite just outside of Coeur d'Alene, Idaho.

Eating canned food and drinking canned beer, we sat or laid on our sleeping bags next to our bikes and around the fire as the light illuminated the tall trees around us. We found it a little easier to talk about the scare we'd had that morning.

Joe said, "Man, I'd like to get my hands on that son of a bitch!"

Curt replied, "He had the sun in his eyes. He couldn't see us."

"No excuse. It was a no-passing zone," Pugh added.

I remained silent, lost in my own thoughts.

Uncle Tom said, "It's over, nothing we can do about it now. We got lucky. And we've got places to go."

The next day we would hit the World's Fair.

The next morning, we felt like we had learned our lesson. Not wanting to ride with the sun at our backs, we stopped early at a diner in Coeur d'Alene and got some breakfast and coffee.

After crossing into Washington State and completing a forty-five-minute ride, we pulled into the parking lot of the 1974 World's Fair in Spokane.

Finding our way to the front of the parking lot near the ticket offices, we parked our bikes in a motorcycle parking area.

As we walked up to the entrance, the people running the ticket booths called security, who quickly showed up in uniform. The security guards informed us we couldn't come in because we weren't wearing 'appropriate attire.'

We looked around at one another – dirty, greasy Levi's, matted hair, bugs in our beards – and started mockingly criticizing each other for not taking better care of ourselves.

Joe turned to Barney and said, "Why the hell don't you take a bath?"

Barney shot back, "Have you looked at yourself in a mirror lately?"

Uncle Tom, the grubbiest one of all, grumbled, "I should know better than to hang around with you fuckers."

We all laughed. Then, seeing that the price of admission was more than we wanted to pay, we defiantly announced that we could have more fun somewhere else for way less money.

"You can keep your World's Fair." We got on our bikes and left.

Heading south on I-90, we retraced my steps from four years ago. At Ritzville, we cut south on US 395 toward the Tri-Cities. We stopped in Pasco for gas, but I didn't mention Kasey, the girl I had known near there. She didn't belong in our world, and unfortunately, I didn't belong in hers.

We rode down to the Columbia River and followed it the rest of the day until we turned west on State Highway 14 on the river's north side. There were smaller roads, smaller towns, and less traffic. Six hours later, after crossing to the Oregon side, we found a campsite on the northern slopes of Mount Hood.

It was another quiet night of hanging out: a canned meal, a few drinks, a few puffs, telling stories, and enjoying each other's company in another paradise of forested trees alongside the highway.

The next day found us skirting the big city of Portland on the south side, then heading for the coast. Southbound along the beaches and later through the redwoods, I was again in familiar territory as we turned south on 101 – Lincoln City, Newport, Coos Bay, and Port Orford.

These were some of the most scenic highways in the country. I wondered if it was better to have a pack of brothers to ride with or do it alone as I had before. I decided both were the best!

I was having a great time. As we inched closer to home, I didn't want it to end.

At one gas stop, late in the day, we had bought provisions for the night at a station with a store. There were some police cars there. The cops were hassling some people who appeared to be Mexican.

We started a conversation with the cops about what was going on. They told us they were arresting illegal aliens. We were surprised to find that they were so far north

We felt sorry for them, having come all this way to find work and a new life, then getting harassed and taken to jail. But there was nothing we could do about it, so we turned back to our bikes.

The police seemed friendly enough, which happened from time to time. With full tanks, we packed up our canned goods, pulled out, and headed south again. Our antennas were up as usual, and before long, we realized that one of those police cars from the gas stop was following us.

Uncle Tom was leading, and I was in the right front position. At first, we kept the speed steady, but when we entered a redwood forest, the light got dim and the road started twisting and turning. We picked up the pace.

Leaning hard around the corners, we strung out into single file to take the curves as fast as possible. It was quite a feeling. The road was smooth, with giant trees and lush ferns on either side, not to mention a string of brothers, all expert riders, lined out behind you. The darker the forest got, the faster Tom went, and, not wanting to look too obvious, the farther the cop dropped back.

Coming around a curve, Tom spotted a sign for a campground off to our left. Frantically waving his hand downward to slow the pack, he hit his brakes hard. I skidded right behind him, waving my left arm while trying to gear down.

We slowed in time and whipped left into the campground. The other five bikes followed as we slowed to idle and coasted into the camp. It was thickly forested with redwood trees and the low growth of long grass, scrub oak, and ferns. It was so green, it almost hurt your eyes. It looked like a Jurassic Park movie

Making a quick right into the campgrounds, we shut off our engines and coasted to a stop. Peeking over the ferns, we watched as not one, but two police cars went flying by very fast, chasing us. No lights, no sirens. As we looked around, we saw numerous campers watching us, wondering what we were up to.

We smiled and waved to them, trying to look friendly. Then we decided that this was as good a place as any to spend the night. We started the bikes back up and rode around the circular camp road until we found two empty spots, side by side. There was a fee for camping there, so we took up a collection and paid for the night.

The long, narrow campground in the deep, dark forest was between the road and next to a flowing stream. We built a fire and broke out the canned goods and refreshments.

The cops never found us.

Soon it got dark. Sitting around the fire, with full bellies and cold beers, not to mention a beautiful forest next to a babbling brook, we thought we were in paradise.

That was, until the mosquitoes came out. Then it wasn't such a paradise anymore. Nobody had bug spray.

The next day was uneventful as we rode along gorgeous beaches and through redwood forests. We made numerous stops to take pictures and enjoy the scenery, which is best done at a standstill. Sightseeing while riding a motorcycle can be fatal.

I had already been through this area, but some of the guys had never seen this part of the country. Once again, some of us wished we could live there.

Late in the day, we camped near Geyserville, California. It was our last campout on this trip, so we tried to make the most of it. The next day, we rode into Modesto to hang out for two nights, doing what they do in Gladiator School.

When we left Modesto, it was our last day of riding. We were lucky, with more good weather. It was the usual tedious slog down Highway 99.

After all of the beautiful country that we had ridden through in the previous three weeks, rolling down the long, straight road seemed almost as bad as a morning commute to work that you did every day. Not that any of us would know how that felt.

In the early evening, our tired bodies steered our long front ends into Orange County. Some riders started splitting off to head home. It had been a good long run. The pack got thinner as riders peeled off with a shout and a wave. Everyone was anxious to sleep in their own beds for a change.

Then it was just Tom and me. When he turned into the alley beside his house on Vine Street, I continued straight, heading to the rented house and the girl I was staying with at the time.

Living the dream. Uncle Tom, Earl, Dale, Curt, Barney & Larry.

Chapter 41
Business as Usual

I was back in Anaheim. Some of our guys were experts at stealing motor-cycles, no matter where they were. I wasn't one of them. I didn't have the nerves of steel that they did.

I didn't feel it was worth the risk, and besides, I wouldn't want my bike getting stolen. I'm sure there would be many funny and exciting stories of their adventures – the drama and, sometimes, comedy. But they are no longer here to tell the tales.

However, one incident that comes to mind is when Barney's bike got impounded by the Anaheim Police Department. They knew us well, and we knew them all too well. For whatever reason, Barney's registration didn't jive with the numbers on his engine, so they confiscated his bike.

It was held in a police impound yard, with locked gates and chain-link fencing all around. They charged Barney with grand theft and set his bail pretty low. He bailed out right away.

They didn't consider one of the brothers named Tom (we had four Toms) and his diabolical mind to overcome any obstacle, especially the police. He, Barney, and another, unnamed, co-conspirator scouted out the impound yard. It was not at the police department, but was a contracted towing service that the P.D. used. It had rained earlier that night, so the ground was wet and muddy.

In the dark of night, approaching from an alley behind the yard, after bending one strand out of the chain-link fence and unwinding the whole thing, they opened the fence and put 2 x12 planks down on the mud toward Barney's bike. Fortunately, surveillance cameras were not common then.

They retrieved Barney's bike and carefully rolled it down the planks, through the fence, and into the alleyway. Getting it up into a waiting van was a piece of cake. They picked the boards up and, using 'come along' pulleys to pull the fence back together, mended the gap, lacing the removed piece of wire back into place. Pulling up the boards so that there were no tracks, they slipped away. No one could tell that anyone had been there.

The next day, Tom's house got a visit from red-faced detectives from the Anaheim Police Department. They were shouting about the theft of the bike, demanding to know where it was and where we had gotten the goddamned helicopter that had been used to lift the bike out of the impound yard.

They were convinced that because there were no tracks in the mud, there was no way we could have gotten that bike out of there without a helicopter.

Playing dumb, Tom and Barney were incredulous and angry that the police had lost his bike. He promised a lawsuit to compensate for his lost property. The detectives slammed their car doors and peeled out in a cloud of blue tire smoke as they left. I wonder if they ever figured it out. Barney finally won a lawsuit for the loss of his bike.

A memorable ride.

By fall, I was up north again. After leaving Gentleman Jim's house in Motown, I was on my way to Sonora. Crazy Jack, one of Jim's Modesto crew, was in the local jail there and I headed to visit him.

I left town on Highway 108. On the back was a pretty young lady named Laurel who had come up with me from So.Cal. At Oakdale, Highways 108 and 120 merged to wind their way up into the Sierra Nevada range's foothills. Gold rush country.

It was one of those clear, blue-skied California days with fall approaching – not too hot, not too cold, with fields of golden-colored grass lining the road when it wasn't the deep amber green of crops of alfalfa or corn.

Traffic was light and the roads were dry, with sweeping turns and a few twisties. In addition to waiting police officers, one of the predators inhabiting this river of asphalt was the giant logging trucks barreling down from the high country where the logging took place.

On their way down the hill, they were always heavily loaded with massive tree trunks. They returned up the mountain empty, but they were always in a hurry in either direction. I was just about always in a hurry too. It was fun to ride that road as fast as I could.

Laurel's long blonde hair was flying in the wind and my long red hair was flying in her face. She weighed about one hundred pounds, so I hardly knew she was back there. I leaned between her slender legs. She was the perfect backrest.

108/120 is a narrow two-lane road with no shoulder, much of it having a double yellow centerline. That means no passing unless you are a young, reckless fool on a motorcycle. Racing up behind one of the empty logging trucks that were heading back up for another load, I wasn't about to slow down. Dangerous passing was something we often did. It was part of our daredevil lifestyle, I suppose. Plus, I felt invincible.

Whacking the shifter down into third gear, I grabbed a handful of throttle. The Shovelhead leaped forward as I swung over the double yellow line into the oncoming lane. Not having been able to see around the big truck, I didn't know that the road was curving to the right. Pouring on the coals, I wanted to get past this guy as quickly as possible.

We were just abeam the back of the tractor pulling the trailer where eight huge wheels power it. At least they seem enormous when you are sitting on a low-to-the-ground chopper. Right then, around the curve ahead of us, there suddenly appeared another logging truck, this one loaded high with thick, heavy tree trunks – but all I could see was the big grill with the Kenworth emblem on the front. Damn, no wonder this was a no-passing zone!

I felt that ice water shock of adrenaline. Things began to happen very fast, with a closing speed of about one hundred and forty miles per hour. But also, everything seemed to slow down in that weird sensation that happens when your life is hanging by a thread and someone else is holding a pair of scissors. I was already leaning right because of the right-hand curve, and the sound of the oncoming truck's air horn got louder as I counter-steered, shoving the right handlebar grip as hard as I dared. I dove the bike right toward those immense, loud, whining, rapidly spinning wheels, the top of which were close to being even with our heads. I felt like a rabbit running next to a locomotive.

Suddenly stabilizing the bike on that double yellow line, I pushed the left grip hard and straightened the motorcycle upright, just for an instant. Pulling in my elbows and knees, I could feel Laurel do the same. She said later that she even pointed her toes inward because everything was so tight between the two trucks.

Though we were about to die, she never made a sound. Just as I got the bike as upright as possible, the oncoming truck flashed past us with no more than an inch to spare on either side. The blast of wind coming off the grill struck us, rocking the bike – and us – viciously from side to side. I fought to keep control of it.

Our senses were overwhelmed. There was the smell of hot rubber and diesel fuel, and even the scent of pine from the tree trunks, not to mention the deafening noise of the two diesel engines and the whining of thirty-six big tires, which drowned out the roar of the Harley.

With the blasting of an air horn from the oncoming truck, Laurel could have screamed at the top of her lungs and I still would not have heard it. But she didn't.

As soon as the oncoming truck passed us, I made sure I had control of the bike. Now that I was free of some major distractions, I realized that we were still alive. The road was still curving hard right and we were still on the double yellow centerline. I got back into a hard right turn to stay in the curve as I grabbed a handful of throttle and raced around the first truck, finally diving back into the correct lane.

Safe at last. Truck number one then gave me a blast of his own horn as if to say, "You idiot!"

Both of those drivers probably thought they had just seen the craziest and stupidest motorcycle rider in the whole world. And at that moment, they would have been right.

Laurel on the back who was with me that day.

Chapter 42
Harleys Still Don't Lean...

We used to like to have runs to Kern County, California. We would ride up Interstate 5, through L.A. and over the Gorman Pass to Bakersfield, then northeast on Highway 178 to the small town and recreational area of Lake Isabella at the southern end of the Sierra Nevada mountain range.

Today much of 178 is a modern four-lane highway, but back then, it was different. We rode on Kern Canyon Road, a narrow two-lane affair, often right next to the Kern River. It had hundreds of twists and turns – a fun road to ride.

A friend of the club, named Jimmy, had a place there. It was kind of a homestead out in the woods. Nowadays you would call it 'off the grid.'

We had been there several times, and it was always a nice place to go once the summer heat wore off. Some of the OKLA chapter were visiting So.Cal. so, as usual, we needed a place to go. About twenty of us rode up to spend the weekend doing the mandatory drinking, having fun, and getting drunk or stoned with our brothers.

Riding our bikes and partying together: Life was good!

This time, someone had brought a smoke grenade. We thought it would be fun to set it off and watch the smoke. Maybe it was kind of like a psychedelic thing. It was one of those canister-type grenades that looked like a soup can with the detonator and the spoon on top. Whoever brought it didn't know what color it was supposed to be. They didn't know much about it at all.

On the afternoon of the first day there, we decided that now was the time, so we walked out of our host's house and found a large rock. Someone placed the smoke grenade on it, then pulled the pin. The spoon popped off and we stood in a little circle around it, waiting for the smoke show.

Just a second later, someone with an unusual degree of common sense said, "Ya know, we should probably stand back a little farther."

Wordlessly agreeing that this was a good idea, everyone, in unison, did an about-face to walk farther back. Suddenly, there was a loud explosion, accompanied by a blinding flash, which was fortunately now behind us. We were all shoved forward as if someone had kicked us in the ass, stumbling to keep our feet under us.

Duh! It was not a smoke grenade! It was either a concussion or a flash-bang grenade. Our ears were ringing. Several brothers who didn't have shirts on under their cuts, including Earl, were peppered with little black burn marks.

The backs of their arms and the bare parts of their backs got the worst of it. We figured it was from burning bits of black powder. Fortunately, there were no severe injuries from the housing of the grenade, which had vaporized.

After the immediate shock, with our ears ringing, we all started laughing about what might have happened. It was a damn good thing we weren't looking at that thing when it went off.

Someone asked, "Who brought that fucking thing anyway?"

Earl didn't find it so funny, as he was in a fair amount of pain from the powder burns. He put on a show for us with one of his famous rants: "God damn fucking Nixon made motherfucking cocksucking son of a fucking bitch!" That is just a sample; he had a way of making it last all afternoon, or evening, as the situation warranted. True to Earl, he always gave it all he had.

Otherwise, the party at Jimmy's was great.

Lake Isabella, California. 1974.

The next day, coffeed up, packed up, and saddled up, we were ready to be on our way back. We said goodbye and thank you to Jimmy and his Ol' Lady before bouncing down the dirt road toward town. We stopped to get gas at the local gas station, then lined up into formation and roared out of town.

Back on Kern Canyon Road, the turns and curves made for a great motorcycle ride, especially on a nice day, on your chopper with your bros. There were lots of trees at this altitude and plenty of right and left twisties, mostly pretty level, without the up and down of mountain roads, which were always fun too.

We were having a good time on the ride out of there. The pack shifted into a single file when we hit the curves. Uncle Tom was leading, and I was right behind him, with Joe behind me. The three of us accelerated, cranking and leaning, upshifting and downshifting, braking and accelerating, having a ball. The rest of the pack fell farther behind us and out of sight.

Of course, Harleys actually do lean as long as they sit high enough and don't drag metal, like footpegs, primary cases, exhaust pipes, etc. It's all about ground clearance – or lack thereof.

Like most of us, Joe Heller had a beautiful bike. It had a long front end, lots of chrome, and yellow flames on the blue gas tank. It looked just right. The frame was raked enough that the bike sat nice and level. In other words, it sat low. Riding right behind me, Joe had all the skills necessary to ride the twisties like a pro.

Unfortunately, his bike did not have the ground clearance to allow him to lean as much as he needed to at the speed we were going. I kept hearing a scraping sound as we were in the curves, and I realized that it was Joe's bike dragging in the tight turns. But he was not about to back off. That was not Joe's style.

Faster and faster, he hung in there, right on our asses, scraping or no scraping. It never occurred to me to slow down for him. I was chasing Tom, and we were having fun. Finally, with the river on our right about fifty feet below the road's level and the mountain on our left, while leaning hard into a left-hand curve, I heard that scraping again, only this time it was louder than before.

Glancing back over my left shoulder, I caught a glimpse of a horrifying sight. Joe and his motorcycle were on their sides, leaving the shoulder of the road and flying into mid-air. That was all I saw: a flash of an image like a photograph.

Joe's bike.

Thinking, 'This is probably not going to be good,' I yelled at Tom that Joe was down, then slammed on the brakes and made a U-turn on that narrow two-lane road. I raced back to the curve where Joe had gone airborne.

I slid to a stop on what little shoulder there was, which was about five or six feet of soft sand before a vertical drop of about thirty-five feet.

Throwing my kickstand out and turning off the key to shut down the engine, I jumped off the bike and started climbing down the rocks lining the cliff on the side of the road. Joe's bike was on its side at the bottom of that cliff. Joe was lying next to it, face down, not moving.

I heard Uncle Tom's bike pull up at the top of the cliff. At the same time, the rest of the pack arrived in a flurry of screeching tires, revving motors, and shouts of anger and confusion. I reached Joe, asking him if he was okay. It was kind of a stupid question at a time like that. I could have been more creative and said, "How was your flight?"

Just then, he rolled over, opened his eyes, and looked at me. His face, beard, and hair were covered with dirt.

He said, "FUCK!"

I said, "Stay down, don't move."

"Fuck that," Joe said as he struggled to his feet, grabbing my shoulder for balance. Big, jagged rocks covered the area where he landed. They were from the side of the mountain, which had been dynamited when the road was made.

There was one small bush about four feet high and he had landed right smack on top of it.

Joe remembered looking up and seeing nothing but blue sky and his bike right over him in mid-air. He knew that it was going to land on him, but somehow, he was able to kick out at it and push it away.

That probably saved his life. A six-hundred-pound motorcycle landing on top of you can ruin your whole day.

The rest of the boys came clamoring down the steep cliff. To my surprise, some of them grabbed me and asked if I was okay. I said, "What the fuck, I'm fine. Joe's the one that crashed."

They turned their attention to him. I found out later that after I had jumped off my bike and scrambled down the hill, the kickstand had sunk into the sand and my bike had fallen over.

The rest of the pack, coming around the curve, saw my red motorcycle lying on its side with me nowhere in sight and Uncle Tom just pulling up. They all slammed on their brakes, thinking I was the one who had gone off the cliff.

Hurting in a hundred different places, Joe was upright and conscious, which seemed a miracle given what he had just been through, and with no helmet. He felt his body all over and proclaimed that he had no broken bones. It was not exactly a professional medical diagnosis, but it would do for the moment.

He noticed that he had lost the pistol that he was carrying, so we started an immediate search of the area for it. I took a photograph at the scene during that search, but we never found the pistol.

Looking for Joe's pistol at the bottom of the cliff.

We still had to get that bike up to the road. Like a bunch of ants, we lifted, dragged, pulled, and climbed our way back up that steep, almost vertical cliff of large, jagged rocks with that heavy motorcycle. Finally, it was back up on the side of the road.

Almost on cue, a pickup truck saw all the bikes and stopped. The driver pulled onto the shoulder and asked if he could help. We told him that we had a bike that needed to go back to Anaheim.

He said, "Well shit, I'm going to Garden Grove. That's right on my way." Lucky as usual. We tried to tell Joe he should go to a hospital and get checked out, but he refused.

We loaded his bike into the back of the truck, and Joe carefully and painfully climbed into the passenger seat, settling in beside his new best friend.

The rest of us set off on our long ride back to Orange County: Kern Canyon Road and Highway 178 to Bakersfield, Highway 99 to I-5, up over the Gorman Pass, then down into Los Angeles, and finally back home. It seemed like a hop, skip, and jump, only about four hours with gas stops and good traffic, but we went a little slower this time.

The guy with the pickup truck took Joe to his front door and helped him unload the motorcycle. The next day, his wife, Betsy, insisted that he go to the hospital to get checked out and have X-rays taken. Sure enough, just like he said, no broken bones. Joe was tough, but he was pretty sore for a while.

Amazingly, the damage to the bike was relatively minor. Because it landed almost upside down, there was no damage to the engine and transmission. With Joe's vast supply of spare parts, he was back on the road in a week.

Hangmen Joe.

Chapter 43
The Second No.Cal.

By 1975 Gentleman Jim, being the perfectionist that he was, after years of preparation, had collected people whom he knew – not thought – would make the grade.

Finally, he decided he had enough quality people to form a lasting chapter in Modesto. This was the second No.Cal. charter. The first one had been back in about 1965 when the Richmond Hangmen changed their bottom rocker from Richmond to No.Cal.

He brought his crew down to So.Cal. and members from OKLA showed up too. It was April, a good time of year to ride.

The official ceremony was at Mark's house in Elsinore, about an hour out of Anaheim. The party started on a late Friday afternoon. No.Cal. was now official. Jim and the boys sewed on new patches. We made toasts with bottles of whiskey and tequila as we passed them around.

We partied well into the night, always happy to see people from out of town. Those present were most of So.Cal. and a good showing from OKLA: Greg, Davey, Zero, Spence, Stanley and JV.

There was also the new No.Cal. guys, who were not new. We had known most of them for years.

Gentleman Jim, of course,

Chuck Chapman, solid as a rock, Jim's first VP.

Larry Kiser, brother of So.Cal. Jack, who came in a couple of years later after he got out of prison. Jack was one of the most loyal Hangmen for the rest of his life.

Gentleman Jim with the new No.Cal. rocker.

Also, Mexican Bob, a loyal member of the Motown crew for years.

Butch, as big-hearted as he was big.

Little Phil, who was always ten times bigger than he really was.

Kanaka, the short, stout, badass, but good-natured Hawaiian bull-dozer.

Jimmy Joyce, unpredictable but dependable in a fight. Which he usually started.

Baby Huey. 100% Hangman, all the way, all the time. More than enough for a new chapter in No.Cal. that was long overdue.

The next day we rode out on Highway 74, then stopped at a lookout above Lake Elsinore. We watched hang gliders and took pictures, then got swarmed by the police – in this case, the Riverside County Sheriff's Department. They could find no violations or warrants, so they moved on.

A typical scene.

We headed down the Ortega Highway for some great riding and ended up at a winery where we continued to celebrate. Motorcycle clubs must ride. After all, it's all about the bikes. If a club gets hung up on anything else, it's not really a motorcycle club.

The No.Cal. chapter was a done deal. I knew all the guys very well. After all the time I had spent in Modesto, I was proud to be there for its formation. And Gentleman Jim was the magnet that made it all happen.

No.Cal. Larry, OKLA Greg, Gentleman Jim, Uncle Tom and Mark, So.Cal.

Hangmen MC, OKLA, No.Cal. & So.Cal. 1975

Chapter 44
Learning to Fly

Approaching the ripe old age of twenty-four, I had been wondering where my life was going. I had been riding on the razor's edge for seven straight years in a life where even one year seemed like a combat tour of duty.

Would I be sitting around bars almost every night when I was forty? Or would I be sitting in prison? Would I be dead?

Of course, it would not matter one way or the other.

A buddy of mine, named Jerry, had hung out with the club for years. He didn't ride and was not a member. A Vietnam vet and a surveyor, he had been a high school buddy of Uncle Tom's in Joliet, Illinois. I knew him well.

He had gotten a job on the pipeline in Alaska, where big money was being made. There were stories all over about people making one hundred thousand dollars a year up there, or more, just driving a truck or working in the oil fields.

It sounded too good to be true and I wanted in on it. Besides, it sounded like quite an adventure.

After a stint on the North Slope, Jerry was back visiting Anaheim in March of 1975 with his pretty young wife.

After telling more stories about the piles of money to be made, he was about to head back up again. I was looking to both make some money and create a future that didn't involve prison. I asked him if he thought I could get a job on the pipeline too.

He said, "Maybe. Come on up and give it a try."

I started making plans. I told the club I would take a leave of absence, go to Alaska, make a ton of money, and be back in a year.

Just before I left, one brother said to me, "Wow, you're really going to do it, aren't you?"

"Yeah, of course. I said I would."

"A lot of people say things, but never do them."

"Not me."

In May of 1975, I got on a Boeing 707 and flew to Anchorage.

I stayed in touch with everyone, and a couple of the brothers came up to visit. I never did get a job on the pipeline. I never made a ton of money. And I wasn't back in a year.

However, I did learn to fly. I bought and lived in a log cabin with no running water and a wood stove for several years, going from one construction job to another. Then I worked for a large auto parts company.

I went on many hunting trips for big game, sometimes alone. They tell you not to do that up there.

I got married, got divorced, sold the property for a profit, and bought an airplane without knowing how to fly it.

I knew I could fly. If I could ride a motorcycle or a chopper with a suicide clutch, or operate a forklift, tractor, or big truck, I could fly an airplane. Like a motorcycle or a horse, you just become part of it.

I thought that, perhaps, if I could make money flying, for once I could enjoy what I did for a living. It was a long shot for a high school dropout with an arrest record who was lousy at math and got airsick, but I thought I could at least make it to the exciting, adventurous, and dangerous life of a bush pilot.

I soloed after 4.1 hours of flight instruction. My instructor kept asking me, "Are you sure you haven't had lessons before?"

I went on to get my private pilot's license in record time.

In 1979 I decided to move back to So.Cal. With just one hundred hours of flight time under my belt, I flew the little airplane I had bought – a 1946 two-seat Cessna 140 – three thousand six hundred miles back to California.

Because I was a new pilot and inexperienced, many people warned me not to try it. It was too dangerous, with vast areas of rugged country and too few airports. But I was used to danger, and I went anyway. They were right.

I learned a lot on that trip and almost killed myself at least four or five times. My only navigation was a magnetic compass and maps. Still, amazingly, I made it back into the lower forty-eight states with myself and the airplane in one piece.

I stopped numerous times along the way to visit people I knew, including Gentleman Jim.

Back in So.Cal., things had changed. I had changed. My passion for riding a motorcycle and being a Hangman had changed to a passion for flying airplanes and being a pilot. I couldn't learn enough or learn it fast enough. I was obsessed with it. Flying was all I could think about.

I found odd jobs while continuing my flight training, working on my ratings to qualify as a commercial pilot. I did it on a shoestring financially, sometimes while on unemployment. I could not afford a formal flight school.

I hung out with the club in my spare time for parties, funerals, and special occasions.

It was always good to see the brothers, but I backed way off from going on runs and getting into bar fights or worse. I had a new goal in life.

At least five other brothers were learning to fly or already knew how, so we spent a lot of time flying together. Some of us would fly back and forth between So.Cal. and Oklahoma. It was a lot quicker than riding a motorcycle.

We called it the Hangmen Air Force. I heard the police suspected us of transporting illegal drugs that way, but I don't know anything about that.

I stayed out of jail, got my commercial ratings, got married again, and got one flying job after another. In the early '80s, one of them was flying on the fires in California, which was exciting and fun. It was also dangerous.

Ten of the pilots whom I knew while doing that job got killed over about five years. I was fortunate to not be one of them.

In 1983 I achieved my Airline Transport Rating, sometimes called the Ph.D. of flying. By 1986, after a two-year stint flying Learjets, I was hired by American Airlines. Ten years later, in 1996, I was promoted to captain.

Eventually, after I had been at the job for a while and felt more secure, I started riding with the club more.

Gremlin, Indian Dave, and I started the Arizona chapter in 2005. In 2008 I traveled to Germany to make the first contact with the German Hangmen.

By 2009, I had retired from American and embarked on a five-year part-time career delivering airliners around the world. In 2014 I completed a thirty-three-year flying career. It was something I could never have imagined in my wildest dreams, and something I had certainly not planned. I just went from one small goal to the next.

I was extremely lucky that I had no felony convictions, as that was the only question along those lines that American asked me.

Fortunately, they didn't ask about all those misdemeanors.

Hangmen in Artwork

Master biker artist David Mann.

David Mann, the famous biker artist, did several paintings in which Hangmen were featured. Moose was in 'Tijuana Jailbreak' and the other titled 'El Forastero New Years Party' has Skip standing there holding a noose.

Neither of their patches are visible. David did two paintings with our patch on display. Even though this painting has Ed Roth's name on it, he had paid David Mann for it and copyrighted it with his own name.

"Big Daddy" Roth helped make David Mann a legend in biker art.

According to Wikipedia, Roth commissioned either fourteen or twenty Mann paintings, depending on what source you use.

The picture above is Titled "13 Miles to Bakersfield."

Seven patches are lying in the foreground, Hells Angels, El Forastero, Hangmen, Misfits, Satan Slaves, Hells Outcasts, and Gypsy Jokers. Five of the seven are <u>one-piece</u> patches.

There is a club that started in Southern California in the mid-sixties. I've heard they claim this painting was made for them and the patches in the foreground are ones that they had pulled.

I dispute that.

A new club pulling patches from some of the most prominent clubs in the country?

One of them in the Midwest?

One of the patches belonging to the painter himself?

It is well known that David Mann was an El Forastero.

No way would he paint his patch as a trophy for another club!

Here is another Mann painting with Roth's name on it

The title of this is 'Jacumba,' after a small town in the Southern California desert, a stone's throw from the Mexican border. Many of the So. Cal. clubs used to have runs there in the cooler months.

The three other visible patches are Satan's Slaves, Gypsy Jokers and El Forestero.

The Noose on the Hangmen patch at the far left of the picture is easy to see.

Hangmen Videos on YouTube

There are many videos on YouTube about the Hangmen,
some are old pictures put to music, some are more modern,
and some are a mixture of old and new.

Hangmen MC 1960s by the author
https://www.youtube.com/watch?v=sz3_Meoj0JA&t=1s

Hangmen MC 1970s by the author
https://www.youtube.com/watch?v=sWlrNiBGKCA

Hangmen, Then and Now, by Futon Bob,
HMC National President.
https://www.youtube.com/watch?v=NwryvSS6nuI

Bob expertly uses many of my old pictures to portray the
"Then" part. He has made several videos that have been
very popular. His choice of music is better than mine.

These are just a few; there are many Hangmen videos on
YouTube. If you search, the others should come up.

And finally...

So many people over the years have worn the Noose. It is impossible to mention all of them here.

Too many others have been lost to motorcycle accidents, shootings, cancer, heart attacks, and other maladies, including plain old age.

At one time or another, everyone who wore a Hangmen patch helped to make us what we were then and what we are today.

It is up to the new guys, today and in the future, to determine what we will be. But it may take all your heart and soul. It can take your life.

This club is bigger than any of us and all of us.

Nationwide, the club is stronger than ever, with more and more quality people stepping up to continue the tradition. Just like the U.S. military, it needs new, young warriors to stand up and fight.

To do what needs to be done.

The reputation and legacy of the Hangmen Motorcycle Club continue.

As I write this, sixty-one years and counting.

THE END

Acknowledgments

Thank you to all the members of the Hangmen M.C., past, present, and future, for their respect, friendship, and brotherhood and for making this club what it is.

I would like to thank my agent, my editor, and my publisher, except... I don't have any of the above. I have never written or published a book before, and this effort is all mine.

So, all of the mistakes are mine as well. I realize it is about as polished as a pair of combat boots after two years on a battlefield.

Thank you to my son, Chris Vann, for reading the whole manuscript and providing valuable advice on 'What to leave in, what to leave out' (Bob Seger).

Thank you to Jan Sullivan for the picture on the cover and for giving me a son. You are loved and you are missed.

Thank you to my daughter, Meghan, for always being there, no matter what. And to my sister, Christine, for always believing in me.

And to the women in my life, whose love has helped make me who I am.

The author today, Arizona 2021

My deepest appreciation to everyone who takes the time to leave a written review on Amazon, Barnes and Noble or Goodreads.

You can contact the author at his website.
dalearenson.com
Email, dale@dalearenson.com
Or on Facebook.

Made in United States
Orlando, FL
04 December 2025

73879437R00245